DIFFERENT BUT EQUAL

DIFFERENT BUT EQUAL

Communication
Between the Sexes

KAY E. PAYNE

PRAEGER

Westport, Connecticut
London

Library of Congress Cataloging-in-Publication Data

Payne, Kay E., 1941–
    Different but equal : communication between the sexes / Kay E.
Payne.
        p. cm.
    Includes bibliographical references and index.
    ISBN 0-275-96522-8 (alk. paper)
        1. Sex role. 2. Interpersonal communication. 3. Communication—
Sex differences. 4. Communication in sex. 5. Gender identity.
6. Feminism. I. Title.
    HQ1075.P39 2001
    305.3—dc21   98–31076

British Library Cataloguing in Publication Data is available.

Library of Congress Catalog Card Number: 98–31076
ISBN: 0-275-96522-8

First published in 2001

Praeger Publishers, 88 Post Road West, Westport, CT 06881
An imprint of Greenwood Publishing Group, Inc.
www.praeger.com

Printed in the United States of America

∞™

The paper used in this book complies with the
Permanent Paper Standard issued by the National
Information Standards Organization (Z39.48–1984).

10 9 8 7 6 5 4 3 2

Contents

Introduction

ORIENTATION OF THE BOOK

Different but Equal: Communication between the Sexes really began when I started my studies as a doctoral student at Vanderbilt University, in Nashville, Tennessee. For my doctoral dissertation I needed to write about something for which I felt passion. Without passion I knew I would never complete the project. I decided to write about the role of the corporate wife in America. I played the role of corporate wife, married to a man who had assumed an important position for both the corporation and the family, while I also worked part time and took care of our three children. In my role as corporate wife I had struggled with a number of issues that had tormented me from the beginning of our marriage. I found all of my answers in "faith" issues, but I still wanted to understand and describe the secular perspective of my anxieties. What I discovered, simply put, astonished me! The doctoral dissertation was only the beginning of a life-changing adventure mirroring and encompassing the unique struggles of a whole society coming to terms with social change. The social change was reflected in confusion about restructuring role relationships, the retraining of people who wanted to have an active role in work and play, struggle with power issues between those who had and those who wanted to have, and shifting cultural symbols exemplified in the stories, myths, humor, play, ceremonies, and heroes of American society. This book reflects and describes the communication issues associated with that social change.

The book intends to incorporate the communication issues inherent in social change between the sexes at work and at home. In this regard, it provides theoretical and practical knowledge about gender differences in communication as offered in speech communication, business communication, and related disciplines. Second, it provides basic information relevant to service courses, organizational communication courses, and interpersonal communication courses. Third, the book acts as a useful resource for advanced courses in public speaking, communication theory, group communication, mass communication, sociology, and social psychology.

This analysis intends to present the reader with research and interpretive information from sources with a wide variety of expertise, understanding, and insight by using a pluralistic perspective. Frequently, gender communication books provide only a feminist perspective—depicting females as victims, or females as oppressed—without regard for the impact this has on relational communication. As the social pendulum moved to the extreme Left (liberal) in America during the 60's, 70's, 80's, and 90's, many advances were won for women, but often at the expense of relationships with men both at home and at work. As society began to devalue masculine men and revere masculine women, the social fabric of the country began to unravel. That unraveling of society emerged in the breakdown of the family: children killing children, drugs and violence in the streets and workplace, and the absence of real respect for people, which was replaced by legislated respect for others. The book is intended to move the pendulum back to the center, where we recognize and accept men who want to be masculine and women who want to be feminine, and all people in between. It does not take the point of view that suggests all people should be androgynous.

The subject of gender differences in communication has become socially important. Women have become members of the mainstream work force, thereby effecting enormous cultural change, while men have started to take a more active role in child rearing. The subject has risen to political importance with the issues of sexual harassment and political correctness affecting both men and women and what they can say. The subject has risen to ethical importance because the social and political changes have invoked a crisis in values.

The book also serves as a "reader" for the communication generalist. The unique approach is twofold: (1) to approach the subject of gender differences and communication between the sexes without hostility toward either sex; in the process of providing this approach it discusses some of the changes that have occurred between men and women and how the sexes relate to one another from social, political, and ethical perspectives; (2) to provide expertise from people who operate on the "front lines" of research observing men and women in the work world (in action) to determine their

impressions of gender differences in communication in the cultural, relationship, and task environment of work and play, both positive and negative.

ABOUT YOUR AUTHOR

For most books information about the author would be less significant
than in a book on the subject of gendered communication. The subject
matter and the handling of the research make it significant for you to know
my perspective so you might recognize how your own life experiences differ
from or reinforce my understanding of reality. Our life experiences shape
our perspectives, so, in this regard, the subject of gender will be influenced
by your sex, age, religion, and cultural background. I am a Caucasian,
heterosexual, middle-class woman, who was married in 1961 and remains
in the same committed relationship to this day. My husband and I have
three children, one male, two female, and (at this writing) three grandsons.
I have always worked outside the home in some capacity for pay, but only
since 1987 have I experienced the work world from a full-time position.
My marital status, race, class, and sexual orientation have been approved
by Western culture. Therefore, I have enjoyed the privileges that result from
social approval. However, during my years of love and work I have also
been on the receiving end of hostility from others for a variety of reasons.
Consequently, I know what it's all about to have experienced those kinds
of feelings and that kind of thinking. My position is that we all experience
oppression at some level, but, in the final analysis, it's our response to it
that matters most.

ORGANIZATION OF THE BOOK

The book is loosely organized around three major themes: first, the construction of the gendered self; second, the differences between men and
women as they relate to one another through language, power, and nonverbal communication; third, the effects of gendered communication in
leadership and the media. The book incorporates old and new research,
theoretical and pragmatic ideas, male and female perspectives, and ideologies based in liberal and conservative thinking about gender.

Part I, Chapter 1, describes biological, psychological/sociological, cultural, and religious influences on the development of gender. This chapter
focuses on sex role development, the impact of sex roles on communication,
and the future of sex roles. Chapter 2 examines the rhetorical movements
influencing social views and policies about men and women that have contributed to the cultural conversation about gender. Chapter 3 compares
and contrasts traditional ideologies with humanist and feminist ideologies

as they relate to gendered communication. This chapter also looks at how feminism affects faith and how men and women of faith often compartmentalize their values at work and home.

Part II, Chapter 4, talks about self-esteem and gender communication. The process of developing self-esteem recognizes an internalization of different aspects of a person's biological makeup, his or her perceived opinions of others, the impact of culture on his or her opinion of self, and the religious messages he or she hears about self. The concept a person develops of self, however inexact, fluctuating, and uncertain, functions as a guide in social behavior, often affecting the words we choose to describe feelings and events. Chapter 5 discusses the hierarchical and partnership models of marital communication. This chapter also discusses the impact of gendered communication on courtship, how it has changed the face of marriage and often created gender role conflict. Chapter 6 explains how sexual language affects the perceptions of men and women and how they relate to one another. It includes a discussion about the sexual revolution of the 60's and 70's, pornography, and sex education. Chapter 7 continues the discussion of language by applying it to the stereotypical masculine and feminine styles of communication, verbal aggressiveness, argumentativeness, and sexism. Chapter 8 looks at the power continuum between men and women: who has it, what it looks like, how and when it is used, and how we can each access power. Some of the misunderstandings about power become clarified when examined in this chapter through the lens of gender. Chapter 9 describes nonverbal gendered communication in terms of proxemics, kinesics, haptics, paralinguistics, and artifacts.

In Part III, Chapter 10 looks at gender differences in leadership with attention to the stereotypes and differences in how male and female leaders experience and communicate anger, status, stress, and persuasion. Chapter 11 depicts the images of men and women in the media through magazines, television, newspapers, movies, and popular music. The gradual changes in the portrayal of men and women in the media reflect changes in society.

TEACHING ABOUT GENDER AND COMMUNICATION

Frequently, students enter a class about gender and communication hoping to get ammunition to "shoot down" the opposite sex. Women who advocate extreme feminist views, who have themselves experienced some sort of abusive relationships with men, and/or who are filled with anger against men, for whatever reason, often begin a class like this somewhat disabled. Because they have become so sensitized to their condition, it often is difficult for them to hear the good contributions men make to society and to the lives of women. When these women become overwhelmed by ideas that do not agree with what they believe to be true, they may reach an impasse. It's hard to entertain ideas of reconciliation that would enable them to enter into healthy relationships with those of the opposite sex, whether they be love or work relationships, when they have been indoctrinated with ideas that oppose reconciliation.

This phenomenon holds true for male students, as well. Male students of this decade have listened to considerable denigrative rhetoric about them and their relationship to women. They have been called oppressors, rapists, deadbeat dads, unnecessary to women except for their sperm, selfish lovers, wife beaters, child abusers, and on and on—in some cases rightfully so. When males hear enough of this kind of rhetoric they may fight or take flight. Many men who hear about a class centered on gender communication expect it to be a male bashing class. Unfortunately, when males arrive in class with these attitudes they often fail to comprehend the messages of reconciliation available to them when examining gendered communication.

The goal of a course in gendered communication should be to create an atmosphere in which students can express their anger and hurt, can share their thoughts about unfair stereotyping, and can articulate their struggles with just getting along with people who differ from them. Often this may require an "aha" experience, a paradigm shift, thinking outside the box, the removal of anger, pride, and hurt. Changing the way we think challenges all of us to stretch ourselves, but we often resist. I recommend that when studying the material in this book students try to start from zero and reconstruct the way they think: try to throw away former baggage, get free of their anger, and claim peace with others. This is not a class in counseling, however. The study should release new ways of thinking about old problems; considering gendered communication can be unsettling. It requires courage. It may challenge your thinking, but it will enlarge your awareness of others. You can play an active role in creating personal lives for you and others that exhibit fairness, compassion, discipline, responsibility, and intelligence. This can be accomplished by understanding how men and women may be *different but equal*.

PART I

1

Gender Role Development

I'm like an acorn. I have to decide if I want to grow up and be a big strong oak tree. I have to decide if I want to stand out in the wind and the rain and allow the birds to [poop] all over me. Or, if I want to let a squirrel gather me up and eat me. There is something to be said for living in the nice warm belly of a squirrel.

Anonymous

Several years ago, after safely landing in New York following a transatlantic flight from Paris, a male flight attendant announced that the flight had been their first with an all-female flight crew. A spontaneous eruption of applause filled the aircraft with cheers of astonishment and praise. The obvious evidence of broken barriers for women almost drowned out the secondary comment made by the flight attendant. He said that, although not for the first time in history, we had also had an all-male crew of flight attendants. The gender role reversal caused a continuous round of cheers and applause while the beaming flight crew walked out of the cockpit each with one arm raised high like a winning athlete crossing first over a finish line. As the passengers disembarked from the plane, one comment surprised a few people who heard someone say, "I'm sure glad they didn't tell us women were flying the plane before we left or I would have gotten off. I don't appreciate being deceived in this way. I may never fly with this airline again."

A few years earlier I might have thought the same thing. Presupposing only men could be pilots and females should be flight attendants suggested an adherence to conformity "previously" endorsed by society. However, the eruption of applause by the majority of passengers suggested something much more interesting and forward thinking. Most of the individuals on this particular flight had undergone at some previous time a paradigm shift from an old to a new belief structure. Changes in society make it no longer easy to predict how a person will play out his or her occupational or family roles. The inescapable changes in male/female roles intimately relate to communication, for communication announces social images of gender and seeks to persuade all of us about correct male and female behavior.

Legitimate perspectives about how people should play out their roles secure individuals in sustained practices of what they think of as normal and right. Because individuals often do not question their perspectives, what seems natural to one may impose rigid boundaries on another. In recent years research explaining why people communicate the way they do has focused on the concepts of masculine and feminine rather than male and female. This research has led us away from the rigid boundaries of limiting gender sex role stereotyping. By exploring the similarities and differences between male and female roles more accurate descriptions of human communication behavior have emerged. Increasing awareness and reflecting on gender role theory and communication improve a person's ability to discern the arbitrary from the desirable. As a person enlarges his or her awareness of prescriptions for gender roles, freedom to choose a course of action and identity suitable for that individual produces greater gender role fulfillment.

Gender includes the social construction of masculinity and femininity within a culture, whereas *sex* refers to a person's biological or physical self. Gender reflects the interaction whereby a person incorporates his or her biological, psychological/sociological, cultural, and religious characteristics. Stereotyping an individual according to sex or gender often leads to *sexism*, an action discriminating against a person on the basis of sex. Sexist ideas often account for and justify divisions of labor and family responsibilities by gender.

Communication involves the exchange (sending and receiving) of messages, or information, through speech, signals, or writing. Communication incorporates interaction on two levels: instrumental (task) and maintenance (relationship). Communication both proclaims and reflects the interaction of those characteristics of role development within a specific culture. Four theories of gender role development intimately connected to communication are the biological, psychological/sociological, cultural, and religious. In the next few sections each of these will be discussed in an effort to explain phenomena each of us often observes and experiences in everyday life.

BIOLOGICAL

With the exception of a few people, in most cultures we can easily discern the sex of someone by either the appearance or the voice. X and Y chromosomes act as determinants of sex, the biological quality providing our identity. Our sex remains stable throughout our lives, and as we grow we begin to develop characteristics in our personalities often reflecting our sex. Not giving it much thought, we anticipate our interactions with others, often keeping their sex in mind. Some even claim they talk to people of the same or opposite sex differently, frequently acting more tenderly, less argumentatively toward females than to males. Unlike those of sex, determinants of gender appear to be less stable. At the 1994 World Conference for Women in Beijing, China, attendees defined five genders: masculine male, feminine male, androgynous male or female, masculine female, and feminine female. Researchers argue about the possibility of gender differences between males and females beyond those associated with physiological characteristics. Some argue the similarities so outweigh the differences that gender should not even be a subject of study. Others claim these distinctions are so great that they devote their entire career to understanding the differences. Although sex determines who will bear children, gender accounts for how we play out our life roles, and how our life roles affect our communication.

Biological explanations acknowledge gender role differences most obviously. Physical development, including physical size, anatomical features, and genitalia, offers gender differences explained by biology. Differences in maturation rate between boys and girls show girls' physical development advances more quickly than boys' until the age of about sixteen. Biological theories also focus on how chromosomal and hormonal distributions affect individual features, mental processes, and moods (Moir & Jessel, 1991). The combination of XX chromosomes creates a female child and the XY combination creates a male child. As a child develops in its mother's womb, during the first trimester, external male or internal female genitalia begin to develop. By the fourth month, male genitalia can be observed, photographed, and videotaped to acknowledge the upcoming birth of a male child. When the genitalia do not show up in X rays parents can assume a female child will be born. As the sex of the child becomes clear, the secretion of hormones begins to affect the development of other male and female sex characteristics.

Estrogen, a female hormone, regulates reproduction and develops and maintains female secondary sex characteristics. It causes women to experience an inclination toward nurturing (Ehrhardt, 1984). It causes women's bodies to make blood vessels more flexible than those of men (Shapiro, 1990). Estrogen strengthens the immunological system, making women less susceptible to certain infections and viruses. It also tells the body where to deposit fat, explaining why women have larger breasts and hips. The fat also redistributes as a useful aid in the protection of the fetus during pregnancy (Moir & Jessel, 1991).

Testosterone, on the other hand, controls the secondary sex characteristics in males (Webster, 1984). Tavris (1992, p. 151) writes that men's hormones affect their behavior in a cyclical way, similar to that of a female cycle. As testosterone level increases, males become increasingly more aggressive, violent, and even abusive. High testosterone levels appear to be linked to dominant behavior, jockeying for power, attempts to influence or dominate others, and expressions of anger. Testosterone also contributes to men's higher concentration of muscle mass, giving them more natural strength than women, a greater oxygen-carrying capacity, a lower resting heart rate, higher blood pressure, and more efficient ways of recovering from physical exertion (Stockard & Johnson, 1980).

The distribution of these hormones impacts the development of male and female brains so men and women develop brain-lobe specialization in different ways. Researchers (Devor, 1989; Feingold, 1994; Tannen, 1986, 1991) claim men and women use both lobes of the brain, although men have greater development of the left lobe, controlling linear, logical, sequential, abstract, and analytical thinking. However, when males reach the low points in their hormonal cycle they appear to have better spatial abilities ("Study Links Men's Cognitive Abilities," 1991). On the other hand, women experience greater development of the right lobe, controlling artistic, imaginative, intuitive, visual, and spatial tasks (Gorman, 1995; Devor, 1989; Feingold, 1994; Tannen, 1986, 1991). This may explain, in part, why girls may exhibit neatness in such tasks as coloring, drawing, and handwriting, and boys may exhibit messiness, clumsiness, or ineptness at early motor skill development (Simmons & Whitfield, 1979). The corpus callosum, a link between the two lobes, is more highly developed in females, suggesting they experience more bilateral brain activity. Able to receive and store more sensory information than men do, women enjoy the reputation of being more holistic thinkers, partly explained by their bilateral brain activity (Hartlage, 1980; Lesak, 1976; Walsh, 1978). Because male and female brains develop differently, they also process information in different ways, resulting in different perceptions, priorities, and behavior (Kimura, 1987). Moir and Jessel (1991) claim males dominate females through their innate aggressiveness, whereas females reproduce, historically the most well known biological difference between males and females.

These biological theories of gender provide us with general information about masculine and feminine behavior. They do not, however, explain individual men who may have less testosterone and behave less aggressively than other men, or women who express more aggression than other women. Freud believed a child identified with the same-sex parent as an irreversible consequence of perceived and actual anatomical differences. Although no research disputes the impact of biological processes on the development of sex roles, many researchers claim other factors also play a part in the determining of gender roles, picking up where biological theory stops.

PSYCHOLOGICAL/SOCIOLOGICAL

Freud (1957) explains how the psychological effects of family dynamics encourage the development of gender roles consistent with the same-sex biological parent. The primary caretaker, generally the mother, has most direct influence on later development. Because a fundamental similarity exists between mothers and daughters, daughters identify with their mothers, learning to play their roles within this same-sex relationship. As sons grow up, however, they recognize a difference between themselves and their mothers, leading to development of a separation from their mothers, as sons identify more closely with male role models. Consequently, researchers associate boys with independence and autonomy from their mothers (Chodorow, 1978).

Other research examines the influence of interpersonal relationships on gender role development, including social learning and cognitive development theories. *Social learning* theory (Mischel, 1966) focuses on communicating with and watching others as contributing factors explaining how a child learns to imitate actions and roles of same-sex role models. As this behavior develops, social learning theory suggests that it becomes reinforced by others. Frieze et al. (1978) claim that when children act out gender-appropriate behavior, society rewards them, but when they act out gender-inappropriate behavior, they may be punished. Specific masculine behavior such as rough-and-tumble play, and specific feminine behavior such as thoughtfulness and obedience characterize gender-appropriate behavior for boys and girls (Moir & Jessel, 1991). Tannen (1986) agrees that the differences between boys and girls result from different treatment by society.

Cognitive development theorists (Kohlberg, 1958; Piaget, 1965; Gilligan et al., 1988) claim interactions with others influence the self-definition of males and females differently. This theory differs from social learning theory since as children distinguish sex differences the desire to be competent at their gender creates a more active role in the process of learning appropriate same-sex roles. By the age of six children have a sense that no matter how they change their hair or clothes, their biological sex remains the same. Ruble et al. (1981) say once a child realizes the constancy of his or her sex, he or she begins to adopt and prefer sex-appropriate behavior as a means of reinforcement. Same-sex models become gauges for figuring out their progress. Reinforcement for "appropriate" gender behavior and differential treatment based on sex often continue sex stereotypes.

The 90's created opportunities for understanding sex roles associated with both same-sex and opposite-sex models. As more and more women entered the work force and left the traditional home behind, Crosby (1991) claims children benefited by losing some of the rigidity of their sex-role stereotyping; further, children who attended child-care centers showed benefits in their intellectual and emotional development because they had more contact with children and adults outside the family. On the other hand, Hewlett (1991) argues, children experience developmental problems, in part, as a result of mothers' going to work. She claims parents do not have the time or energy to guide children, often leaving them to fend for themselves. They underperform at school, commit suicide at higher rates, need psychiatric help more often, suffer eating disorders or malnutrition more often, bear more children out of wedlock, take drugs more often, and become victims of violent crime far more often when compared to previous generations. At this point it is important to recognize that the research about the development of gender identity about psychological/sociological constructs consists primarily of studies on white middle-class girls and boys. The effect of "mothers' working" on the sex-role development of children generates little agreement except that the next generation will determine the personality of our culture. West and Fenstermaker (1995) include experiences of race and class as important components affecting gender role and as influences that play a role in cultural development of gender.

CULTURAL

The third area of gender role development relates to the influence of culture on the development of identity. *Social learning* theory (Mischel, 1966) and *cognitive development* theory (Gilligan et al., 1988) claim individuals learn to be masculine and feminine through observation and communication. The process in which alteration occurs in the structure and function of a social system results from the individuals and groups composing it. Culture impacts people, and when they play out their roles the status achieved by those roles also impacts the culture. In fact, status and role reciprocally affect one another. *Standpoint* theory offers insights into how a person's status within a culture shapes his or her life role. The status or position we hold in a social system may be formal, like that of a business person, or informal, like that of an opinion leader. These roles entail different expectations by the culture. Should an individual deviate too far from the prescribed set of behavior, his or her status may be challenged. In our discussion of gender, masculine and feminine may be affected by status views held by a particular social system.

Studies by M. Mead (1968) discovered various ways other cultures define masculine and feminine roles; in one culture sex roles were reversed, in another extremes of what we consider masculine and feminine were encouraged, and a third promoted femininity in both men and women. In his *symbolic interactionism* theory, G. Mead (1934) claimed individuals learned socialization and became competent at their sex roles through interacting with others and learning the status, values, and expectations of a society. Labels such as *strong* or *graceful, rambunctious* or *demure, mean* or *kind* help children identify with the appropriate self-image expected by the culture. Finally, standpoint theory (Collins, 1986; Harding, 1991; Ruddick, 1989) acknowledges the importance of an individual's status and position in society, focusing especially on race, class, gender, and affectional orientation.

Katz (1982) described an African ethnic group having no fixed hierarchy. The central theme of the culture revolved around Kia, a boiling emotional energy derived from *num*, a powerful trancelike energetic jumping dance induced from the ground up root of a special plant (Katz, 1982, p. 55). The dance encouraged healing through the reduction of tension. Within this ethnic group power derived from how a person received num and controlled rapidly boiling num, and from the drama and effectiveness of his or her curing techniques during the dancing. When Western culture began to influence this ethnic group the central theme of the culture broke down, as increases in alcoholism, disease, hunger, oppression, and tension developed. Where harmony had been a central force, sedentism, a system of squatters and serfs, and exchanges of services for money began to surface. The development of a hierarchy signaling a more male dominated society and a decrease in the mobility of women began to emerge.

Gilligan (1982) describes the differences in male and female children resulting from cultural pressures affecting personality development. Reflecting on Chodorow (1978), who says boys separate and girls identify with mothers, Gilligan claims males often feel threatened by emotional intimacy, whereas females feel threatened by separation. Consequently, as social pressure interacts with personality development, males experience difficulty with relationships and females tend to experience difficulty with individuation. Women often define themselves in terms of their ability to care; men often define themselves on a hierarchichal set of principles determining right from wrong, or determining what is justice. The impact of communication on these culturally based assumptions is revealed in the way people talk about their lives and react to the real world as they perceive it.

Growing up in the 40's and attending college in the 50's left women and men with relatively few role choices. Women expected to become wives and mothers or perhaps nurses, teachers, home economists, secretaries, or cooks. Men also expected to marry, but they expected go to work to earn money for the family, to act as the contact person for the family with the

outside world. Few women and men in the first half of the twentieth century branched out into more "opposite-sex-specific" roles, but when they
did, people often regarded them as anomalies. Our culture promotes and
upholds certain values for the roles of women and men with sex specific
values, expectations, meanings, and patterns of behavior (Weedon, 1987).
Each of us accepts or rejects these gendered images. Communication artic-
ulates the cultured images of women and men, teaching the "correct" way
of behaving. When we hear stories, watch movies, listen to musical lyrics,
read magazines and newspapers, and talk to our relatives, these cultured
images are reflected. For example, when we see a beautiful slender woman
or a muscular, handsome man, unfortunately both women and men measure themselves against this person as a standard.

Because these cultural images pervade our lives, we often accept them
without much thought. Learning to evaluate and reflect on the messages
reinforcing cultural views of men and women, accepting the workable, and
rejecting the ideas that hinder people, empowers individuals to take control
of their own lives, choose roles suiting them, embark on careers formerly
thought appropriate for only one particular sex, and generally increase their
freedom to chart their own course. Determining the workable aspects of
sex roles for a society and discarding those that individuals find oppressive
requires focused energy and discernment.

RELIGIOUS IDEOLOGY

Many thinkers, despite the great variety existing within and among the
various world religions, regard religion as having the common feature of
patriarchy (meaning projection of male concerns with the subjugation of
women). To understand sex roles and their patterns of complementarity,
we must examine a complex set of information about religion and attempt
to boil it down to provide a simple understanding. Among all the religions
of the world, sometimes at the core, and sometimes at the margins, individuals have had sex role choices within "degrees of human freedom, of
options taken and refused, of the exercise of aspiration and will, even if
sometimes within patterns of severe constraints" (Guisso & Johannesen,
1981, p. ix). Sanday (1981) claims tribal religions did not exhibit universal
male dominance. But rather, male dominance existed among religious
groups when antecedent conditions of an outer orientation, a separation of
the sexes, and a situation of cultural stress existed. An *outer orientation*
occurred when one pursued power "out there," as when one hunted animals or sought dominion through war. Because these activities took men
away from the camp or home, a male bonding and separation of the sexes
began to develop. The separation of the sexes became exacerbated during
the stress of war. Judaism, early Brahmanism, and Confucianism developed
extreme male dominance at a time of great stress. Sagan (1985) found

Polynesian and African religious societies experienced radical transformations in their value systems as their kingdoms developed into more "complex societies." Sanday (1981) thinks male dominance developed at a relatively late point in human history; by contrast, simpler societies exhibited conceptual symmetry in sex roles.

When the Jews returned to their homeland after the Babylonian captivity, the tensions entailed in reestablishing the kingdom increased anxiety about women. The establishment of kingdoms within the culture of any religious community can be an extremely violent stage of history. Efforts to ensure the male line would not be polluted by a philandering wife became important in setting up the kingdom. Increasing rigidification of the role definition for a woman often involved protection of her by her brothers, father, and husband to ensure her virginity before marriage and her fidelity during marriage, and at this time the idea of "wife as property" often developed. Within the establishment of extreme male dominance men had to be brave, tough, and aggressive. Places for men to congregate often developed; frequent quarreling, fighting, wife beating, rape, and raiding of other groups for wives became factors in establishing kingdoms. Often the exclusion of women from decision making and separation of places for men and women to eat developed; segregation of the sexes in education often developed "male-only" schools (Sagan, 1985).

Searching for sex role differences in male/female roles by looking at religious groups in relation to gender role development often involves much more than how sex roles develop and goes to the larger issue of how each person "should" live according to religious tradition and how society should be organized. To suggest that there might be a way we should live assumes a society holds common social values. In a complex society one set of values seems impossible to define. In societies where a variety of religions coexist, the confluence of these religious groups seems to agree on many of the basic values of a healthy society. Those basic values include the importance of the family unit as the foundation of a stable people. In the family unit, just as in the workplace, people play specific roles to accomplish the necessary tasks to make the family work. People often gravitate to the roles in which they exhibit the most skill or have time to fulfill their obligations.

Many religions provide instruction, indicating that their "written code" has a specific role for wives in society in relation to their husbands, and God honoring women will obey the words of their God(s). Dobson (1991) advocates the Christian view that women's enjoyment of the capacity for reproduction gives them a greater appreciation for stability and security. Because of the fragile nature of the male's ego, requiring respect, and the intense need of the female's ego, needing love, Dobson says, society should not tamper with the time-honored relationship of husband/protector and wife/recipient of protection because it works best. He claims the God of

Christians determines the husband's leadership role in the family, meaning his decisions prevail in times of differing opinions. However, he emphasizes that the role does not mean heavy-handed disregard for the feelings and needs of wives. Dobson claims this arrangement works best for the majority of people. But when Christian women choose to play their roles in agreement with what Dobson advocates they often experience a lack of fulfillment. Even among Christian males and females the ideology of male leadership in the family stirs strong emotions. Feminists disagree with these role definitions and for decades worked to enlighten both men and women to recognize other options within the context of marriage providing them with greater freedom of role development. Hubbard (1990) agrees, asserting that other than differences in reproductive organs no significant physical differences exist between the sexes. Any differences that do exist, she said, result from social or cultural conditioning created by males who were determined to keep women in roles that promoted the well-being of men. She believes enough variability exists among men and women to construct a society where both sexes could contribute in whatever useful way suit their talents.

Powell (1993) asserted that the U.S. work force in the year 2000, if trends continued, would show increases in the number of women at work from 45 percent in 1990 to 47 percent in the year 2000. Tang (1999) reports 67 percent of women at work in October of 1999, so the Powell statistics have been exceeded. White males were expected to represent only 40 percent of the work force. But Tang (1999) reports 75 percent of men at work, which is a drop from 86 percent in 1950, but still higher than the predicted 40 percent. *Women & Work* (1995) projects a similar trend in the Australian work force. The population of women in South Africa is represented by 52 percent of the people. As South African democracy develops, trends of increased participation of women in the workplace are expected to follow those of other developed nations. In a democracy, individuals make their own decisions about whether to work and about what kind of work they will do. As women emerge as the dominant work force, men are likely to play more important roles at home.

COMMUNICATION AND THE IMPACT OF GENDER ROLES

Canary and Hause (1993) and others (Ragan, 1989; Putnam & Wilson, 1982; Smythe & Meyer, 1994) argue that gender and communication behavior affect each other little and research based on gender differences reflects information that solely examines stereotypes. Other researchers (Tannen, 1994; Gray, 1992; Bate, 1992) claim that if theorists ignore the obvious differences between the sexes, their gender roles, and communication patterns, they will overlook an important variable. How society defines roles for women and men provides expected behavior and the values associated with them, including how individuals communicate with one another. Gender, as described earlier, is how we play out our life roles. How we learn the behavior and communication appropriate to these roles has long been a subject of research. In the early 70's, Bem (1974) developed an inventory for measuring sex roles, and although it has been criticized by some, it remains a relatively useful tool for self-assessing one's gender role identity in terms of the degree of masculine or feminine attributes an individual perceives himself or herself as possessing.

Bem (1975) describes masculinity as independent, assertive, and forceful, whereas the perception of femininity includes affection, sensitivity to the needs of others, understanding, and gentleness. Masculinity and femininity affect perception of phenomena. When we perceive information we engage in at least three activities: selection, organization, and interpretation. If we learn gender roles from the variety of theoretical prospectives outlined earlier and our goal involves playing out our sex role competently, according to expectations of society, then it seems logical that we will receive and process information in specific ways, accepting some and rejecting other information. *Perception* involves the selective process of attending to, hearing, and remembering information that may agree with what we already believe to be true. Given this, it follows humans will selectively process information relating to what they need to fulfill their goals, in this case, gender roles (Peck, 1978). How we select, organize, and interpret information may be affected by our sex or the way we play out our gender roles (Payne & Payne-Houchen, 1999).

Gendered communication includes information about and between men and women. Not only do men and women reflect gender roles through communication, but they are impacted by communication about gender. People perceive differently because they experience life differently; consequently they abstract different information from a scene that they find useful in processing information. Physiological aspects of gender affect perceptions, as do those of psychological and sociological life experiences and cultural and religious ideas. Our feelings and the circumstances of a situation affect how we perceive information and these may be, in part, determined by our gender roles.

Gender role theories traditionally lead us to conclude that stereotypically feminine women (Bem, 1974, 1979) will communicate by using a passive/assertive style in efforts to achieve rapport, connection, relationships, equality of status, support, inclusiveness, responsiveness, and self-disclosure. Stereotypically masculine men (Bem, 1974, 1979) will communicate by using an assertive/aggressive style in efforts to accomplish tasks, achieve status, dominate the talk stage. Masculine men will act forceful and instrumental, with more abstraction, less concreteness, and less responsiveness to others. Regardless of sex, a person can engage in different levels of masculinity and femininity or fall somewhere in between. Someone whom Bem (1974, 1979) referred to as *androgynous* would posses "both expressive and instrumental abilities" (Hudak, 1993, p. 281).

GENDER ROLE TRANSFORMATION

Sometimes, individuals who fail to conform to rigid gender stereotypes receive lower evaluations than those who do conform. Pressure to conform as masculine males and feminine females continues to exist. This supports the theory of sex role congruency, arguing people who conform to a socially constructed gender role will be perceived more positively. Harris (1977) and Stoppard and Kalin (1983) suggest individuals who conform to societal expectations are viewed as better adjusted, more likable, and more competent communicators than feminine males and masculine females. On the other hand, in a study by Smith (1985) individuals formed reliable impressions of a speaker's masculinity, femininity, and androgyny by listening to tape recordings. The androgynous male received the highest ratings for competence and the masculine female received the lowest ratings.

Clearly, traditional roles for men and women fluctuate from decade to decade, family to family, culture to culture, and even religion to religion. In fact, in the twenty-first century it may not be so easy to continue to define "traditional" roles without sounding antiquated. So, how will the roles of the future compare with those of the past? What impact will a person's sex have on the biological, cognitive, experiential, cultural, and religious aspects of his or her role development? Women in America will probably never leave the workplace now that they have tasted the pleasures of independence. Although women still carry more of the responsibility for household tasks, men now share some of that responsibility. Also, though men carry more of the responsibility for providing the economic security necessary for families, women now contribute to their families' economic security.

Pleck (1977, p. 182) described gender role as "the psychological traits and the social responsibilities which individuals think are appropriate behavior for them because they are male or female." Those who oppose traditional views of gender role development believe these views limit an individual's options in terms of variations in sex role identity. Pleck (1977) envisions an extended stage of gender role development that occurs at a point when individuals experience difficulty "fitting" the more traditional roles because the rules of behavior do not make sense to them. Consequently, these individuals often "transcend the norms of stereotypical gender role" and develop both expressive (feminine) and instrumental (masculine) attributes of role development (Bem, 1974), referred to as *androgynous*. When individuals transcend the norms of tradition they often share responsibilities in the home and workplace. Not all individuals, however, vary from traditional roles and ideas of what society views as male (masculine) and female (feminine).

So, are men and women better off with shared responsibilities in the workplace? The Business and Professional Women's Foundation of Washington, D.C. (1992), claim that although women have made unprecedented strides into the workplace, a subtle form of discrimination still holds them back from breaking through the "glass ceiling." To combat this, women engage in lawsuits against companies who fail to promote them fast enough, an action that generates fear of, but not respect for, women in the workplace (Farrell, 1993). Gilder (1995) argues that when *anyone* reaches the summit, "the slopes are slippery." Qualified men on occasion also find themselves shut out of jobs, but they smash the ceiling the old-fashioned way, by leaving the company and starting their own businesses. Farrell (1993) says people who succeed monetarily *and spiritually* think of men not as having all the power but being more willing to pay the price of power. Some disagreement seems to exist about whether or not men and women as a society are better off with women in the workplace.

Are men and women better off with shared responsibilities at home? Berne (1995, p. 131) claims women who can share such responsibilities experience more "freedom of choice in career, mate, offspring, and lifestyle." The opportunities for women today to define their roles as individuals and women far surpass those of any other time in history. Barnett and Rivers (1992) argue working women experience greater emotional satisfaction, increased self-esteem, and greater happiness than their domestic counterparts. But career women who delay childbearing while they pursue their career find the experience of staying at home raising their children enormously fulfilling, much more so than their former belief of balancing job and family (Pearcey, 1995). In contrast, Julty (1995, p. 146) said even men reap "the benefits of the realignment of gender roles." Men can define their roles in ways varying from the stereotypical "macho" male role model to more stereotypically feminine types of role models, including daily child care provider. On the other hand, Bly (1990) argues today's men have become too soft, out of touch with their masculinity: soft boys who no longer understand the process of breaking from their mother. He further explains that without male role models in the home to help them break from their mothers, boys often resort to violence to demonstrate their manliness. Farrell in 1993 asserted that all was not well for males in the culture of the 90's: that as a direct result of feminism, government passed quotas taking away jobs from men who needed to provide for their families. Fierce competition from a federal government that in 1987 offered more money and services to women with children than nearly 30 percent of single men could provide (Mackey & White, 1993) discouraged would-be fathers. Farrell (1993) went on to say feminism not only excluded the "now unimportant male" from his family but encouraged the government to tax him beyond his ability to keep up. It was not females, but males who experienced discrimination in the workplace, being denied equal rights. Even males who choose to play the role of child care provider agree they receive a subtle stigmatization by society as a result of being "unemployed."

CONCLUSION

Identifying the processes involved in coming to grips with gender roles presents a complex tapestry of issues. When good and honest people disagree about how roles should be played, it becomes increasingly important to respect and appreciate the public debate. In a democratic society, we can learn from those with whom we disagree as we question our differences, especially when the inquiry leads us to become more broadly educated. How we play our gender roles in a democratic society appears to be the choice of the individual, the guidance given by his or her family, the biological factors given by sex, the cultural expectations, and the religious underpinnings of such a person. At this time of transition, we all operate in a state of somewhat confused anxiety about gender roles, but learning how gender roles come into existence goes a long way to helping us shape our future.

By the time children enter school, they know their sex, and they have a basic understanding of what society expects of boys and girls. This chapter has focused on sex role development, the impact of sex roles on communication, and the future of sex roles. Most successful males and females want to succeed at working or living together as a necessary part of life. Not only that, but both men and women want to play their roles well, want to reduce the noise and confusion they hear from different groups, and want to be able to predict how their roles should be played with maximum satisfaction.

Cadden and Galifianakis (1995) published a view of women, work, and home after conducting a survey revealing more women would choose to be homemakers rather than having outside jobs if they could. On the other hand, Friedan (1981) compared the condition of being a housewife to living in a Nazi concentration camp, indicating housewife roles can create a sense of emptiness, nonexistence, and nothingness in women. Stroh and Brett (1994) say men whose wives do not work earn more money than men whose wives do work. Related to this, in October 1995 Farrakhan called black men to Washington for a "Day of Atonement." Various speakers at that rally charged men to go home and take responsibility for their family.

Additionally, the Promise Keepers movement (Schmidt, 1994) motivates men toward Christ-like masculinity by telling them to go home and "take charge of your families, while honoring your wife." Traditionally, men were in charge at home and women played a housewife/mother role. A number of theories affecting gender development exist. Each of these theories seeks to explain different dimensions of gender, but none is the definitive answer to explain gender. Rather, these theories each help us see the influences on gender from unique perspectives, each sharpening our focus of how biological, psychological/social, cultural, and religious influences impact gendered communication. The biological dimension of gender helps prompt or restrict individuals to act in certain ways, whereas the psychological/sociological dimension acts to enable people to internalize information about gender. The cultural dimension of gender impacts how we come to understand our maleness or femaleness in terms of status within the context of society; the religious information we receive confirms or denies our reality. Each of these theories describes communication as central to the development of gender. Communication both reflects and impacts our view of gender. No one theory should be accepted as the complete explanation of gender roles, but rather should be thought of as part of a tapestry of ideas that together form a complete picture.

2

Persuasive Attempts at Shaping Gender Roles: Women's and Men's Movements in America

> In the battle of the sexes, you never meet what you can truly call a conscientious objector.
>
> Anonymous

Biological, psychological/sociological, cultural, and religious influences on gender identity usually do not entail much conscious effort. Social movements try to persuade masses of people to realign their thinking; gendered social movements attempt to realign public thinking about gender identity. Women's and men's movements in America have had such agendas. Women's and men's groups have effectively come forward to influence cultural views of masculinity and femininity and have in turn made an impact on cultural perspectives. For example, in the early 50's men were thought of as masculine and women as feminine. In the early twenty-first century, however, shifting images of men and women no longer immediately conjure up masculine images of men and feminine images of women. In fact, we often find masculine or androgynous women and feminine or androgynous men, as well as the stereotypical images of former years.

Cross-cultural studies depict gender roles in different ways that provide a broad spectrum of perspectives. For example, among the Arapesh ethnic group of New Guinea, both men and women exhibited what historically had been described as maternal, womanly, unmasculine parental roles and somewhat feminine sexual aspects. Both men and women exhibited personality attributes described as peaceful, cooperative, other-centered, and helpful and also showed a sense of reciprocity, responsive to the needs and demands of other people (Mead, 1963). The ideal Arapesh couple "is the mild, responsive man married to the mild, responsive woman" (Mead, 1963, p. 279). Just one hundred miles down river, both the men and women of the Mundugumor ethnic group of New Guinea presented sex role behavior consistent with what historically have been described as masculine in the Western world. Their behavior patterns depicted individualism, self-centeredness, a lust for power and position, ruthlessness, violence, virility, fierceness, distrustfulness, competitiveness, contemptuousness, and an open hostility among members of the same sex (Mead, 1963). The ideal married couple of the Mundugumor ethnic group would be "a violent aggressive man married to a violent aggressive woman" (Mead, 1963, p. 279). Living along a lake just a short distance from both the Arapesh and the Mundugumor ethnic groups were an artistic group called the Tchambuli people. The social structure of the Tchambuli operated under a patrilineal organization with clear distinctions of sex roles portraying feminine males and masculine females. Despite the patrilineal structure, the Tchambuli women held the real power and acted as the dominant marital partner, and men played "a less responsible more emotionally dependent" role (Mead, 1963, p. 279). The married couple ideally paired individuals whose personalities opposed and complemented one another within a complicated tapestry of polygamy. In yet another ethnic group, the Kali Hari people of Western Africa, clear distinctions of male/masculine and female/feminine gender role identity existed, but no inequity occurred between the sexes until after Western civilization took hold (Katz, 1982). In some South American cultures public male authority and power, a necessity for the machismo image, often masked the true domestic power and authority of women (Sanday, 1981).

Changes in depictions of sex-role identity in the United States demonstrate the power of gendered social movements. For example, in the fairy tale *Cinderella* the main character acts out a feminine role of a demure, passive, hardworking, long suffering, servant-type stepsister who bows to the authority of her domineering stepmother and stepsisters and waits for someone to rescue her. In a newer version of the same basic story, the movie *Ever After* showed the character of Cinderella as independent, tough, feisty, competitive, and aggressive about what she wanted, refusing to put up with the condemnation of her stepmother and stepsisters. In a second example of the effects of a gendered social movement, the movie *Gone with the Wind* depicted the character Scarlett O'Hara demonstrating a public feminine role and a private more androgynous/masculine role (Jerome, 2000). The sequel, *Scarlett*, depicted the title character's acting out her private and public roles in a more masculine or androgynous style. These role changes have been impacted by the persuasive efforts of a powerful gendered social movement.

Money and status have long been measures of masculinity used to attract a desirable wife in hopes of carrying on the family name. Over time, however, gendered social movements have persuaded women to join the work force and therefore gain their own sense of status and independence. The idea of femininity has also changed from the perception of frail and uninformed women during the Victorian age to more modern times with tougher women who often operate on the cutting edge of information. These changes did not happen without the persuasive efforts of the women's movement, which altered cultural understandings. Because of this impact any attempt to understand gender roles and communication between the sexes must include an awareness of the rhetorical movements informing the social perceptions of maleness and femaleness.

A *rhetorical gendered social movement* is an organized attempt to persuade society to change the status quo with regard to issues of gender through language and action. This gendered movement began with women and took the name *feminism*. A dissatisfaction with the status quo, which women viewed as oppressive, motivated women to band together, usually against the common enemy. The common enemy against which feminist first began to organize was the patriarchal system: not men, per se, but the system. Because women had no voice (Kramarae, 1981) the system had organized itself around the ideals of men. The original goals of the movement included removing the oppressive influences on women that appeared to emerge from the Victorian era.

Myriad scientists from the Victorian era thought that not only did men and women differ, but women were inferior. The scientists based their claims on "scientific evidence" derived from anthropology, biology, psychology, and medicine. For example, Darwin (1900) claimed white men represented the most advanced life form; women were simply underdeveloped men. Physical anthropologists believed that women's smaller heads were empirical evidence of female mental inferiority (Broca, 1868). Lombroso (1894) said women of genius were rare exceptions, who on close examination were found to have some virile qualities. Campbell (1891, pp. 46, 47) emphasized the point by saying, "Genius of the highest order is practically limited to the male sex." Clarke (1874) explained how reproductivity in women drained them to such an extent that engaging in university studies would atrophy their womb. Finally, Spencer (1897) viewed women and men as physiologically suited to only certain types of labor, thus relegating men to the marketplace and women to the home.

Early feminist advocates pursued varying objectives for women based on differing analyses of what they saw as oppressive forces. All members of the movement, however, shared the belief that the status of women must be improved, and women and men should be free to decide their own careers and life patterns. Adherents advocated social change ranging from moderate to radical. Rhetorical approaches differed between groups: some argued that women and men differed but were equal; others asserted women and men did not differ.

The concern for equal rights for women in England dates back to the late eighteenth century, when Mary Wollstonecraft in 1792 published *A Vindication of the Rights of Women*, in response to the widely held belief in women's submissiveness, their desire only to please men, their passivity, and their lack of intelligence. She advocated education of women, equal work opportunities for men and women, involvement of women in politics, and application of the same moral standard to men and women. She argued from the position that women and men were basically the same. This belief smacked the face of commonly held views of society, so her influence varied over time. Wollstonecraft had long-term success in influencing women across Europe, including her own daughter, Mary Wollstonecraft Shelley, an independent woman herself, the author of *Frankenstein*, and the wife of the poet Percy Bysshe Shelley. Orr (1997a) has described Wollstonecraft as having a somewhat negative influence on the society of her own time, setting back the cause of women, because her reputation as a radical or extreme Leftist (Jacobin) and an advocate of immorality (an immoralist) generated considerable criticism. These arguments against Wollstonecraft emerged from the general rejection of her major premise that women and men did not differ. Other critics not only rejected her public image, but dismissed and attacked her rhetorical arguments, claiming they were "not well planned" (Tomalin, 1974, p. 136), lacked "logical structure" (Urbanski, 1980, p. 55), and were "ill arranged, repetitive and too full of digressions" (Brownmiller, 1975, p. 4). Griffin (1996, p. 273), however, claims that when Wollstonecraft's opposition could no longer "refute the content of her arguments, they refuted the form of her argument," employing a form of ad hominem criticism.

THE FIRST WAVE OF FEMINISM

In the United States the movement for women's liberation was begun by Lucretia Coffin Mott, Elizabeth Cady Stanton, Lucy Stone, and Susan B. Anthony, who focused on a woman's right to vote, a right provided by the Nineteenth Amendment to the constitution. However, none of the organizers of that first convention, held in 1848 in Seneca Falls, New York, ever lived to see women vote: it was not until seventy-two years later, in 1920, that women gained that right in the United States. During the period preceding the twentieth century, voting and all other political activity were the domain of men. Women stayed at home managing domestic issues, and men dominated the political world. The debate in the early twentieth century centered around whether or not women should share power and control in areas traditionally controlled by men. The argumentation included the proposition that men and women differed.

Opposition to the right to vote rallied around the arguments that women's voting would "distract women from their domestic duties and would harm the nation by having those ignorant about government making decisions" (Martin, 1916, pp. 312–314). Martin (1916, pp. 320–326) as-serted that suffragists believed that with the vote they could transform so-ciety by changing the "savage and barbarous world" of men into a softened, civilized world. Martin argued that women operating in a man's world would not soften the man's world; rather, it would harden women. Arguing against these popularly held social beliefs about women, suffragists failed at their attempt to gain the right to vote until forty-eight years later, as a result of another issue.

In attempting to implement social change, a speaker who pushes too hard, too fast, may cause an audience to reject his or her argument, or even become more entrenched in its original position (Sherif et al., 1965). When cultural feminists attempted to cause social change on the subject of the vote, they approached it by beginning with a commonly held belief of the time. They argued that differences existed between the two sexes in fun-damental ways. They claimed women were more pure, moral, nurturing, and committed to harmony than men. They did not challenge the domestic roles assigned to women, as suffragists had, but rather celebrated the "cult of domesticity" as the ideal of femininity or true womanhood (Welter, 1966). These rather Victorian conceptions of women actually led to the securing of women's right to vote. One platform used to achieve this right emphasized the higher morality of women in efforts to curb the corruption of political life. This rhetorical strategy carried them to victory in 1920 in amending the Constitution to grant women the right to vote (Campbell, 1973). Despite the win, few women actually voted and the women's move-ment in America remained dormant for the next thirty-five years.

After World Wars I and II America's attention focused on creating fam-ilies and enjoying America's world dominance. The prevailing conservative political views did not produce much political, social, or professional in-terest in women's rights. Also, since the overriding voice of the voting rights issue was that of the cultural feminists and they affirmed women's tradi-tional roles, broader reforms in cultural views of women declined (Wood, 1994). It was not until the second wave of feminism that interest in broader issues began to take hold. During the 60's and 70's women's liberation groups spread rapidly in the United States and in many European countries, Australia, New Zealand, and Japan. Although specific issues varied from one country to the next, similar concerns tended to prevail everywhere.

THE SECOND WAVE OF FEMINISM

From the 1960's until the mid-90's, a second wave of feminism increased the numbers of women who wanted to claim a voice in defining what they wanted, what new customs should be born, and what chorus should sing out the identity of women. Friedan (1963) kicked off the second wave with the claim that women who dedicated their lives to a career as wife, nurturing a husband's career and tending to a house and children, were feeling unfulfilled. Consciousness raising groups and informal discussion groups were intended to increase awareness of sexist attitudes and behavior against women. Many saw the need to end the traditional psychological stereotyping of women as passive and dependent, and of men as active and independent. Traditional family roles and patterns of marriage were criticized as basic factors in perpetuating inferior treatment of women. Their acceptance by women was also criticized. As in the first wave, both liberal and cultural ideologies coexisted within the second wave. In 1966 Freidan founded the National Organization for Women (NOW), which acted as a "voice" opposing various oppressive influences within the workplace and family. The liberal feminists accomplished many advances for women during the second wave period. The diverse goals of the various ideologies, however, caused fractures in efforts to form a coherent definition of who feminists really were. Consequently today few women under the age of thirty identify themselves as feminists because they disagree with its premises or are unclear about what being a feminist means. They have not experienced the same problems getting good jobs as previous generations did.

The feminist movement operated from a core ideology, but not as an ideological monolith. In the earlier part of the second wave of feminism the women's movement became identified with three main ideological strands: liberal feminism, radical feminism, and socialist feminism (Ryan, 1989; Buechler, 1990). Today, feminist ideology advocates diversity, which in turn requires an acceptance of differences in ideology among various orientations that differ in the scope of change they advocate and their views of inequality and oppression of individuals based on class, race/ethnicity, and sexual orientation. The great diversity of feminism at the end of the twentieth century created a perspective that suggested to some that feminism, as we know it, might be finished. A brief review of the diversity within the second wave of feminism helps explain the unique perspective of each group. A review of some of the backlash groups provides insight into why younger women felt the need to prepare for the third wave of feminism. Despite the fractured appearance of feminism, a retrospective examination reveals a number of accomplishments on behalf of women that resulted from the efforts of liberal feminists.

Liberal Feminists

The major liberal political view that an "individual's sex is irrelevant to her rights" (Jaggar, 1983, p. 27) presupposes that male and female differences do not exist in nature. The dominant rhetorical argument of liberal feminism emphasized egalitarianism and argued for compensation for past injustices and a redistribution of wealth to rid society of oppression against women (Crowley-Long, 1998). Liberal feminists also argued for gender-neutral standards once equality was established. Crowley-Long (1998, p. 113) suggests that most academics tend to emphasize and support research that "supports the liberal political view that there are few significant differences between women and men."

Liberal feminists latched on to Friedan's (1963) notion of the unhappiness of the role of housewife. Friedan defined the problem as a political issue, deploring the confinement of women to home life, which prevents women from developing personal and professional interests. Middle-class white wives and mothers found validation in the message of liberal feminism. Gaining strength from radical feminists, liberal feminists, headed by Friedan, started NOW working to secure political, professional, and educational equity for women. The central ideology that declares women and men are alike in important respects and therefore entitled to equal rights and opportunities is reflected in the organization's work. NOW has been responsible for considerable legislation on behalf of women, and liberal feminists have contributed to the advancement of women in such actions as the following: Title VII of the Civil Rights Act of 1964, which establishes the illegality of sex discrimination and states that sexual harassment constitutes sex discrimination; Title IX of the Education Amendments of 1972, which prohibits sex discrimination in educational institutions that receive federal funds; the discovery and removal of sexist language in textbooks and public communication, stimulated by academic research and advocacy; equity for women in sports; reforms in banking and credit laws; advancement of women in public and appointive political positions; and increased awareness of women's issues (Wood, 1994). The rhetorical strategies of this group included lobbying, speaking at public forums, drafting legislation, supporting feminist research, and holding conventions to develop strategies for the future. Liberal feminism does little, however, for women who believe women and men differ in distinct ways. And Crowley-Long (1998) suggests that liberal feminism does little to address the issues of race, class, and ethnicity that radical and socialist feminists have raised.

Radical Feminists

Radical feminists emphasize differences between men and women. Daly (1992) claims the cultures of women and men differ along biological and reproductive lines, and especially result from patriarchal oppression. She argues women nurture and use more creative energies than men, who act out aggressive behavior, such as that in competition and war. Radical feminists root their arguments in these differences, depicting how society elevates men and subjugates women. But, they argue, women value personal relationships, an essential human element, and men are therefore "culturally deprived" (Burris et al., 1973, p. 59). The theory of differences based on biological characteristics enables radical feminists to advocate the development of a whole new social order based on the values of women.

Consciousness raising acted as the war cry of radical feminists imploring women to become enlightened about the cause of fighting discrimination. Women organized and began to hold national meetings in 1968 to define and determine the rhetorical strategies they would use to represent their principles and practices (Campbell, 1973). They protested anything that they saw as objectifying women, especially beauty contests, makeup, high heels, and bras. Shopping, cooking, cleaning, making coffee at work, and acting as the primary care giver of children became sources of tension. Radical feminists achieved temporary solidarity among women and empowered grass-roots political support for women's issues. Their rhetorical strategies focused on empowering and affirming women and shedding old images of "feminine" women. Positioned even further along the radical spectrum are another group, the socialist feminists.

Socialist Feminists

Marxism refers to the economic and political ideas of Karl Marx and Friedrich Engels, who developed a system of thought that gave a primary role to class struggles in leading society from capitalism to socialism and then to communism (Webster, 1984). Marixist feminists subscribed to Engels's assertion that the oppression of women resulted from the breakup of tribal collectivism, in which women were the equal to men. However, the decline of the matriarchal clan and the subsequent development of a class-divided society made women a class that was not equal to the class of men. Marxist feminism argues that the oppression of women resulted from these changes and advocates replacing capitalism with a communist system of structuring society with the intention of eliminating class divisions.

Socialism refers to a social system in which the producers possess political power and the means of producing and distributing goods (Webster, 1984). Socialist feminists believe the sexes differ along biological lines and extend the Marxist argument, asserting that classism results from the division of labor. Socialist feminists believe that the decline of the matriarchal clan and the rise of a patriarchal class caused the historic decline of women's status, as a caste system that subordinated women (Reed, 1970) and revered men. Socialist feminists argue for a whole new society in which all forms of sexism, racism, classism, and heterosexism cease to exist. They advocate the destruction of capitalism, superseded by socialism: a society in which all people are free of exploitation, manipulation, and prejudice. Other feminist groups of the twentieth century held diverse views about women's identity and had diverse goals.

One of the leading proponents of socialist feminism, Hillary Rodham

Clinton, "retracted, disguised, and repackaged in more benign wrapping" her views (Olson, 1999, p. 103), which contradicted democratic principles. The Carnegie Council report, of which she wrote several chapters, advocates that "teachers, pediatricians, and social workers . . . socialize the task of raising, supporting, and nurturing children" (Olson, 1999, p. 103) in the future Clinton idealizes. Her earlier writings revealed "a leftist ideologue" who proposes replacing the traditional role of the nuclear family, assigning to children center stage as "levers with which to extract political power" (Olson, 1999, p. 105) to "force judicial mandates and legislative change" (Olson, 1999, p. 109). In the 1992 presidential campaign Dan Quayle advocated family values, the antithesis of socialist feminist ideology. During that campaign Hillary, operating as a major tactical player in her husband's presidential race, skillfully used a rhetorical power tactic whereby a speaker picks his or her target, personalizes it, polarizes the debate, and crushes the opponent (Alinsky, 1971). The tactical strategy successfully shut down Quayle, characterizing him as fantasizing family values. Olson (1999) interprets the phrase "fantasized family values" as meaning that the government is the real provider of values, an idea consistent with socialist feminism ideology.

Ecofeminists

The American feminist theologians Dorothee Solle, Rosemary Reuther, and Mary Daly turned some women in a slightly different direction in response to oppression. The ecofeminist worldview emphasizes the feminine aspects of God as Goddess. The central idea of some ecofeminists emphasizes solving environmental problems; others combine this focus with spiritual ritual. Ebeling (1991, p. 1) states that many ecofeminists "hate men and want women to control the world." Ecofeminism establishes a new religion especially interested in Gaia, the earth goddess in Greek mythology, and with the Minoan Cretan civilization that existed before Christ. Ebeling (1991) claims ecofeminists believe they are God and exist in a cosmic consciousness with all other forms of existence. Adherents of this philosophy argue against the timber industry as they organize events and blockades to stop the removal of trees; and "hoot, hiss, and holler at rallies if a timber industry representative tries to speak" (Ebeling, 1991, p. 4). They advocate tribal existence of hunting and gathering food that grows wild and emerges from the bounty of the goddess Earth and deify everything female (Ebeling, 1991). Julia Butterfly Hill, an ecofeminist who lived in a tree for two years, descended from her tree in December 1999. The love of the tree, which she named Luna, sparked a debate energized by the logging industry, which claimed Hill and her love for her tree constituted a religion. The industry filed a lawsuit against the government claiming that when the Forest Service protected Hill and her concerns they were mixing government and religion.

A relatively new faction, dating from about 1974, when d'Eaubonne published *La Feminisme ou la Mort*, Feminism or Death, provided the philosophical foundation for ecofeminism, ideas that energized another group in the second wave of feminism, lesbian feminists.

Lesbian Feminists

The lesbian feminist Paglia (1992, p. 23) has described lesbianism as a "product of the intolerable pressures and repressions of the affluent, ambitious nuclear family, marooned by the breakdown of the vast, multigenerational extended family, still powerful only among the working class." Whereas gay men are promiscuously seeking sex without emotion, "lesbians often end up in emotion without sex" (Paglia, 1992, p. 24). Two groups of lesbian feminists have defined themselves. One claims lesbian feminism represents sharing and support among women; the other emphasizes sexuality between women as the core of lesbianism.

Lesbian feminists describe society as benefiting the rich and the white male (Bunch, 1975). They advocate a rejection of male sexual and political domination, often even rejecting men, gaining a sense of self, including sex, around the concept of woman. Because of the division of labor, as men hunted and women gathered, lesbian feminists believe men conquered women. They engage their rhetoric around a theme that attacks and rejects male supremacy by withdrawing from heterosexual sex. Wittig (1979) denies that: "One is not born, but becomes a women"; it is civilization that "produces this creature" (Wittig, 1979, p. 1). The political goal of lesbian feminism opposes women as a subclass and seeks to suppress men as an upper class. Once the male class disappears, women as a class will also disappear; then, Wittig (1979, p. 2) claims, there would be no "slaves without masters."

The rhetorical energy of lesbian feminism centers around the various battles over job discrimination, insurance coverage, housing, and property rights in defense of sexual orientation. Much of the rhetoric of lesbian feminism rallies them around the defense of their life-style and choice of partners, particularly against the church, "the media, and the public," and other feminist groups (Wood, 1994, p. 87). Lesbian feminists often band together to argue against the prevailing hostile, heterosexual ethic of American society.

Gender Feminists

Hoff-Sommers (1994) describes feminists of the second wave in terms of gender and equity feminists. Hoff-Sommers (1994) characterizes gender feminists as bonding together under the banner of rage against men. At a rage conference held at the Graduate Center of City University of New

York in October 1992, Hoff-Sommers noted gender feminists collectively described the rage women experienced as a result of how men keep them down. Anger panels and anger sessions acted as themes and titles of organized rhetorical events. Those who spoke at the sessions articulated their rage in the following terms: "Women are under seige," "Women are in a gender war"; they are "victims of mass persecution" and should watch out for the "impending male backlash"; they are "angry and struggling." One claimed she was "angry, the alternative is depression" (Hoff-Sommers, 1994, pp. 19–20). The women attending the conference represented "tenured professors at prestigious universities who had fine and expensive educations" (Hoff-Sommers, 1994, p. 21). In the early 90's women students had experienced protection under Title VII of the Education Amendments of 1972 and represented larger numbers at universities than men students (Hoff-Sommers, 1994). She described these feminists as "unreasonable, unjust, ideological" (Hoff-Sommers, 1994, p. 53) and wondered why they expressed so much anger though they were such a privileged group.

The gender feminists of academia created women's studies programs and advocated feminist classrooms. Equity feminists explained the decline of higher education as resulting from an academic feminism that subordinated scholarship to ideology (Hoff-Sommers, 1994, p. 274). On the other hand, Hoff-Sommers found equity feminists to be more reasonable and just.

Equity Feminists

Equity feminists, as described by Hoff-Sommers (1994), are similar to first wave feminists in their goal of equity without discrimination. Equity feminists support the great gains of women in the second half of the twentieth century and point to Elizabeth Cady Stanton of the 1854 movement for women's suffrage as the greatest proponent of the equity feminism cause. Equity feminists describe gender feminists in perjorative terms, especially in academia, where, Pogash (1992) says, they misrepresent statistics to suit their views. The frequent misrepresentation of statistics, expanded definitions of rape, and fuzzy accounts of other crimes against women often led to legislation activated by gender feminists. Equity feminists believe that gender feminists give feminism a bad name.

Black Feminists

Ladner (1987) attracted attention to the differences between white and black feminism. She found disparity between her own experiences growing up as a black woman and her socialization by white feminism. In particular she claimed black females viewed child rearing positively, whereas many white feminists viewed it negatively; black females saw themselves as strong and autonomous, whereas white feminists viewed themselves as victims.

Davis (1982) pointed to economic problems for black women who fought both racism and sexism. She pointed to child rearing among black slave women as not an oppressive experience but rather one in which black women anchored themselves in a community. Walker (1984) has coined the term *womanist* to describe black women who love other women. She provides historical documentation of the violation of black women by black men and white men. Yet she primarily focuses on everyday life such as the value of music, dance, and quilt making among black women. Activist bell hooks (1990) has criticized much of white feminism, which she claims excludes many African-American women.

Women of Color

Women of color is a specific designation of a group of nonwhite feminists. Anzaldua (1983) described how marginalized Chicano women do not fit into feminism. Morales (1983) raises the voice of Puerto Rican women and the unique rites of passage experienced by women of color through immigration, desperate economic conditions, and political struggles. Yamada (1983) draws in the perspective from Asian Pacific American women. As a visitor to a feminist women's meeting she became disillusioned because the group seemed to be pushing their own agenda rather than letting the needs of the group determine the direction of the organization. She expressed a general mistrust of the women in the feminist movement and explained this as a pervasive feeling among many marginalized groups of women. Women of color may also include black feminists.

Separatists

Separatists choose to "remove themselves from the mainstream and live in tune with communal values and respect for life, including life of people, animals and the earth" (Wood, 1994, p. 84). Separatists have been so named because they have adopted a revolutionary goal of forming all-women communities where feminine values could flourish without intrusion from men and the aggressive, individualist, oppressive values of capitalism. They seek interdependence in life-style communities and approach living with mutual respect for one another and harmony. "As a result of their withdrawal from mainstream society, they contribute little influence" (Wood, 1994, p. 84).

Structural Feminists

Ruddick (1989, p. 130) has described motherhood as involving women's traditional "caring labor, mothering, production and preparation of food, kin work, housework, nursing, teaching, and care of the frail elderly" causing them to develop more nurturing and supportive roles, in contrast to the competitive values men learn through participation in the workplace. Unlike separatists, "structural feminists believe in the roles traditionally prescribed by society with women's place in the home" (Wood, 1994, p. 84). Structural feminists rarely take a public voice but will speak out for the protection of mothers and children and speak out for femininity. Donovan (1985, p. 62) has described women's (domestic) political value system derived from traditional women's culture and has attempted to apply it to the public realm.

Revalorists

The goal of the revalorists is to reestablish traditionally feminine skills, activities, perspectives, and contributions to cultural life. They want to establish women's contribution to history and literature within the curriculum of American schools. Campbell (1989), Keller (1985), Gilligan (1982), Belenky et al. (1986), and Donovan (1985) all represent revalorist efforts to highlight women's achievements in a variety of fields. Revalorist rhetoric focuses on seeking public forums to raise awareness of and respect for women's ways, including art, and the beauty and "integrity of women's traditional roles" (Wood, 1994, p. 88). Wood (1994) suggests that women's traditional arts such as weaving and quilt making act as symbolic rhetorical strategies that speak louder than words. Tensions exist between liberal feminist perspectives and those of revalorists because celebrating traditional activities of women often appears to value activities resulting from oppression (Janeway, 1971; Miller, 1986). The revalorist response to this criticism is that not celebrating women's traditional activities ignores generations of cultural contributions. Wood (1994) claims that revalorists play an important role in rewriting history to include the contributions of women.

THIRD WAVE FEMINISM

First and second wave feminisms were marked by large, distinct activist movements. The first wave concerned itself with women's suffrage, and the second with radical reconstruction or elimination of sex role stereotypes and the struggle for equal rights of women and men. The third wave of feminism does not represent a distinctive activist movement but seems to be more of an academic construction (Alfonso & Trigilio, 1997), whose emphasis grew out of a political and theoretical discussion of problems of race and sexuality of the early eighties. A group of about one hundred young feminists gathered in New York City and organized themselves into an activist network, "The Third Wave" (Orr, 1997). With a vision of becoming a national network for young feminists from diverse cultural and economic backgrounds, to straighten the relationships between younger and older feminists, and to consolidate a strong base of members who could mobilize for specific issues, political candidates, and events (Dulin, 1993) the new activists rallied the group. Among the first and most cited published works were anthologies by Walker (1995) and Findlen (1995) of "next generation" feminism.

Some assert that this movement emerged from students in women's studies programs at American universities who heard war stories from their embattled professors but who could not identify with their struggles. Others argue that the movement emerged from the political agenda of postmodernism. Still others suggest that the third wave of feminism identifies with and sanctions the production of new sexualities without providing the political strategies for evaluating them. Madonna represented this constantly changing identity, resisting definition, transgressing boundaries, but not clearly articulating any positive feminist philosophy. In general, the rhetoric of this movement is still fluid, and the feminists in it seem to belong to generation X. Third wave feminism seems to want to learn the art of freestyle thinking, to think outside the box, to color outside the lines, but they are still trying to define themselves and learn from the waves of feminism preceding them.

THE MEN'S MOVEMENT

Men have been living through a cultural revolution as powerful and contentious as any in the history of the world, and it has not been easy (Baber, 1995). They have responded to changes in both cultural and social relations of gender. Some of these changes have been provoked by feminism, some by antisexist gay liberationists, some by academic men who support feminism, some by Christians seeking to understand biblical perspectives, and others by divorced and angry men seeking father's rights (Messner, 1995). Some of the groups in the men's movement support feminism, some resist feminism, and some attempt to avoid feminist issues altogether. Some men recognize that they enjoy institutional privilege, some have become aware of the costs of masculinity, and some want to return to the wild man to recover their lost manhood. Feminists targeted men as the enemy and caused them to begin to question their masculinity. They failed to make a distinction between patriarchy and masculinity, and as a consequence caused men to become ashamed of being men rather than questioning the validity of patriarchy (Bly, 1995). Targeting men (not patriarchy) as the enemy hurt not only men but society, as well.

Nothing intimidates a man faster than the mockery and disapproval of women. When a woman laughs at a man, when she critiques him without pity, when she mocks him, he is usually emasculated and silenced (Baber, 1995, p. 155). "Manhood is an honorable condition, and it seems clear men need help today perceiving themselves as men" (Baber, 1995, p. 155). Among the first men to oppose the excesses of feminism, Baber, author of the "Men" column in *Playboy*, expressed views rejected by rational men, careful men, men who did not share his desire to provoke. He nevertheless continued speaking against excesses in feminism in his column for over fifteen years. At the Women's Freedom Network in the fall of 1995, he found an audience of sympathetic women. Men, he said, "cannot do much without the support and blessing of the women in their lives. We are needful, driven, frightened and lonely creatures, and we do not endure the anger and criticism of women at all well."

Two threads of the men's liberation movement describe essentially two directions in which men have focused their discussions. The first thread favors women's liberation and attempts to abandon the language of sex roles in favor of a more egalitarian language of gender. The second general thread includes men's groups that became disillusioned with feminism or that watched the woman's movement from the sidelines and saw it helping women, but hurting men. The first group ranges from antimasculine to profeminine; the second reverses the focus, from antifeminism to promasculinism. The diversity of issues varies with each group, but the general intent is to address major feminist rhetoric against men.

Profeminist Men

In the spring of 1971, four radical feminist men initiated an outcry of men against sexism in *Brother: A Male Liberation Newspaper* (Messner, 1997). In the early 80's at the First National Conference on Men and Masculinity a male radical feminist advocated that men renounce their masculinity and give up their male privilege in an effort to unite with women for the betterment of society (Messner, 1997). Profeminist radicals focused on the costs of masculinity and the institutional privileges afforded men. Many male feminists wanted to change the social expectations of masculinity that caused them to repress their feelings (Hudson & Jacot, 1992). They organized in efforts to establish a network of support for men and to identify and talk about problems and frustrations inherent within the cultural perception of masculinity (Doyle, 1989, p. 307). Within these groups men learned how to talk openly with other men about their feelings, historically discouraged from discussing topics like these because they were thought to be unmanly. As the movement progressed, the costs of masculinity led to discussions of personal feelings about masturbation, which led to feelings of guilt, an emphasis that changed the focus of the group. Deemphasizing the costs of masculinity, profeminist radicals then centered their discussions on the ways men derived power and privilege within the patriarchal society and how they could assist women in restructuring an egalitarian society. Litewka (1977) described how men become socialized to objectify women, to fixate on portions of the female body, and to conquer through sexual intercourse, with rape the ultimate domination of women. At this point profeminist males changed the focus of their rhetoric again, joining feminists in opposing rape, pornography, and battering of women (Messner, 1997). A rhetorical tactic used by profeminist men to add more men to their group was the use of personal persuasion at work and in private to convince other men to stop discriminatory practices against women.

Promasculinist Men

Promasculinist men believe feminism caused many of the problems faced by men and contemporary families. They see feminism and its ideology as in conflict with men's interests (Freedman, 1985) and assert that the legitimate social, psychological, and spiritual needs of men have been ignored by feminists (Kipnis, 1995). They believe profeminist men denigrate men and contribute to negative stereotyping of them. Some of the promasculinist rhetoric centers on anger and feminist backlash. They claimed that feminists have tried to conceal who has real power and that men have experienced oppression in the form of shorter life span, health problems, military conscription, and divorce and custody laws that favor women (Goldberg, 1976). They believe feminist ideology and men's shame have combined to cover up stories of men whom women have physically abused (Logan, 1985) and murdered (Panghorn, 1985). Although many men initially hoped feminism would lead to human liberation, not just women's liberation, they discovered the women's movement sought only unilateral liberation for women (Adams, 1985). Promasculinist men want to regain some of the turf that women have taken from them and want feminists to recognize ways in which males suffer, risk abuse and neglect. They want men to regain control as family leaders and argue for a reconstruction of society so that men can assume full rights to care for and nurture children (Messner, 1997). The majority of promasculinist rhetoric centers on father's rights, often situating them within the terrain of antifeminist politics (Messner, 1997) and closely aligning them with the mythopoetic men's camp and other promen's groups.

Mythopoetic Men

Bly (1990) claims that men have forgotten how to be men and therefore how to teach their sons to be men. Becoming a man does not consist of biological factors exclusively, but requires hard work, personal courage, and the support of older men. Moore and Gillette (1992, p. 179) assert that when a society does not support and facilitate this achievement, the warrior energy of men would "turn up outside in the form of street gangs, wife beating, drug violence, brutality to children, and aimless murder."

Mythopoetic men claimed men had been ripped asunder by modernization, the Industrial Revolution, and feminism. When men were taken away from their farms and became isolated within industrialization they became separated from their families. Boys lost fathers who could teach them about manhood and who could teach them how to relate to other men. Bly disagrees with profeminist men's desire to become more like women in learning to be sensitive and caring. Rather, he thinks, feminism has made men "soft" and decidedly unmasculine. Allis (1990) charges that feminists have castrated American males, who want their manhood back. Mythopoetic men want to reclaim courage, aggression, and virility as masculine birthrights and qualities put forward in the service of worthy goals. Bly's (1990) book *Iron John* acted as a powerful rhetorical statement to mythopoetic men. It maintained a place on the national best-seller list for over thirty weeks, indicating a strong resonance among men.

The term *mythopoetic* derives from the use of old fairy tales and poetry to guide men on spiritual journeys aimed at rediscovering their masculinity. The rediscovery of their masculinity, however, largely ignores men's relationships with women (Kimmel & Kaufman, 1994). Messner (1997) says that the mythopoetic men's movement has brought men together in a way that both nurtured the wounds feminists inflicted on them and mutually empowered them through the emotional bonds established by the movement.

Promise Keepers

After listening to feminists turn *masculinity* into a perjorative term, and with a growing concern about the feminization of men, Christian men gathered to pray about their roles as early as 1990 under the leadership of Bill McCartney. The organization began with only 72 members, but with a growing yearly attendance, by 1995 their group had swelled to over 700,000 Christian men. The growing concern among Christian men revolved around the idea that American men had abdicated their responsibilities in the home, had abandoned their children, and had given over their authority to women. The central theme of their movement corresponds with the tenet of feminism that men have not kept their promises to women as providers and protectors and have not treated women with respect. Their rhetorical energy focuses on asking God to forgive them, asking God to direct them, and asking God to enable them to reestablish their roles as husband and father within the context of the nuclear family. Until 1996, Promise Keepers appealed to mostly white heterosexual men. In 1996, however, the theme of their rally centered around breaking down walls, with the intention of including all men. Clatterbaugh (1997) describes this movement as a threat to feminism: as right-wing conservatives who want to reestablish their position of authority over women, urging women to submit to their husbands as obedient servants.

The rhetorical strategies of the Promise Keepers movement explain, in part, how the group so forcefully and quickly became energized. First, their members shared a common way of looking at the world. Second, they used preexisting structures and practices within the Christian church. Third, they utilized state, regional, and community designated leaders in a "carefully trained and prescribed chain of command" (Clatterbaugh, 1997, p. 179). Fourth, they utilized preexisting groups such as those of Edwin Louis Cole (1982), who had already been organizing Christian men and holding separate retreats for them. Fifth, they organized their rallies around familiar formats commonly found in other evangelical gatherings such as the Billy Graham crusades (Clatterbaugh, 1997). Sixth, they acknowledged and tied in to such historical figures as Billy Sunday, who had led a wave of Muscular Christianity at the turn of the twentieth century. Sunday had held evangelical rallies similar to those of the Promise Keepers depicting Jesus as a model of masculinity.

Free Men

Free men also aimed at restoring men's pride in being "real men," as depicted in the traditional macho images of Clint Eastwood, John Wayne, Sylvester Stallone, and Arnold Schwarzenegger, who in the movies acted tough, rugged, decisive, invulnerable, and self-reliant. Free men see profeminists as soft and effeminate (Gross, 1990). They believe the inequities of society have caused men to suffer too, especially in the provider role. Ehrenreich (1989) discusses how men learned to define their masculinity in terms of their ability to make a living and support a family. Consequently, Farrell (1991, p. 83) claims, men are relentlessly oppressed by the "24 hour a day psychological responsibility for the family's financial well-being." In order for men to attract women, whereas women may become sex objects, men must become "success objects" (Farrell, 1974, pp. 48–49). Many men believe women will not love them if they do not provide for them financially.

One of the rhetorical strategies of this group has been to lobby for reform of discrimination against fathers in custody of children and in child support. They want a discussion of father's rights and responsibilities to children before couples divorce so that fathers understand what is at risk. They agree with Promise Keepers, who advocate the regaining of their headship within the family.

The New Man

In attempting to predict what the "new man" of the 90's would be like, Ehrenreich (1989) claimed that the most striking characteristic would be that he would no longer define his maturity by his ability to be the family breadwinner. Consequently, he again became the target of women, who complained that men were commitment phobics, refusing to grow up and postponing marriage or avoiding it altogether. She described the new man as one who would work hard to establish and maintain a good career, work out at the gym, collect art, become a gourmet cook, decorate his own apartment, and adamantly refuse to be a meal ticket for some woman. He would explain on a first date that there would be no commitments. Instead of equating marriage and settling down with maturity, the new 90's man would enjoy other legitimate options and would describe them in terms of growth (Ehrenreich, 1989). Whereas a masculine man of earlier years often displayed his status through the size, beauty, and taste of his wife, the new man would demonstrate his own status through a new male consumerism. Ehrenreich (1989) described him as an elegant dresser, a cautious drinker, who was well educated, had good muscle tone, and was knowledgeable about the food he chooses at restaurants. The new man of the 90's thus redefined himself in ways that many feminists would describe as shallow and status-conscious rather than less aggressive and more emotionally accessible.

In the summer of 2000, an incident occurred in Central Park, New York, in which a number of young women were assaulted by a group of young men who attempted to rape and molest them. This incident sparked enormous controversy in the news media and among feminists who claimed this incident was another example of conventional macho male socialization run amuck. Hoff-Sommers (2000) describes several other similar incidents. In the late 80's in the South Bronx, the "whirlpoolers," a group of high school boys, surrounded girls in public swimming pools and sexually assaulted them. In Glen Ridge, New Jersey, some high school athletes raped a retarded girl. In Lakewood, California, high school boys who called themselves the "Spur Posse" kept score on the number of girls with whom they had sex as if it was a game. And the shooting incident at Columbine High School in Littleton, Colorado, and the various other shooting incidents in high schools across America in the late 90's and early 2000's sparked a defining moment in America which started a cultural conversation about the welfare of young boys. Hoff-Sommers (2000, pp. 181–183) claims that the problem with these young men was not male socialization but, rather, its absence. Of course, these examples typify "some" boys and do not take into account all the many young boys who lead moral lives.

So, what do these incidents tell us about the new man of the twenty-first century?

Messner (1995) states that both femininity and masculinity continuously shift along relatively unequal power relations. He claims that multiple forms of masculinity exist but notes that we are also witnessing the emergence of the man who places family relations ahead of career. At the same time, he suggests that men say, rather than actually do, the new fatherhood thing in an effort to protect their public image. Yes, they help with the children more than their predecessors did, but child care remains the domain of women. Hoff-Sommers (2000, pp. 196–197) claims that parents, churches, and schools need to come together to provide and enforce traditional moral standards and discipline, and to stop denigrating masculinity in our boys and men.

OTHER GENDERED MOVEMENTS

Many positive changes in women's lives have resulted from the various movements concerning gender, among them economic opportunities, antidiscrimination policies, and positive self-esteem for women. Yet the successes of feminism have led to an intense countermovement, or backlash (Faludi, 1991; Wolf, 1992). Both Faludi and Wolf report a widespread conspiracy against women to prevent them from making use of their hard-won freedoms, to punish them for liberating themselves. Despite their outcry, no real organized effort of antifeminism groups exists for the purpose of attempting to undermine the confidence of women, nor obstructing their efforts toward equality. However, in the early 70's Morgan's (1973) book *The Total Woman* suggested women should return to their traditional attitudes, values, and roles in life, ideas opposed by feminists. Andeline (1975) advocates that women return to embodying moral purity and being submissive to their husbands. Schlafly effectively stopped the Equal Rights Amendment (ERA) in 1970 and defeated feminist efforts to gain recognition of women's equality on a constitutional level.

Faludi (1991) describes two themes of backlash: the first defines feminism as the source of women's problems, as well as broken homes, tension between spouses, and delinquent children; the second argues women never had it so good and should stop whining and enjoy their new freedom. Feminists have generated much antidiscrimination legislation that opened many doors, and women no longer need them to fight for them. This idea resonates with many women under the age of thirty because they have not experienced oppression in the same way as the older generation of feminists, explaining in part third wave feminism.

Generally, the backlash against feminism operates as disparate ideas emerging from individuals dissatisfied with the turn of feminism within the late 80's and early 90's. Although individuals voiced their dissatisfaction with feminism, no real organized following developed until about the middle 90's, when Hoff-Sommers's (1994) *Who Stole Feminism?* expressed strong opposition to certain feminists. Hoff-Sommers, a feminist herself, argues that radical feminists veered way off course in efforts to trump up charges of problems that did not exist, at least not to the extent feminists claim they did, for the sake of getting legislation passed. She claims feminists falsified research findings, misinterpreted statistical reports, and lied about problems just to make a point. Hoff-Sommers (1994, p. 24) defines these women as "gender feminists" who have "taken a divisive, gynocentric turn," an emphasis that has placed women in a political class whose interests are at odds with the interests of men. "Women must be loyal to women, united in principled hostility to the males who seek to hold fast to their patriarchal privileges and powers" (Hoff-Sommers 1994, p. 24). Hoff-Sommers says once women believe they experience life as a subjugated gender, they are primed to be angry and resentful against men as oppressors; prepared to believe the worst about them and their harming of women: "They may even be ready to fabricate atrocities" (Hoff-Sommers, 1994, p. 42); she claims, "radical and socialist feminists showed the old ideals of freedom, equality, and democracy as insufficient." Hoff-Sommers (2000, p. 14) claims that feminists have made it "fashionable to attribute pathology" to healthy male children.

The Women's Freedom Network formed in an effort to represent women who disagree with the feminism of the 90's, opposing the notion of woman as victim and man as enemy. Their effort involves uniting men and women and emphasizing rational judgment. A more extreme conservative group, Concerned Women of America, focuses on fighting the liberal, anti-Christian agenda, often taking on feminism as an enemy, particularly on the abortion issue, but this group also rallies against homosexuality and advocates submission to the husband as the head of the home.

The Million Man March, promoted by Louis Farrakhan and Benjamin Chavis, acted as a ritual renewal for black men. The gathering was intended to express a determination to make permanent changes in black communities. The march succeeded in countering stereotypes of black men as violent, bereft of mainstream values, with no interest in spiritual or moral matters, blaming social structures or blind forces for their problems (Dyson, 1995). The prevailing objection by feminists (especially womanists) called attention to the failure to address the issue of the treatment of black women by black men or to express repentance for misogyny, sexism, and patriarchy. The appearances of Dorothy Height, Maya Angelou, and Betty Shabazz attempted to counter complaints by black women who wanted to be included; instead their inclusion was seen as a token gesture. Black men marched to proclaim their desire to be better sons to their mothers, better husbands to their wives, better fathers to their daughters. Womanists argued the march was a throwback to the times when women were expected to stay on the sidelines to cheer on the men. For many women, the march was an effort to reconstitute patriarchy (Dyson, 1995).

The male-only gatherings of Promise Keepers also angered feminists, especially Patricia Ireland, head of NOW, who harshly criticized it. Her "dark warnings about patriarchy and a right-wing political takeover" (Leo, 1997, p. 16) denounced the Promise Keepers as a militaristic, antiwoman organization posing a great danger to women's rights (Kersten, 1997). Her comments may have been prompted by the Pauline tradition of male leadership in the home. Many feminists believe conservative Christian women become the dupes of their male oppressors in the patriarchy by accepting such roles.

Antifeminists claim the family acts as the most fundamental unit of society, not the individual. More than any other force, it shapes the values, attitudes, and beliefs of children. When the family collapses, children suffer first; then the community itself does. Once communities begin to decay, governments often step in and offer policies that represent different things to different people. To orthodoxy the policies may appear to promote indolence, promiscuity, readily available abortion, and parental indifference to the task of child rearing. To feminists, the policies may appear to promote freedom from oppression. Additionally, many women who prefer to be homemakers feel their role has been diminished by feminists, who characterize it as a career choice that makes slaves of women (Friedan, 1981). By discouraging women from having children or encouraging them to postpone motherhood until they have established a career, have had multiple abortions, or have waited until pregnancy was a risk to their health, feminism impacted the family negatively. Obsessed with self and fulfilling material and personal needs, feminism appeared to many women to be seeking to enrich some women at the expense of others, not unlike many other values in America.

CONCLUSION

Rhetorical movements aimed at changing social views and policies about men and women have contributed to the cultural conversation about gender. Articulating the concerns of women, feminist views advocated two movements, one promoting women's equality with men and one proclaiming women's difference from men. Curiously, these diverse views combined to secure many basic rights for women, including suffrage. Feminist activists first rallied around the suffrage movement in 1840; they were later known as the first wave of feminism. The second wave began around 1963 with the publication of Friedan's *The Feminine Mystique*. Feminist activists rallied around rhetorical strategies aimed at defining women's nature, rights, and roles in opposition to the "traditional" wife role. The third wave of feminism, floundering for a definition, began in the late 80's as younger academic feminists were unable to identify with the problems of the first and second waves of feminism, partly because they were marrying later and enjoying more independence than their predecessors. They now advocate a vision of becoming a national network for young feminists from diverse cultural and economic backgrounds, consolidating a strong base of membership who could mobilize for specific issues, political candidates, and events.

Men's movements articulated a variety of views ranging from profeminist to ultramacho. Many men joined forces with women to speak for equity and freedom from oppressive social expectations for men. Some of these men became discouraged by the oppressive strategies of the women's movement against men. Others believed men had forgotten how to be men and needed to rediscover and cultivate a distinctively male mode of feeling and relating to other men. Large male gatherings such as those of the Promise Keepers and the Million Man March articulated views of men who wanted to take responsibility for their homes and families. Some feminists feared these ideas would set women back into patriarchal oppression.

The backlash movement appeared critical of feminism and attempted to blame it for many of the social ills in American culture. From some groups criticisms about masking hidden political agendas, falsifying research findings, falsifying reports leading to legislation and generalizations about hysterical feminists caused many women to regard feminism as something they wanted to avoid. Some feminists described a fear of the backlash as a "melange of messages" (Wood, 1994, p. 120) from disorganized voices aiming to stop further feminist efforts and reverse some of the victories won through women's activism.

3

Gender Communication and Religion

Let those who do not practice all they preach stop preaching long
enough to catch up.

Anonymous

PORTRAIT ONE

Suzanne dreamed of marrying, having a family, and being at home taking
care of her children. After a few years of what she thought was complete
happiness she and her husband divorced and Suzanne then had the responsibility of raising the children alone while working full time. She
claimed that she did not receive equal pay for equal work and would have
sued the company if she had been smarter. Later she remarried and began
working in her home to contribute to the financial status of the family. She
expected equity in work roles for women and equity in roles at home. She
did not believe she could ever submit to her husband's authority, either in
a spiritual or in a secular sense. In fact, she believed women, more often
than not, acted as the spiritual leaders of their homes. She believed women
took more time to read and understand Scripture, and men focused more
on work matters. Suzanne believed women of faith should follow extremely
restrictive rules in the church. She believed that women in the church had
substantial power and influence and could witness in many other ways than
in the pulpit.

PORTRAIT TWO

Nazum lived with her parents and she remained a virgin until she married. She attended the university and studied sociology, received her master's and doctoral degrees, and planned to teach in a university. Her parents arranged her marriage to her husband, but she could have refused their choice if she had found the man disagreeable after meeting him. The couple became acquainted with one another after the engagement through exchanges between the families, information collected from others, and specifics related to issues of character. They periodically met while chaperoned and graciously accepted one another with a spirit of adventure. Having both been raised Hindu, both accepted the traditional method of finding a spouse. Nazum became a teacher, raised three children, and accepted her husband as the authority in the home. Living in India would have prevented Nazum from enjoying many liberties she enjoyed in America. Both she and her husband advocated equal rights for women in the workplace. Nazum's husband always accepted her arguing her case in any situation that caused controversy between the couple, but his word was accepted as final.

PORTRAIT THREE

Homa always wanted to marry a man who would give her a stable lifestyle. She did not want to work outside, but rather to care for the children in their home. She thought women possessed more skill in child rearing and fit into that role more naturally than men. She believed in traditional roles for women of faith, agreeing with the Holy Qur'an (Koran), which was interpreted as saying women should not hold leadership positions in the faith. Homa felt that her religious beliefs guided her life at home because the hierarchy of the relationship was defined by Scripture. At home she took complete charge of all domestic work unless her husband disapproved, and that rarely happened. She believed the female body should be covered, but she did not wear the traditional Islamic chador. She believed women deserved equal pay for equal work and should have an equal opportunity to strive for any job. She, however, did not work. She participated as a contributor to and decision maker for the family, yet recognized that in any complex relationship final authority must rest with one person. She contentedly relegated authority to her husband, father, or other male relative in the family structure and appreciated the support and protection it gave her and her children.

PORTRAIT FOUR

Karen always wanted a career. When she married she went right to work in her career and over time advanced to a management position with her company. Her work role provided her authority over men and a substantial salary. When Karen's husband lost his job, she played the role of major breadwinner. In her work role she advocated a feminist ideology and used a team approach when operating her department. At home Karen and her husband shared responsibilities and decision making equally. She believed her faith advocated that men and women be partners. She chose not to have children because she did not want to experience the conflict between work and family. Karen believed that because of their faith, she and her husband, Tom, had experienced a wholesome partnership, always reconciling after difficult disputes, enabling them to see one another with a forgiving spirit. In addition, she believed her faith provided her life with a blueprint, a structure promoting order in both of their lives. As people of faith, they both worked toward the mutual goal of protecting their personal relationship.

THE PROBLEM

These four women represent a variety of attitudes and roles experienced within the marital structure. Each woman expresses adherence to two apparently opposing ideologies at the same time: traditionalism and feminism. In the second half of the twentieth century great changes occurred in the roles of women and in the American family structure. Inspiring these changes, two opposing moral visions of American society still struggle to win the culture war. That war characterizes *traditionalism* as commitment to an external, definable, stable, transcendent authority and characterizes *progressivism* as a tendency to resymbolize historic faiths according to prevailing assumptions of contemporary life. This includes an authority structure emerging from individual rights and choices, shifting over time. The four women described here reflect roles drawn from these two opposing ideologies. The two sides of these opposing ideologies have both faith and secular adherents, but the culture war cuts across all boundaries (Hunter, 1991). Any modernizing society includes primary values from both a progressive-secular (in the late twentieth century it was called *humanistic-feminist*) and a traditional-sacred (faith) worldview, and these worldviews often contradict each other. As societies modernize, the work of maintaining so-called traditional institutions has typically been assigned to members of the population defined as relational (women), as members of the population defined as rational (men) have enacted the values of the progressive-secular worldview (Beck, 1996). As women demanded equal work opportunities in progressive terms, many women took over the progressive-secular worldview. The traditional-sacred view laid the responsibility for the moral education of children mainly on women, not because it was required, but rather because it just happened. So, as women became increasingly humanistic-feminist in the late twentieth century, society was left without anyone to care for traditional institutions or dependent people.

The transformative power of the overall feminization of America and faith traditions has led to tension in various faiths and in relationships between men and women. Given all this, both sides of the culture war between humanist-feminist and traditional-faith adherents portray one another as exceedingly dangerous forces in American life. Consequently, individuals who hold values from both humanistic-feminism and traditional faith often experience cognitive dissonance (Festinger, 1957). *Cognitive dissonance* occurs when individuals act in ways contradicting their beliefs or hear information conflicting with their existing belief system. They experience dissonance, or psychological discomfort, which motivates them to change some of their beliefs and behavior or avoid the situations and the information that are aggravating the dissonance. Festinger, however, believes people can hold two opposing views at the same time.

PURPOSE

This chapter describes the communication strategies employed to alienate the proponents of traditional-sacred and feminist-secular ideas from each other. It examines the roots of the traditional-sacred/humanist-feminist debate, comparing and contrasting traditional ideologies with feminist ideologies. It analyzes the communication strategies humanistic feminists use to influence and refute traditionalists, as well as those traditionalists use to refute humanist-feminists. The roots of the traditional/feminist debate are examined in terms of religious contexts, and the resulting culture war is discussed with regard to the decline of the family. Finally, this chapter explains various cognitive dissonance strategies used by women and men to reconcile feminism with traditional ideologies.

ROOTS OF THE TRADITIONALISM/ HUMANISM-FEMINISM DEBATE

Women and men around the world experience life differently across various religions, cultures, and periods. In understanding sex roles and their interrelated patterns, extreme aspects of historical stereotypes provide some measure of truth. One common feature of the great variety of world religions is the patriarchal nature of their belief systems. But what does that mean? Does characterizing them as patriarchal mean the various faiths project supremacy of the father in the clan or family and the legal dependence of wives and children without right of inheritance, or does it merely indicate descent and succession of social organization as traced through the male line (Webster, 1984)? History provides evidence that men prepared the written sacred Scriptures, with divine inspiration (depending on the religion). Although the original Scriptures indicate equality of the sexes, other factors contribute to a reinterpretation of those Scriptures challenging the egalitarian nature of the relationship between men and women. What then changed the nature of the relationship?

Sanday (1981) claims social organization helps men and women orient themselves as males and females. Although the culture decides the sex roles of its members, the choice of how individuals play them out is determined by the needs, desires, and power of the members of that society. Ancient concepts of sacred power often determine power roles between the sexes (Sanday, 1981, xv). Though male deities often set a pattern for male dominance within cultures, a study of world religions often negates this correlation. For example, early Buddhism had deities of both genders, yet it advocated and organized society according to a patriarchal organization. Hindu, Taoism, and Confucianism followed a similar pattern of deity worship with some female deities but inherited a male-dominated social system (Young, 1987). Some of the most important temples of worship for the Chhattisgarhi Hindus were devoted to Goddess worship (Babb, 1975).

During the formative period of the world's older religions, "Judaism, Brahmanism (early Hinduism), and Confucianism, which influenced the others by defining the prevailing social structure, extreme male dominance developed at a time of great social stress" (Young, 1987, p. 9). Sagan (1985) argues that societies evolved over time, from those based on kinship orientation to those organized around centralized leadership, which had the power to reward or oppress. As societies became more complex, leaders began struggling for more land and power, warring with other ethnic groups, imposing new ethnic identities on them, raping their women, and destroying their way of life. Taking a woman away from another man or another kingdom not only defiled the woman but polluted the genes of the defeated kingdom. Increasing anxiety about women, maintenance of protection and dominion over women, increasingly rigid role definitions, exclusion of women from political and economic decision making, all contributed to the rise of kingdoms and the overturning of egalitarian role relationships between women and men.

In the rise of kingdoms, men expressed their dominion over their wives by being authoritarian. "He had the best of the food, which she kept waiting at his wish" (Sanday, 1981, p. 164). Separation of the sexes and creation of specific sex-linked tasks also became features of the social structure. Schools were the exclusive sphere of males, men and women could not eat together, women became property, and women could not inherit. Sagan (1985) describes how boys were required to separate themselves from their mothers, producing an intensity of separation anxiety for both mother and child. Boys then identified with their fathers through initiation ceremonies into male society and other exclusive male domains, helping them disengage from their mothers. Men then faced death as warriors and envied the privileged position of women, who, because of their primary role in the reproductive process, had to be protected (Young, 1987). How does the concept of role differentiation play itself out in various world religions?

The primary purpose of all religions is to provide salvation for their adherents. What constitutes salvation and how one achieves it vary among the many religions of the world. That the term *salvation* can be used in connection with so many religions indicates that it is a distinguishing notion common to a wide range of cultural traditions; the term refers to the saving or delivering of humankind from some dire situation. The fact that humanity is in some dire situation itself implies a series of related assumptions about human nature and destiny. The first of these assumptions relates to the way human beings ended up in this dire situation. The major world religions take two distinct views on this issue: (1) Humankind shattered a previous ideal state by rebellion against God, which caused death to enter the world: a moral error that indicates that humankind is basically bad; (2) humankind plays out a role in the battle between two opposing forces—good and evil, light and darkness, life and death—in which they make an intellectual error that can be corrected on Earth: humankind is basically good. Additionally, religions view humankind as essentially a psychophysical organism: salvation separates and then reunites body and soul, or the intrinsically evil physical body corrupts the soul, and salvation releases the soul from the body. The phenomenon of sexual intercourse plays an important but ambiguous role in issues of salvation. On the one hand it provides the means for reproducing life; on the other, it provides pleasure, which has the potential for distracting both the moral and the intellectual aspects of humankind from the pursuit of salvation. Consequently, women are often seen as the seducers of men, who must be controlled to prevent men from falling into sin, and risking the loss of salvation.

An examination of the main world religions helps identify the source of some of the arguments on the opposing sides of the traditional-sacred versus humanistic-secular worldviews. This chapter will look at when and where the religion first came about, what people adopted the philosophical or religious ideology, who founded it, and how one acquires salvation. The distinctive role of women in each religious ideology reflects some aspects of the patriarchal theme. The religions discussed—Hinduism, Buddhism, Confucianism, Taoism, Judaism, Christianity, and Islam—have impacted the culture war in America, the melting pot, by providing arguments for both worldviews.

Hinduism

Most Hindus live in India and parts of Pakistan, Bangladesh, Sri Lanka, Nepal, and Sikkim. The Rgveda, the earliest literary text of Hinduism, reflects a sacrificial religious system known as *Brahmanism* or *Vedism*, the text of which consists mostly of hymns (Kadoduala, 1997). Chiefly composed during the second millennium, the Rgveda originated from a nomadic tribal people, previously inhabiting the steppe country of southern Russia and Central Asia, who called themselves *Aryans*. Much of early Hinduism emerges from the period of Brahmanism with strict adherence to a patrilineal tradition. With men working the herds and warring to hold back the northern invaders, separation of the sexes became inevitable. Survival rather than oppression determined the early importance of men because the society needed male children to preserve the group and to protect the community (Young, 1987).

Gradually, male importance became slightly modified with a new appreciation of the "couple" and recognition of the importance of females to reproduction. Unfortunately, the importance of feminine purity to the reproductive process, which reflected on the status of fathers as well as husbands, mandated male control. "The valued though potentially dangerous sexual and reproductive powers of women are rigorously controlled by men through such extreme institutions as child marriage, purdah, no divorce for women, a prohibition against widow remarriage, and either the social isolation through stigmatization or the burning of widows" (Allen, 1982, p. 8). Consequently, marrying off daughters early, even before menstruation, helped protect families from the threat of a female's becoming unchaste and released parents from their responsibilities for the daughter (Young, 1987).

The concept of transmigration, or the doctrine of rebirth, became a central theme in Hinduism. The growth of asceticism (renouncing the world and attaining *moksa*, or liberation from rebirth) became the "psychology of masculine thinking, but women were to be oriented to rebirth" (Young, 1987, p. 69). Status for women was defined by the absence of learning, yet to maintain her husband's status a woman needed to be cultured in aesthetic dimensions of the home. Obeyesekere (1984) asserts that a Hindu woman was expected to treat her husband as "the supreme and only one," a "god," to speak to him without anger or hostility, only with gentleness and amiability (Shastri, 1969). This "human god" no doubt sometimes disappointed her, leaving her to look to more ideal surrogates, such as gurus.

Various communication strategies led to improvements in the life of women. Advocates for change said that a practice that was not specified in the Rgveda must have resulted from social evolution and should no longer be practiced. Other tactics to effect changes were the arguments that a specific action was not to be practiced in the present age and that norms for behavior should be set by the "good people" of the region (Young, 1987). No one introduced more change beneficial to women than Gandhi, who released women from a domestic orientation to one that allowed them full participation in education, economics, and politics (Kalelkar, 1960).

Confucianism

Confucianism represents a way of life founded by Confucius in the fifth and sixth centuries B.C. and has been followed by Chinese people for more than two millennia. Its influence has spread to Korea, Japan, and Vietnam. Some people regard Confucianism as a religion, but generally it is viewed as a system of learning moral values and human relationships. A central core teaching of Confucianism entails a hierarchy based in the cosmic order of things: the yin and yang. The three points of central doctrine in Confucianism are that heaven created life, everything in life is relational, and all life should be harmonious. "The cosmic order did not involve worship, but rather engendered learning from the heavens, imitating the behavior of the gods, forming a human order modeled upon the cosmic order" (Kelleher, 1987, p. 136). The family became a revered sacred community as the source for the renewal of life; appreciation of the parents, and of their parents became the basis for ancestral worship. Specific ceremonial behavior for every conceivable human interaction provided a pattern for people to follow in daily life and in special rites of passage.

The hierarchy of the cosmic order is applied to human relationships. Parents and husbands occupy superior positions; children and wives, inferior positions. In fact, the man is so important that he is often spoken of in the same breath with heaven and Earth to form a triad. Women play a central role in Confucianism by virtue of their place in both the cosmic order and the family. The role of wife is the focal point of a woman's life, and marriage usually occurs when she is twenty. She ensures her status in the family by having sons. Although Confucianism does not represent a way to achieve a place in heaven, it does represent an opportunity for the realization of the fullness of life by a total immersion in humankind through service to society. That immersion provides an identification with the cosmic order in such a way as to contribute to the powers of heaven. Males can achieve this through becoming "sages," whereas women achieve it through being submissive to their husband and obedient to their in-laws and making contributions to their family. Confucianism lends itself to the victimization of women through such practices as foot binding, female infanticide, prostitution, and the slave trade, but it also gives women a sense of self-discipline, appreciation for education, and respect for public service, enabling them to contribute to society (Kelleher, 1987).

Confucianism underwent a series of evolutions throughout the various Chinese dynasties. Confucious believed in the goodness of humankind; evil was acquired. He said the superior person understands right from wrong; the inferior person understands what is profitable. Later, Hsun-tzu declared that "the nature of humankind is evil; goodness is acquired" (*Encyclopaedia Britannica*, 1979, p. 1094). During the Han dynasty and for seven centuries thereafter, both Taoism and Buddhism took hold and appeared to appeal specifically to women. Various attempts to marry Confucianism with other schools of thought brought about a variety of undesirable effects. The greatest reforms for women occurred when the Communists formed the People's Republic of China. Women then joined the work force, began to hold public office, and made contributions to society through public service.

Buddhism

The spread of Buddhism over India, Sri Lanka, Central and Southeast Asia, China, Korea, and Japan began in the sixth century B.C. with the teaching of Siddhartha Gautama, the Buddha (Cush, 1997). The influential role Buddhism played in the spiritual, cultural, and social life of much of the ancient Eastern world endured throughout the late twentieth century, attracting increased interest and some followers in the West. The works regarded as the sacred literature of Buddhism consist of original teachings of the Buddha, as well as the various philosophical and religious works of all major forms of Buddhism. The literature emanated within the community of monks (little evidence of writings from women exist) and helped them realize a goal. The central theme of Buddhism is that its adherents strive to realize Nirvana (a state of oblivion to care, pain, or external reality) (Barnes, 1987).

An agnostic philosophy, rejecting both the concept of a personal creator and personal immortality, the nexus of Buddhism centers around the quest for release from all that is worldly: the emptying of the self. The Buddhist saint transcends worldliness in one of two ways: through self-concentration (curiously, one empties the self by focusing on the self) and through self-sacrifice of behalf of others. To transcend all human imperfections and attain enlightenment, a Buddhist may be required to live more than one, if not many, lives.

Most of the main schools of Buddhism thriving today advocate full egalitarian doctrines. A doctrinal effort to prove women were karmically inferior to men and therefore unable to reach the stage of enlightenment failed because it was generally believed to be "antithetical to Buddhist doctrine" (Barnes, 1987, p. 131). Buddhist doctrine holds that all human beings are made up of a psychology that includes both maleness and femaleness. Women can reject the traditional role of wife and live together as "laywomen in communal groups or live in Buddhist run communities" (Topley, 1975). Most of the problems among Buddhist women today originated in "deeply rooted social values" (Barnes, 1987, p. 131) rather than the tenets of Buddhism.

Taoism

The sixth-century-B.C. Chinese philosopher Lao-tzu founded Taoism, a major political, social, religious, and scientific influence on China, and all cultures influenced by China, especially those of Vietnam, Japan, Taiwan, Hong Kong, and Korea. Its later commentators, Chuang-tzu and Lieh-tzu, also influenced what has become known as the *Tao*, or the Way (McFarlane, 1997). Characterized by a positive, active attitude toward the occult and the metaphysical, Taoism focuses on longevity and immortality, humankind and the universe, simplicity and happiness, and primitive, spontaneous behavior, yielding to and following nature. Writings advocate breathing exercises, special dietary habits, alchemy, and specific sexual practices designed in the context of the theory of yin and yang for the purpose of extending life (Reed, 1987). They make use of *shamans* who use magic to cure the sick, divine the hidden, and control events. The Way refers to a code of behavior and a doctrine, an effort to restore order to nature by imitating the Way of Heaven (McFarlane, 1997). The Taoist canon (sacred literature) is both philosophical and esoteric (designed and understood by the initiated).

Taoism advocates the harmony and equality of all opposites, including male and female. Important female images represent creative powers, and the status of women is equal to that of men. Women fully participate in Taoist leadership and ordination, except at the highest rank, Divine Lord (Maspero, 1981). Originally intending complete harmony between the sexes, Taoism has experienced some transformations resulting from its close association with Confucianism and Buddhism in China, both extremely patriarchal in nature. In Taoist thinking, *yin* represents the dark side, inwardness, the cold, the shade or cloud, the damp, passivity, the female (Reed, 1987). *Yang* represents the sunny side, brightness, stimulation, vigor, movement, the hot, the dry, the male (Reed, 1987). The ideal involves balance, not the victory of one over the other. Taoist harmony differs from the Western view of dualism: good over evil. In Taoist harmony, the two sides (yin and yang) depend on each other for their existence. Balancing the two sides, the mutual interaction of the two forces produces harmony in society and nature. Taoism today is based on the power of the female and interdependence of male and female. "The creative principle is symbolically female because Tao is like an empty womb, the origin of all things. However, the former positive views of women's sexuality and public leadership have been modified by Chinese Buddhism and Confucianism" (Reed, 1987, p. 181).

Judaism

The religion of the Jews, a specific ethnic community (membership in which is constituted by birth, or conversion), is based on the belief in a unique divine revelation, election, and covenant with God. The historical account of Judaism distinguishes it as a unique religion in that its members have experienced God's presence in human events, as a people special to God to be set apart to reflect (through good works) and be a witness to God's holiness. The presence of God—in person—revealed the pattern and structure of communal and individual life to his chosen people. God created a covenant with Israel requiring obedience to the Torah (the sacred Scripture) of the Jews; God would remain sovereign over the people in his promise of salvation through a Messiah (Lancaster, 1997). The concept of salvation has been primarily conceived in terms of the destiny of Israel as the elect people of God but includes those who have been "grafted" into the faith: the Gentiles.

History proved the impossibility of living in accord with obedience to the law, and over and over again the Jews failed, were called back to the covenant through the prophets (humans who spoke on God's behalf), were warned about possible retribution, repented, and were forgiven. The purpose of the law was to instill in Jews the recognition of their complete dependence upon God's mercy. Jews believe the choice to obey God rests in an ethical, intellectual decision; the Jewish tradition traces this choice to one of humankind rather than an individual assisted by heaven. At the appointed time God will judge the wicked and relegate them to *sheol* (hell), whereas the righteous will be transformed and transported into a new world where creation will be restored (Lancaster, 1997).

The covenantal relationship between God and Judaism gives Jewish people a strong ethnic self-consciousness throughout their long history. Holiness became a preoccupation for men, often causing negative attitudes toward women. The Pharisees thought of women as inferior to men, evil, filled with the spirit of fornication, plotting against men, and gave men stern warnings to take care. The preservation of the kingdom led "Jewish women to sacrifice personal fulfillment for the sake of national survival" (Poupko & Wohlgelernter, 1976, pp. 48, 49). The importance of ethnic purity led girls to marry at a very early age to ensure virginity (the same was not true of boys). If the husband could prove his wife was not a virgin, he could have her stoned. Male property rights included the wife, so violation of property rights was incorporated within the concept of adultery. The imagery of the Hebrew God embraced both masculine and feminine, but as Jews interpreted the Talmud, it severely restricted women's roles and offered them an ambivalent self-image (Carmody, 1987). Efforts to upgrade the status of women have focused on reinterpreting the talmudic legislation (Berkovits, 1978). Current Jewish feminists have devised new religious rituals excluding men such as during the Jewish seder. Another new ritual replaces and downplays Moses' role in the opening of the Red Sea by God with a celebration of the supportive role of his wife Mirriam. In the ritual, the symbolic Mirriam provides a chalice of red wine.

Christianity

Christianity began about two thousand years ago in what is now known as modern Israel, inspired by Jesus of Nazareth. Believers recognize Jesus as the Messiah predicted in Judaism, who provides salvation through his incarnation, perfect obedience to the law, sacrificial death, and resurrection. Christians believe that Jesus died on the cross for the sins of *all* people and that when a person comes to believe that, he or she becomes a Christian. Christians believe Jesus is the *only* way to heaven. The basic belief in the divinity of Jesus is central to the doctrine of Christianity. It is recognized as the largest of the world religions, with more than 1 billion adherents throughout the world. The soteriological evaluation of history finds expression in the Christian division of time into two periods, before Christ (B.C.) and after Christ, "in the year of the Lord" (*anno domini*) (A.D.) (*Encyclopaedia Britannica*, 1979). After three centuries of persecution, Christianity became the official religion of the Roman empire. The center of the Catholic church remains in Rome to this day (Holmwood, 1997).

Christians believe humankind is deserving of damnation for the original sin inherited by descent from Adam, and for individual personal sin. They believe doing good is made possible by the indwelling power of the Holy Spirit (God/Jesus in spirit form) and cannot be accomplished apart from God and therefore glorifies Him. They believe all good done by humankind apart from God reflects on humankind, rather than on God; therefore, to God such works are of no value. Because of what Christ has done on behalf of humankind, Christianity has been described as the most desirable salvation religion because it is the only religion in which salvation has been accomplished on behalf of humankind without any "assistance" by human beings.

Protestantism emerged out of the Reformation, a time when reformers adopted what some describe as a patriarchal reading of the Pauline tradition enjoining silence and submission on women both within the order of creation and as a means of discipline for the sin of Eve (Ruether, 1987). The interpretation suggests Adam and Eve enjoyed equality in the garden of Eden, but the doctrine changed because of Eve's primacy in sin, when women lost their original equality with males and began to suffer subjection to the rule of husbands. Other perspectives describe the silence of women and their absence from leadership positions within the church as forms of protection for them. In the nineteenth century, people became confused by the different but complementary natures of men and women, as opposed to the feminist idea that men and women were basically the same. Some progressive denominations ordain women, but many traditional denominations do not (Ruether, 1987). Christianity often fails to explain adequately the combination of the tradition of a benevolent hierarchical order and a partnership relationship in marriage. Roles for women within the public worship service continue to arouse conflict and debate.

Islam

Islam arose in Arabia during the seventh century A.D. as a result of the preaching and teaching of Muhammad, who is believed to be the last prophet in a long line of prophets sent from God. Moslems (Islamic people) live all over the world but are concentrated in the Middle Eastern countries, as well as Pakistan, India, Africa, Indonesia, and China. The sacred Scripture, the Qur'an (Koran), is regarded as the Word of God delivered by the angel Gabriel to the prophet Muhammad, who inculcated a sense of brotherhood and a bond of faith within the entire Islamic population that generated an emphasis on community. Anyone who attempts to harm the interests of the community receives harsh punishment. Moslems believe they have been commissioned by God to carry the religious and social character of Islam, along with its value system, to the world through the jihad (holy war) (*Encyclopaedia Britannica*, 1979).

The basic aim of Islam is salvation, avoidance of future punishment at the Last Judgment. Submission to God (Allah) is the means to salvation, for Allah is thought to be merciful. Adherents must accept the basic beliefs in (1) angels (hence the message from Gabriel), (2) the sacred books (Jewish, Christian, Zoroastrian, and Hindu, in addition to the Qur'an), (3) a series of prophets, and (4) the Last Day of Judgment (*Encyclopaedia Britannica*, 1979). Moslems are required to perform specified actions: praying five times a day, paying a welfare tax called the *zakat*, fasting, and making a pilgrimage to Mecca.

When some Islamic women attempt to diverge from tradition, most men and women resist the idea, even when confronted with contemporary ideologies. Many women want to take part in the full functioning of society, to take advantage of educational and professional opportunities. On the other hand, male attitudes conditioned by the tradition of Islam, although not necessarily supported by the Qur'an itself, have been and continue to be influential in determining what opportunities are available for women. In extremely conservative Islamic traditions women must cover their faces and bodies when they are in public places and must never defy the rule of their husband (Smith, 1987). The movie *Not without My Daughter* depicted such a relationship.

Traditional and Feminist Ideologies

The struggle between traditional-sacred and secular humanistic-feminist ideologies creates tensions in many world religions. Exactly what does each of these ideologies represent? The traditional-sacred belief system is based on God, creation, morality, the fallen state of humankind, redemption through faith, often the free enterprise capitalist system, and specific but flexible roles for males and females. Secular humanism believes in the actualization of the self. The theory of evolution, amorality, the basic goodness of human beings, and often a one-world socialist system. In secular humanism, individuals observe their own changing values, and society is blamed for the consequences of the actions of its members. Humanism generally advocates equality of opportunity for the sexes, and many of the more radical tenets of feminism agree with those of humanism. For example, some feminists agree with humanists who believe that no certainty or truth exists because of constant change (evolution), or because of personal perception, and therefore law must be continually changed. Traditionalists, on the other hand, believe the law derives from a higher, unchanging source. Rowe (1985) describes the major differences between traditionalists and humanists as follows: Traditionalists believe men and women differ, whereas humanists believe men and women do not differ. Traditionalists believe faith and sex belong together within marriage for the purpose of procreation, which happens to be pleasurable. According to Rowe, humanist groups believe that pleasure is the purpose of sex, which happens to lead to procreation. Traditionalists believe in absolute rights and wrongs; humanists believe individual choice operates as the basic determinant of rights and wrongs. Rowe says that traditionalists believe the family is the basic unit of society, whereas humanists believe the individual is. Traditionalists believe homosexuality is wrong; humanists believe it is not wrong. Traditionalists believe abortion, suicide, and euthanasia are wrong, and humanists think choices such as these should be up to the individual (Rowe, 1985).

Traditionist believe that children need the moral education associated with "Aristotelian ethical theory and Judeo-Christian religion and practice" (Hoff-Sommers, 2000, p. 192). Humanists believe children are born without sin and it is society that corrupts them, so democratizing the classroom leads to social justice, consistent with theories of Rousseau (Hoff-Sommers, 2000 pp. 191, 192). These differences in the basic ideologies of traditionalism and humanism lead to cognitive dissonance for traditional women and men of faith who have been exposed to humanist philosophies, often in much of feminist rhetoric. Radical feminists also feel dissonance when confronted with traditional women and men who believe in interdependence with their mates and dependence upon faith. One traditional woman told me about a conversation she had with a feminist: "I told her I had to pray about a particular decision that weighed heavily on me." The radical feminist told her, "I have no respect for someone who is that dependent on someone else." The traditional woman thought, but did not respond, "I have no respect for someone who acts that independent of God." The two appeared to be operating from polar ideologies and concepts about the interaction between faith and self.

Traditional gender norms maintain patriarchal notions governing the role of women within the home and the church, including the wife's submission to the authority of the husband and teaching of moral values in the role of care giver (Brown, 1984). Traditionalists consider complete abdication of authority over one's own life (relinquished to the husband) excessive. Generally, traditionalists resist women's ordination and promote "family values." Women may exercise their prerogative of working outside the home to contribute to its economic support (Glenn, 1990), and they may pursue university education (Weissman, 1976). In the traditional family, doctrines of male authority are subject to each person's relationship to God. Traditional norms advocate the definable, transcendent authority of God, whom the patriarchal male supposedly models himself after in the family. The survival of the "traditional family" and maintenance of patriarchal gender roles within it are thought to be essential to a healthy society.

Humanism is characterized by a tendency to resymbolize historic religions according to prevailing norms of contemporary life. Daly (1968, p. 19) says, "If God is male, then the male is God," suggesting that the concept of God as male serves to define men and male roles. Characteristics associated with God, such as strength, wisdom, and dependability, are typically associated with men, whereas the corollary values applied to humanity, such as weakness, vacillation, sin, and ignorance, are stereotypically applied to women (Eve). Consequently, feminist philosophers of religion often reject the idea of a transcendent God in favor of a totally immanent God. They often replace god with goddess, suggest changes in the linguistic structures of sacred texts, and reconceptualize the suppositions about the nature of reality itself (Suchoki, 1994). Feminists argue that the traditional family oppresses women and reveres men (Friedan, 1981). The idea of patriarchal authority in the home angers many feminists, who adamantly oppose it. Consequently, feminists have encouraged women to participate in the public sphere, reducing the importance of their roles as wives and mothers. Stacey (1990), however, claims that women entered the workplace as a result of economic necessity and increased opportunity rather than acceptance of feminist ideas.

THE INFLUENCE OF FEMINISM ON THE CHURCH

The impact of feminism on society has penetrated systems of faith; traditionalists resist that impact but cannot escape its influence. Each religious group (Judaism, Protestantism, Catholicism, Hinduism, Buddhism, Islam, and Taoism) has dealt with feminism within its own denomination in different ways. Feminists have challenged the authority of Scripture and tradition, the legitimization of the subordination of women, and the support of the exclusion of women from ritual and religious leadership. In the larger society, traditionalists oppose feminism, but within systems of faith it poses a much greater challenge. Feminists within those systems press for changes in women's roles within the church, especially ordination. Additionally, they press for marital partnership rather than male headship, as interpreted in written texts of faith.

As a strategy for accessing women of faith, feminists publish articles in religious periodicals, where many women first encounter feminism (Bendroth, 1993). *Christianity Today* publishes many articles promoting feminist concerns, but many church leaders still preach male headship. In the Catholic church, Rome's push for higher education of its nuns to help them become more effective teachers exposes them to a wide range of new ideas, including feminism. Feminist nuns press for inclusive language, a larger role in church leadership, and ordination, causing a deep split within the church. The liberal orientation of many Jews makes them receptive to feminism; among the most prominent Jewish feminists are Betty Friedan, Gloria Steinem, and Bella Abzug, each speaking more from a secular feminist perspective than from a Jewish one. Religious Jewish feminists have achieved goals that include women's ordination (in reform Judaism in 1972), a widely accepted bat mitzvah for girls, Jewish women's prayer groups, and admission to Yeshiva University (in 1993) (Carmody, 1987). Although feminism has impacted the Jewish community of believers, it remains a minority view.

Feminism's strongest political opponent is the conservative Right, who insist on a literal reading of headship. The prolife position is also identified with the conservative Right, who often oppose feminism. Urging change, feminists ask the conservative Right to reject the characteristics that make them unique. The response to feminism within the ranks of the conservative Right strikes a curious posture. Characteristic of the kind of apologetic offered by the conservative Right are arguments such as that traditions of faith consider women to be equal, if not superior, to men; American society does indeed undervalue women's work, but feminism intensifies the problem whereas conservative faiths solve it; men often are emotionally inexpressive and insufficiently involved with child rearing, but conservative Right communities encourage greater male sensitivity and involvement with children; and faith traditions celebrate sexuality within marriage and provide strong scriptural role models for women. Advocates of the conservative Right discouraged feminism among their members characterizing feminism as rejecting Scripture and promoting selfishness. They attempt to co-opt feminism by arguing that tradition characterizes women as equal or even superior to men (Kaufman, 1991; Lienesh, 1993; Rousseau, 1991). When feminists complain that women are undervalued and men oppress them, the conservative Right acknowledges this as true in secular society, but not in homes of faith. The solution to the problems feminists want to resolve, they say, is a return to traditions of faith. Individuals who endorse an intrinsic (devout) orientation to their faith evidence less sex role stereotyping, fewer negative attitudes, and less prejudice toward women (Allport & Ross, 1967) than nonfaith persons. Disagreements among clergy in various conservative Right groups represent a schism that makes it difficult for them to repress feminism. Within the various faiths feminism has inspired the formation of a variety of groups—including the Christian Coalition, Concerned Women for America, the National Council of Catholic Women, the Eagle Forum, and the Moral Majority, as well as a prominent public role of televangelists like Pat Robertson and Jerry Falwell.

THE DECLINE OF THE FAMILY

Women use a variety of strategies for resolving the cognitive dissonance associated with holding bipolar sets of values, feminism and traditionalism, at the same time. One way of thinking about these two sets of values entails compartmentalizing: feminist ideology and the workplace in one compartment, and traditional ideology and the church in another. But where does the home fit into all of this? Some would say the family primarily acts as a field where ideologies of faith are acted out. Others argue that confusion about gender roles has arisen in response to the increased participation of women in the marketplace. Traditional gender roles see males and females as different: females largely responsible for care of the home and children and males generally responsible for financial stability. When women work outside the home, maintaining these gender distinctions becomes increasingly difficult. As the distinctions become increasingly difficult to maintain, some feminist groups support observing no sex distinctions, a pivotal idea within a large part of the feminist movement.

Balancing such conflicting ideas requires choice rather than duty. Often groups of faith interpret their written Scriptures to suggest wives should submit to husbands, but Dobson (1982) suggests a more modern interpretation: mutual submission. LaHaye (1976) asserts that the competition of women and men in the job market is detrimental to both the economy and men's self-esteem. Asking men to participate in household tasks while women contribute to financial stability helps to emphasize a more egalitarian approach. Many women revere "stay-at-home moms" and male leadership in the home as an ideal yet do not seem to allow their husband much actual authority (Manning, 1995). Women who work full time often claim they "wish they had a wife." Usually these women cite the need for additional income when explaining their career-over-home choice. Still they see themselves as homemakers first, despite their love of their jobs. Not until they return home from work exhausted do they challenge the idea that they have additional responsibility for housework and child care as unreasonable. Traditional gender roles no longer make sense as they reflect on the reality of their lives. At this point most advocates of traditional gender roles ask for assistance from their husbands.

In one Christian family who believed in traditional gender roles, the woman had a closer relationship to Christ than did her husband. When joint decisions were made and they disagreed, the woman claimed her husband was not divinely inspired since he did not engage in Bible study, prayer, Christian fellowship, and other manifestations of the spirit. As the more spiritual member of the family, she would tell him to pray about their decision until he agreed with her. She actively drew on the notion of a superior spirituality of women in an effort to undermine the authority of her husband. Despite this, many Christian women do believe in actually submitting to their husband, in theory, and feel that it enhances the relationship. For example, submitting to Christ saved the marriage when the road became rocky for three women in a small Lutheran church. Learning to submit to Christ enabled these women to see their husbands differently, making it possible to love and forgive them as Christ had in reconciling the whole church to God. Learning to submit actually empowered these men and women in their relationships because they began to see one another as on the same team rather than as competitors. Mutual submission enabled them to accept traditional gender roles, while maintaining flexibility in their attitudes toward feminist gender role ideas.

A father's involvement in child rearing has become an issue of great concern to many traditional families. The breadwinner role has taken men out of the home for longer periods in business travel, and later at night with heavier responsibilities at work while climbing the corporate ladder. As a result of professional as well as home maintenance responsibilities and some much needed leisure activity, men have been left with little real time or energy to become involved in child rearing. Many male groups such as Promise Keepers and the Million Man March encourage men to refocus their energies, to go home and take responsibility for their children, to regain headship in their families with mutual concern for the well-being of the family as the basic unit of society. Robert Bly (1990) says that boys have forgotten how to be men; Rekers (1996, p. 11) postulates a "gender identity disorder" among maladjusted individuals who have attended to the message of "eliminating all distinctions based on sex." In pathological cases, children who deviate from the normal pattern of exploring masculine and feminine behavior often develop inflexible, compulsive, persistent and rigidly stereotyped patterns: maladaptive supermasculinity or effeminacy in boys or maladaptive hyperfemininity and hypermasculinity in girls. Rekers (1991) asserts that well-adjusted, secure male identity and female identity role models provide positive examples for healthy family life and have a positive impact on repairing the declining family in the larger culture.

RECONCILING FEMINISM WITH TRADITIONALISM

Many women turn from feminism to traditionalism, others turn from traditionalism to feminism, still others generally believe in traditionalism but listen to feminist rhetoric and make a deliberate rational choice (Neitz, 1987) to accept something from each ideology. Aware of their choices, unlike their predecessors, who saw only one choice (that of homemaking), those who select traditionalism do so because it meets their needs for meaning and order, marriage and family, and community. Since those needs are primary, they willingly accept patriarchal structures, often rejecting other viable choices. Either coming from feminism and adding to it some traditionalism or accepting traditionalism and reaching for feminism, the rhetoric of each causes both of these groups of men and women to experience dissonance. The life experiences of men and women shape their role choices and conflicts in role restriction, subordination, status seeking in society, and any number of other spheres, producing dissonance. A variety of methods for dealing with the resulting conflict have been described in the literature.

DISSONANCE REDUCTION FOR MEN AND WOMEN OF FAITH

Davidman (1991) finds some women of faith insulate themselves from the larger society by forming closely knit groups with others who have made the same choices. Other women compartmentalize their lives by submitting to male authority at home, though not at work. Kaufman (1991) finds women balance patriarchal norms by emphasizing traditions elevating women as superior. Greeley and Durkin (1984) find many women angry with the treatment of women by the organized church who resolve their dissonance by emphasizing the value of loyalty to the organized church but reducing their financial contributions. Roof (1993) studies Baby Boomers who selectively disregard disagreeable norms within the organized church. Neitz (1987) advocates dissonance reduction by reinterpreting those norms requiring more emotional expression and family commitment from husbands and accepting the idea of keeping the marriage intact as a more pragmatic value. McDannell (1989) writes that in many families husbands abdicate headship and leave religious responsibilities to wives. In such families, norms of behavior exhibit a public patriarchal and a private matriarchal structure. Though the husband wields official authority, the wife has the real power in the home. In other families, Lawless (1988) observes a pattern of "mutual submission" that interprets written Scriptures to mean men and women submit to each other, exchanging responsibilities for child care with work roles for women as a means of contributing to family finances.

Conflict arising from the bipolar values of traditionalism and feminism varies, depending on who is talking. Catholics oppose birth control, whereas both Protestants and Catholics oppose abortion and homosexuality. But some more liberal Protestant and Jewish groups do not oppose abortion and appear divided on the issue of homosexuality. Disagreements also exist within these groups with regard to ordaining women as pastors, priests, or rabbis (Hao, 1993). Most religious groups stress the importance of personal responsibility and accountability for sin. But each of these groups of faith takes a slightly different view as to what *is* sin. All of the groups of faith do agree, however, that an authority higher than the self determines right and wrong behavior and they must answer to that authority after life.

CONCLUSION

This chapter has compared and contrasted traditional ideologies with humanist and feminist ideologies. It has also examined the influence of feminism on faith and the decline of the family. Many men and women blame the feminist movement for almost every social ill: abortion, homosexuality, decline of the family, and divorce. During the second wave of feminism, one often heard the complaint that feminists turned women into men, and men into women. Finally, we have looked at various ways women reconcile feminist ideologies with traditional ideologies. If one examines the political landscape of the culture wars, it would appear the solution to the problem of holding bipolar, dissonant ideologies at the same time varies. Both feminists and traditionalists would prefer to reduce the tension by evangelizing their values to the rest of society. Festinger's (1957) theory of cognitive dissonance suggests that when individuals act in ways contradictory to their beliefs or receive information conflicting with their existing belief system, they experience dissonance and psychological discomfort. This often motivates them to change some of their beliefs and behavior, or avoid certain situations and information that aggravate the dissonance. But many people appear to deal with dissonance in a different way: so long as the dissonance provides a coherent meaning system, they appear to be content with the apparent contradictions. When people draw values from cultures that appear to promote greater well-being, the dissonance can be arrested by the strategies used by the women and men discussed in this chapter. When two opposing cultures overlap, as feminism and traditionalism often do, and people live in both worlds without being required to give up one for the other, the symbol systems of both provide pragmatic resolutions. Regardless, women and men usually have one primary identification, either feminist or traditional, and the adoption of the secondary identification merely serves some pragmatic end.

PART II

4

Self-Esteem and Gender Communication

Self-esteem is built up by a total pattern of successful experiences. Self-esteem can neither be quickly developed nor quickly destroyed. It deserves to be carefully guarded because it is often the difference between success and failure.

Eugene E. Jennings

The roles for men and women have changed over the last twenty years, becoming more chosen than imposed, less isomorphic with gender than in the past, less segregated as to function, and less often in separate worlds. Also, men and women appear less married now than previously. Single-parent families, divorced or widowed adults, individuals between marriages or not looking for commitment lead more households today than in the past. Whatever their situation people meeting and interacting with other, both professionally and personally, view each other through the lingering filter of traditional sex role stereotypes. Psychology views the developmental struggle to separate and individuate (Gilligan, 1982; Miller, 1976) as progressing along linear and predictable stages. Males typically separate from the mother and assume their own unique personality (Freud, 1963). Females sterotypically identify with the mother, also assuming their own unique personality, but less independent. Newer roles for both men and women depict males identifying with mothers (as well as fathers) and females with fathers (as well as mothers), thus creating new gender types of feminine males and masculine females, or androgynous individuals, and development of new roles (Cook, 1985). Whenever individuals attempt to create new gender roles, the psychological stereotypical model of what they see as normal and desirable affects their self-image. The reformulation of roles has implications for communication, as well as for other fields of knowledge, such as sociology, biology, physics, religion, archaeology, history, medicine, law, and language (Eisler, 1987; Gimbutas, 1982; Capra, 1983; Chopra, 1991; Keller, 1985).

Self-esteem is the evaluative regard, acceptance, respect, and worth one has of himself or herself (Blaskovich & Tomaka, 1989; Mullin, 1983; Rosenberg, 1989). Raimy (1948, p. 154) believes self-esteem results from "present and past self-observation." This includes the interactive component of one's biological makeup, the perceived opinions of others, the impact of culture on one's opinion of self, the religious messages one hears about self, all combining to form one's opinion of self. Rogers and Dymond (1954) argue self-concept affects and regulates our behavior and often represses or lessens our awareness of experiences. The cognitive component of self-esteem involves mastery of the environment (Woodworth, 1958), control of rewards (Ziller et al., 1969), sense of social adequacy (Janis & Field, 1959; Dittes, 1959), and sense of interpersonal competence. All of these definitions entail a sense of power and independence in the social sphere. This chapter examines the impact of gender roles on self-esteem in terms of biological, psychological/sociological, cultural, and religious fields of knowledge.

BIOLOGICAL IMPACT OF GENDER ROLES ON SELF-ESTEEM

Biological differences (sex and race), rooted in genetic makeup and affected by cultural influences, involve socioeconomic stratifications. The social and psychological processes involved in sex or race identification resulting from biological differences especially influence individuals because they cannot easily leave their group. Social scientists (Hogg & Abrams, 1988; Liebkind, 1992; Tajfel, 1978) argue gender identity in one of these groups strongly influences a person's self-concept and psychological functioning. However, Tajfel (1978) claims an individual can symbolically or psychologically leave a group he or she perceives does not contribute positively (lower power and status) to his or her social identity by regarding himself or herself as not being a typical member of the group. In fact, some women have shown strong prejudice toward their own group (Goldberg, 1968; Hogg & Abrams, 1988). Masculine hair styles, masculine dress, and aggressive communication styles help women leave their own sex group and identify with masculinity. These women believe their lower status and lack of power result from illegitimate rules and discrimination (Miller et al., 1980; Spence et al., 1985), so they symbolically or psychologically leave the group. Social movements such as feminism acted to challenge illegiti-mate status inequities between men and women, attempting to alter their effects. Other women refuse to comply with gender group discrimination and display more gender group favoritism, work to promote a sense of group unity, and adhere to and promote the value of femininity.

Self-esteem, as it has been traditionally described, overlaps with mascu-linity, but more recently women researchers portray it in terms of feminin-ity, discussing the opportunity for an individual to feel "proud" and "act like a leader" as corollaries of nurturance, relationship, and empathy, terms not historically used together in this "role-blending" manner (Schwartz, 1983). The way femininity is viewed correlates negatively with self-esteem, especially because of the denigration of femininity from highly masculine women's groups, but femininity correlates positively with marital satisfac-tion (Antill, 1983), nurturance (Bem et al., 1976), and empathy (Thomas & Reznikoff, 1984).

PSYCHOLOGICAL/SOCIOLOGICAL IMPACT OF GENDER ROLES ON SELF-ESTEEM

When self-esteem in men and women is compared, women express lower self-esteem than men (Koffman & Lips, 1980; Maccoby & Jacklin, 1974). Prager (1983) describes masculinity as the predictor of higher levels of self-esteem. Taylor and Hall (1982) say that masculinity positively relates to psychological health in 91 percent of associations and femininity positively relates in 79 percent of associations. Whitley (1983) claims high scores on both masculinity and femininity are conducive to maximum psychological well-being. After a metaanalysis of self-esteem scores on scales of congruity theory, Whitley (1983) finds the high self-esteem scores of androgynous individuals attributable to the high masculinity component. Whitley (1983, p. 775) also notes two other variables relevant to the relationship between sex role and self-esteem: "the centrality of sex-role to one's self-concept" and "the degree of congruence between one's ideal and real sex-role ori-entations." Spence (1983) notes gender role identity varies as to proximics, context, expectations of others, beliefs of the individuals, and situational cues. If one's gender identity varies on the instrumentality-expressiveness (masculine-feminine) dimension over time and in various situations, then the connection between self-esteem and the same scales might be less clear.

The sociological perspective of self-perception, or self-esteem, relates to positive social interactions (Vaux, 1988) and resilience to stress (Neeman & Harter, 1986). It develops within the social context of family, peers, education, culture, and religion. The evaluative feedback received from par-ents and others outside the family provides the structure of self-esteem. As people develop, they encounter social evaluation and incorporate this information into their judgment of self (Ruble et al., 1980). Parental styles have been considered to be important for the emergence of adult self-esteem (Gecas & Schwalbe, 1986; Graybill, 1978; Hopkins & Klein, 1993; Thomas & Raj, 1985). Parents with a high control style, expecting their children to meet extremely high standards, often have a negative impact on children's self-worth. Parents with a high responsiveness to children, behaving in highly accepting and responsive ways in relation to them, allowing open discussions, often promote higher self-worth in their children. Using the sociological perspective, permissive parenting has a positive relationship to children's self-esteem when it is done by fathers, but not when it is done by mothers.

Jones, Chernovetz, and Hansson (1978) find highly masculine males are more secure, less neurotic, less sensitive to criticism, and more internal in locus of control and have fewer problems with alcohol than less-masculine males. Highly masculine females express more feminist attitudes, have higher levels of political awareness, act more extroverted, express more heterosexual involvement, and enjoy more popularity with the opposite sex. Smokler (1974) finds adolescent females with the highest self-esteem tend toward an interest in acquiring competence in androgynous characteristics, those with moderate self-esteem express interest in more femininity, and those with the lowest self-esteem act least competent at feminine tasks. Recely (1973) finds a positive correlation between self-esteem and masculinity in both male and female subjects. After an exhaustive metaanalysis of sex role and self-esteem, Whitley (1983) concludes that a stronger correlation exists between masculinity and one's sense of well-being. Even so, other researchers find androgyny correlates with greater adjustment (Burchardt & Serbin, 1982; Golding & Singer, 1983; Hinrichsen et al., 1981; Orlofsky, 1977), more behavioral flexibility (Bem, 1975; Bem & Lenny, 1976; Bem et al., 1976), and greater assertiveness (Kelly et al., 1981). The blend of masculinity/femininity within the context of androgyny does not account for these positive attributes; rather, the higher level of masculinity as commonly understood in society today does. However, femininity should in no way be discounted as having a positive influence; it simply demonstrates a weaker correlation.

The commonly documented social attitudes about women's roles and abilities impact female achievement motivation in two ways. First, external barriers such as reduced job opportunities, lower pay, and other discriminatory practices may deny women success. Second, these attitudes may internally influence how women perceive themselves and evaluate their chances for success. If a woman internalizes common social attitudes relating to female incompetence, she may reduce her expectations for success and thus her motivation. Or, if competence does not reduce her expectations, femininity itself may deleteriously affect achievement for no specific reason. Gelbert and Winer (1985) find women are strongly affected by fear of success and fear of failure. If they are successful, women risk losing highly valued relationships; if they fail, they fear appearing incompetent (Brenner & Tomkiewicz, 1982). Pfost and Fiore (1990) find both women and men perceive women who succeed in "masculine" occupations as less desirable romantic partners and friends. Because of the lingering filter of traditional sex role stereotypes, women often perceive themselves as at greater risk of failure, humiliation, and isolation if they pursue success outside the traditional female realm.

Chronic low self-esteem increases a person's vulnerability to the deflating effect of criticism, but chronic high self-esteem results in raised self-esteem after praise (Wells & Marwell, 1976). A negative correlation exists between self-esteem and anxiety and neurotic behavior (Wylie, 1974). Low self-esteem correlates with low life satisfaction, loneliness, anxiety, resentment, irritability, and depression (Rosenberg, 1985). Women report depression at a ratio of about two to one to men (Hammen & Padesky, 1977). Women express depression through indecisiveness and self-dislike; they deal with it through talking to a close friend or on the negative side with some affective disorders, such as overeating, hostility, self-deprecating statements, or writing about their feelings (Funabiki et al., 1980). Men tend to withdraw socially and become involved in more physical activities designed to distract them from their depression. A positive relationship correlates high self-esteem and the ability to perform effectively under stress and failure (Schalon, 1968; Shrauger & Rosenberg, 1970). High self-esteem correlates with academic success (O'Malley & Bachman, 1979), internal locus of control, higher family income, and a positive sense of self-attractiveness (Griffore et al., 1990).

Women who describe themselves as liberated appear to differ on measures of self-esteem. Traditional women measure their self-esteem more in relation to friendships and family involvement and less to interests and abilities. Liberated women measure their self-esteem through personal growth and achievement, self-determination, education, and occupation. Since liberated women measure their self-esteem with predictors similar to those used by men, liberated, unmarried women also appear to possess a greater level of self-esteem than married women (Gigy, 1980).

Weitz (1982) studied adult female consciousness raising group participants, noting subjects increased in both feminism and self-esteem during their time with the group. Kincaid (1977) found older married women who took consciousness raising classes developed a more inner-directed orientation both in them and in their ideal woman. Consciousness raising groups appeared to increase a woman's feminism and her trust in herself. Curiously, Kincaid (1977) found the most sexist subjects showed the greatest movement toward feminism.

People who gravitate toward feminism tend to be women, liberals, and gays and lesbians. These groups include people who have large numbers of feminist friends, people who have taken women's studies classes, people who have performed some sort of feminist behavior (like attending a feminist rally), and people who say they know a lot about the women's movement. Kerens (1989) did not find an association between feminism and self-esteem, satisfaction with one's work life, or other areas of one's life. Feminists do not exhibit more androgynous behavior than anyone else, though many researchers believed they would. In fact, feminists often claim they do not allow gender to matter for them. As subjects become more feminist they often become less androgynous because they become aware of the big role gender plays in contemporary American society. Consequently, feminists become more gender schematic, ever vigilant, ready to respond to any situations in which they observe that gender may be affecting a decision. They recognize gender, see it matters, wish it were not so, but do not apply it to their own life. Feminists differ from traditional women as to their perceptions of internal locus of control (Minnigerode, 1976; Ryckman et al., 1972), high ego strength (Gump, 1972), low dogmatism (Whitehead & Tawes, 1976), low defensiveness (Albright & Chang, 1976), low religiosity (Etaugh, 1975), high self-esteem (Harrison et al., 1981), high self-actualization (Hjelle & Butterfield, 1974), greater well-being (Logan & Kaschak, 1980), and high expectations of success (Wiegers & Frieze, 1977).

Fassinger (1990) finds college women oriented toward high-prestige, nontraditional career choices more likely to possess higher levels of agentic, instrumental (masculine) personality characteristics and liberal sex role attitudes. Erdwins, Tyer, and Mellinger (1982, p. 222) say achievement motivation varies throughout the life span. During "child-rearing" stages women report lower measures of achievement motivation relating to career success outside the home. During middle years (ages forty to fifty-five) achievement motivation becomes important, but only after other identity issues are resolved. Wide variations in ways women handle life-span changes such as child rearing/career options indicate the complexity of self-esteem for motivational researchers. Some women continue to pursue career aspirations at the same time as they rear their children, others scale back their ambitions, still others discontinue their careers. How internalizing sex role stereotypes affect self-esteem during these life changes remains an intriguing question.

CULTURAL IMPACT OF GENDER ROLES ON SELF-ESTEEM

Curiously, conservative females do not manifest lower self-esteem when placed in a subordinate position, but liberal women do. In a study by Langer and Benevento (1978) liberal women showed performance decreases on a task when they perceived a social implication of lower status, whereas performance increased on tasks when they felt a social implication of interpersonal superiority. Conservative women, on the other hand, seemed to refuse to accept the implications of these labels, behaving in ways contradicting the status labels: Those with lower-status labels increased in task performance; those with higher-status labels decreased in task performance. It appears an individual's position on a conservative-liberal continuum affects self-esteem when given a superior/subordinate status. Also, subordinates under female supervision do not suffer performance deficits as the result of a cultural bias against female supervisors (Langer, 1979).

Bains (1983) suggests self-esteem biases sometimes operate to preserve a particular worldview. Arkin (1988) claims in the interest of protecting our biases we often present the public self in a way that will help us to establish a stable and favorable private view of self. In other words, we often exhibit behavior in public we expect others will know about at some time in the future. Such behavior attempts to influence public impressions, to gain social approval, to enhance persuasiveness, and, therefore, affects our ability to control our environment. Arkin (1988, p. 14) claims control over our environment produces stability and provides us with a "sense of possibility" or "hope for the future."

Steinem (1992) explains the concept of high self-esteem as important to confidence, career goals, scholarly interest, and a sense of self-worth. She says low self-esteem affects the ability to learn and to achieve. Hoff-Sommers (1994) reports that an American Association of University Women (AAUW) survey shows African-American boys score highest on all indexes of self-esteem, African-American girls next, then white boys followed by white girls. She asks how "those who scored highest on the AAUW's self-esteem measure are educationally at risk, while the group with the lowest confidence did so well? White girls are getting better grades and going to college in far greater numbers than any other group" (Hoff-Sommers, 1994, p. 150). She argues, "If one takes the AAUW's way of measuring self-esteem seriously, then one should now begin to take seriously the suggestion there is an inverse relation between self-esteem reports and success in school" (Hoff-Sommers, 1994, p. 150). The American Association of University Women (1991) published the brochure *Shortchanging Girls, Shortchanging America*, and Representative Patricia Schroeder (1991) testified in support of a bill that would become or be part of the Gender Equity in Education Act before the House Education and Labor Committee Subcommittee on Elementary, Secondary, and Vocational Education. The objective of the study was to promote self-esteem in young women, but Hoff-Sommers (1994) argues that it was plagued with methodological errors. Nonetheless Congress acted on it at the behest of the AAUW in efforts to raise the self-esteem of young women to the benefit of the culture at large.

Young and Wiedemann (1987) resent the androcentric thinking equating

masculinity with independence and attributing it to men, whereas femininity receives no such unqualified endorsement despite its necessity within a
society. Women, they say, must adapt and accept behavioral norms for
their sex (femininity), concentrated in relational aspects, even though society regards them as less socially desirable. The extent to which a society
values these relational gifts determines the degree of empowerment women
experience. Miller (1976) argues the American culture not only does not
value these attributes but interprets them as weaknesses. This attitude trans-
lates directly into lowered self-esteem for feminine women. Kaplan (1986)
characterizes the devaluing of relationships and expressions of emotion
concerning those relationships as causing women to feel inadequate and
unable to measure up to the culturally valued masculine norms. Stanley
and Wise (1983) describe women as "nonmen" falling at the other end of
a bipolar scale from men's experience.

RELIGIOUS IMPACT OF GENDER ROLES ON
SELF-ESTEEM

Another area often associated with self-esteem is the idea of locus of
control. Persons who believe they control the outcome of incidents in their
own life tend to characterize themselves as having an internal locus of
control. Those who attribute the outcome of incidents in their own lives
to luck, chance, powerful others, or other factors outside their control characterize themselves as at the mercy of an external locus of control. Baker
and Terpstra (1986) find demographic factors of gender, including age,
education, and religion, act as better predictors of sex role attitudes than
self-esteem or locus of control. When the family organizes according to a
patriarchal model, many women see themselves as under the power and
control of their husbands. As women become dependent on their husbands
they often begin to rely on them or their children to provide meaning and
structure in their lives: in other words, to provide an identity. The dependency often creates a situation whereby women fail to mature fully or experience the desirable effects of independence (Gilligan, 1982).

Power in a relationship evidences persuasive influence (Raven, 1974) in
efforts to effect change in a partner's attitudes or behavior. Relational
power, however, cannot be thought of as persuasive influence alone but
incorporates such resources as knowledge, money, status, and respect (Lips,
1981). An integrated approach to relational power is one whereby individuals, resources, situations, and actions all come together to produce an
effect. In the religious context, men and women view events as determined
by both divine authority and personal initiation (Friedberg & Friedberg,
1985). On the one hand, trust in God to guide and protect affects the
choices people make (Sexton et al., 1980); on the other, individuals who
have faith recognize their personal accountability for their decisions (Rus-

sell & Jorgenson, 1978). Reliance on God denotes external locus of control, whereas individual accountability denotes internal locus of control.

A partnership model of marriage relationships acknowledging male headship uses such an integrated approach, giving women opportunities to effect change. Submitting to husband's authority as choice, not coercion, places all the power and control in the hands of the one who submits. How so? Because at any point in the relationship if the male head fails to live up to his role of partner, he jeopardizes his authority, especially if his wife loses trust in him. When partners lose trust, relationships break down. The person who submits, therefore, has all the power because withdrawal of compliance can occur at any time. As Lefcourt (1973) describes it, the perception of power and control reduces anxiety (Stotland & Blumenthal, 1964) and acts more as an "illusion of control." An earlier study of women (Feather, 1967) found an external orientation to locus of control, whereas a later study (O'Reilly, 1988) found a significantly higher internal locus of control for women than men. The perception of having no power in a relationship, however, reduces one to a slavelike mentality and produces low self-esteem.

Self-esteem also relates to the kind of person one makes of himself or herself—the kind of character he or she develops. How to determine this becomes a question for philosophers. Wheelwright (1960) claims the development of good character cannot be the same for all, but rather appears to be culture bound. He claims as a culture changes, so do conceptions of the ideal self, as well as conditions for its development. Aristotle (384–322 B.C.) claimed moral virtue stemmed from a person's natural ability to control his or her natural impulses and appetites. He or she achieved moral excellence to the extent his or her rational control of appetite became a habit and so became the expression of an enduring character. To will oneself to moral character without ambivalence, one must consistently apply the same rule to the self as one applies to others on difficult occasions, as well as on easy ones, when other people might observe and when alone; such application is a clear expression of enduring character.

Roberts (1993) describes the subject of self-esteem of men and women of faith. He says faith affects self-esteem in one of three ways: First, people of faith disagree with the psychologists who advocate the promotion of human self over obedience to God. Second, people of faith see obedience as the key to a correct reading of the central message of faith, promoting psychological health, salvation, and the well-being of the soul. Third, people of faith believe much good can be derived by the science of psychology, but are appalled by what it sometimes does to people, replacing the profound shape of the life of faith with something that by comparison seems meager, cheap, and shallow such as the focus on self. This group says they feel unsure of what to make of psychology and the notion of self-esteem. People of faith, he says, see the original self as created in the image of God for obedient fellowship with him, but the subsequent self as fallen to the image of sinful Adam. The second component of obedient fellowship entails perfection in worship, obedience, and service to others. Since perfection was impossible in the fallen image of Adam, people of faith acknowledge their need for a Savior who enables them to be seen as perfect from God's perspective and who helps them to act out God's will by the enabling work of faith. Self-esteem can be seen only through the lens of humility brought about by faith. They believe this to be the essence of positive self-esteem. They believe the only "correct" self-esteem results from viewing God, not ourselves, and seeing ourselves through his eyes. The sight is not flattering, but it changes lives and turns people from self toward others.

But take the concept of self-esteem out of the realm of faith. Judgments about right and wrong cause people discomfort because individuals do not want others to judge them; nor do they want to experience guilt. A generation priding itself on determining its own standards of right and wrong, and doing its own thing, ought not to care about the opinions of other people. But suppose it is true that right and wrong actions actually exist. Suppose, however, individuals believe they are powerless to base their actions on the good. People know they do wrong but cannot stop themselves. Individuals then struggle with a pair of painful thoughts: "I am doing wrong" and "I cannot change." People want to think well of themselves but fall short of their own standards. It then becomes tempting to focus on moral skepticism: "Maybe my actions are not so bad after all." Skepticism of this type protects people from the inner turmoil arising in the mind when they realize they do not, and cannot, live up to their own standards. Healthier thinking, for the sake of self-esteem, would involve remembering the human condition is filled with imperfections, limitations, and sometimes out-and-out wrongdoing. When people do wrong, nothing is wrong with them; they are normal human beings, facing normal problems of the human race. If a person's self-esteem depends upon the premise that he or she can do no wrong, then that self-esteem will always be fragile (Hart, 1992; McGrath, 1992).

Research focusing on self-esteem for men and women has had mixed findings. Some studies find no differences (Seidner, 1978; Drummond et al., 1977; Zuckerman, 1980), and others determine that men experience higher self-esteem than women (Stoner & Kaiser, 1978; Smith & Self, 1978; Gold et al., 1980; Loeb & Horst, 1978; Judd & Smith, 1974; Berger, 1968; Bohan, 1973). These differences may be accounted for by differences in the processing of information from similar experiences. For example, males scored higher on personal self, or how they view themselves as people without regard for others; social self, or how they view their connections with others; self-criticism, or how they view themselves or their ability to identify problems in their behavior. Curiously, no differences in self-esteem between men and women were found with regard to body image, moral–ethical perceptions, family self, identity, or self-satisfaction, all having to do with achievements (Stoner & Kaiser, 1978). Females tend to be more open-minded, more easily persuaded, lower in performance specific self-esteem, but not lower in general self-esteem. Since males and females view the self differently, views of self reflect those differences. For example, males evaluate themselves on the basis of goal achievement, task completion, and other more instrumental activities. Females evaluate themselves in terms of relational criteria such as emotional warmth and sociability (Stake & Stake, 1979).

CONCLUSION

The process of developing self-esteem requires an internalization of different aspects of biological, psychological/sociological, cultural, and religious processes. It exists partly in self-image and partly in artifacts of self-image, such as house, car, clothes, success, good deeds, and as each individual internalizes and organizes his or her perceptions of how other people communicate with him or her either verbally or nonverbally. The concept one develops of self, however inexact, fluctuating, and uncertain, functions as a guide in social behavior. In other words, people tend to act in ways that operate as mechanisms for preservation of their desired image of self. We do not, however, view ourselves in the same way all the time, with everyone, and in all situations we encounter. On one occasion we may feel more positive and at other times more negative. People can raise their self-esteem through consciousness raising, discussion, and other forms of communication interaction. Self-esteem appears to correlate negatively with seeking help from or offering assistance to others, behavior traditionally associated with femininity, and correlate positively with masculinity, including instrumentality, achievement, and goal orientation.

5

Gendered Communication in Close Relationships

For many people the drive for power and the will to love represent opposite poles of human existence and are great sources of human conflict. In their most perverted forms, power becomes domination and love becomes manipulation, and if you use power to get love or love to gain power, a relationship becomes destructive.

Anonymous

When examining close relationships gender roles raise two questions: (1) How closely does a person adhere to gender role stereotypes for his or her sex as prescribed by the culture? (2) In what way does the gender role a person plays relate to communication? Determining who will wash the car, do the yard work, clean the garage, prepare the meals, do the laundry, and care for the children is often affected by gender role stereotypes. Cultural scripts help make most heterosexual relationships predictable in this regard. For example, we still expect the man to "make the first move" by inviting a woman out, and the woman either to turn him down or to accept. Further, the man usually attempts to increase the level of sexual intimacy with his sexual partner, while (at least in the United States) the woman's responsibility involves "refusing his advances" and upholding the moral high ground or "accepting his advances" for whatever reason suits her. We view communication in relationships as either instrumental or relational. Males stereotypically use an instrumental communication, and females stereotypically use a relational model. Women tend to establish a "nesting" influence in relationships, preferring one loyal partner, whereas men often fantasize about a variety of partners or sexual loyalties more closely associated with what has become known as *serial monogamy*.

In the 60's and 70's feminists campaigned against the idea women should have sexual loyalty to one partner. They said promiscuous men were known as "studs" (a positive term) whereas promiscuous women gained reputations as "sluts" and "whores" (negative terms). Instead of applying pressure to promote fidelity among men, feminists advocated infidelity among women, changing the cultural norm. They said women should experience as much freedom as men to explore a repertoire of sexual partners and experiences.

In this chapter the focus is on the changing role of "traditional wife." The hierarchical and partnership models of marriage relationships, courtship, the changing face of marriage, and gender role conflict are discussed, as is Fitzpatrick's (1988) marital relations model. Views of the traditional wife are discussed as the role has moved through a transition toward a more adapted/independent model. Laced throughout the discussion is the impact of the leveling of power toward a more egalitarian approach in marital relationships.

INTRODUCTION

Power acts as the capacity to get things done; *love* means caring for others. People who can integrate and balance the two can attain the highest degree of personal development. Historically, males have had the power in society; females have been the supporters and nurturers. These roles agreed with what gender role theorists assigned as biologically, psychologically/ sociologically, culturally, and religiously correct. This version of how to play marital roles emerged from a traditional way of looking at relationships stemming from the religious view of what God had in mind for maintaining order between man and woman. This Christian-Judaic view of marriage took the perspective that God created man (Adam) in his own image and then created woman (Eve) as a companion or helpmate for man. God intended for this relationship of man and woman to be as perfect as God's relationship with Adam and Eve. Once sin entered the world, man and woman then became created in the image of Adam and Eve, sinners, producing friction between man and woman, just as it did between man/ woman and God. For the first eighteen hundred years of Christianity, the patriarchal view, that men have authority over women, dominated. But, in the early part of the nineteenth century women began to protest against their civil and political degradation, or their unequal position in the relationship. Women wanted their roles to change, and since tradition seemed to promote sexism, women advocated a general and critical study of the biblical texts. Many women rejected the hierarchical model of the man/woman relationship in favor of a model of partnership.

HIERARCHICAL OR PARTNERSHIP MODELS

Protestants and Catholics often argue in favor of a combination of the hierarchical model, placing men in authority over women in marriage, and the partnership model, placing men and women in an egalitarian relationship except when disagreement over spiritual matters exists. Men and women, they claim, may be different yet are equal. Spouse abuse clinics advocate against any type of hierarchical model because many clergy unfairly tell battered women to go home and submit to their husband out of religious duty, only to have the women return to the abuse clinic in the same shape the next week. Spouse abuse clinics suggest women need to leave abusive relationships or men need to stop abusing.

As men and women decide how to distribute power/love in their gendered relationships, they cannot help but acknowledge the stereotypical patterns associated with the hierarchical model of relationships. In this model, females tend to act considerate, quiet, loving, emotionally expressive, obedient, and socially able (Beckwith, 1972; Clarke-Stewart, 1973), and males act independent, competitive, and aggressive and are problem solvers (Cherry & Lewis, 1978). To the extent stereotypical views of femininity and masculinity become internalized, women and men tend to develop gendered ways of experiencing and expressing closeness. The meanings of closeness and ways of communicating affection often create misunderstanding and hurt. Considering these differences in stereotypical male and female styles of relating, what shift in thinking would enable people to switch to the partnership model, if they believed it might be more satisfying? *Close relationships* in this discussion are those enduring over time between a man and a woman, that is, usually marital relationships.

Differences exist in the ways women and men approach and experience closeness. They have different expectations, communication patterns, and ways of interpreting the way others interact with them. For example, feminine individuals appreciate connection with others, higher levels of self-disclosure, nurturing, responsiveness to others, and talking to build and sustain relationships. Masculine individuals appreciate independence, lower if any self-disclosure, instrumental activity, aggressiveness, and talking to build status and power. Tannen (1994) suggests men and women want the same things out of a relationship but express their desires in different ways because of their concerns with socially constructed ideas of masculinity and femininity.

Wood (1997) describes two models of understanding these differences in relational perspectives. The first she describes as the *male-deficit model*, which maintains that men do not disclose emotions, reveal personal information, or engage in communication about intimate topics. The implication of this model is that men's lack of expressiveness condemns them as inadequate in relational intimacy. Tannen (1994), however, says men simply express intimacy in different ways than women. Wood (1997) describes this as the *alternate paths model*, which does not presume men lack feelings or emotional depth. Tannen (1994) suggests our ways of recognizing intimate communication emerged from a female model that failed to consider how men simply communicate intimacy in different ways. For example, men communicate love in more instrumental ways by giving flowers, taking out trash, requesting hugs, and offering problem solving directions as ways of communicating emotional closeness. They prefer to do things rather than talk about things. In fact, gender role development often inhibits men from feeling comfortable talking about feelings and emotions. Interestingly, research (Reissman, 1990; Swain, 1989; Tavris, 1992) suggests that talking about problems may actually be less effective than diversionary activities in relieving stress and enhancing feelings of closeness for men. To prevent misunderstanding both men and women need to become alert to the unique expressions of intimacy. These expressions begin during the courtship stage of intimate relationships.

COURTSHIP

Exciting, emotionally exhilarating, wonderful, confusing, and challenging is the experience of falling in love. Because of the strong emotions tapped in romantic relationships, the communication within them becomes critical and complex. Not getting it right means individuals embark on this adventure many times before deciding to make an effort to understand the tensions. A variety of potential misunderstandings can produce tension that may develop to confuse members of a romantic relationship and extend to marital partners in enduring relationships. Bell and Buerkel-Rossfuss (1990) describe these potential misunderstandings in the form of alternatives, such as (1) honesty versus the protection of feelings (Do I tell you what I think, or do I spare your feelings?), (2) self-disclosure versus privacy (Would you like to know my secrets?), (3) personal autonomy versus interdependence (Is it all right if I spend time with my friends?), (4) integration versus differentiation (Should we dress alike, think alike, talk alike, agree on everything, or differ in these things?), (5) reciprocity versus generosity (Do I do things for you because I love you, or do I want something in return?), (6) commitment versus voluntarism (Do I do things with you so I am allowed to do the things I really want to do?), and (7) novelty versus predictability (Do you like to know how I will react, or is it okay for me to act more interesting?).

Wood (1982) describes the stages of growth as a relationship develops.

First, the individual exists outside the couple or intimate relationship. This follows an invitation stage or a trying out stage of contact including a variety of people. The next stage engages people in exploration through talk to determine compatibility. As the likelihood of compatibility increases, individuals may become more intensely interested and may even experience euphoria. During this stage the "other" becomes idealized and expressions of talk become more intensely intimate. At this stage a person may become totally immersed in the other. As an individual begins to "come to," he or she may revise earlier opinions or reevaluate the other person. During this stage termination may occur, but if it does not, the chances of the relationship's succeeding increase. The final stage of coming together commits the couple to a future of intimacy with each other, usually a public display. One person may be ready for this earlier than the other.

The maintenance of the relationship process occurs after the couple bond, dealing with the search for a workable structure for the ongoing relationship. Structure always involves goals, and certainly roles. If successful negotiating of the structure fails, a relationship may begin to deteriorate. If deterioration begins a person may look for the following stages of relational breakup, as described by Knapp (1984): First, individuals begin to differentiate, meaning one or both members of the couple begin increasingly to focus on the self instead of the pair. The next stage, circumscribing, involves restricting communication to safe areas. During this stage, the couple talks less often, depth of substance is reduced, number of communication attempts decreases, and poisonous exchanges occur. Couples may not even be aware or may not wish to admit that a change in the relationship is occurring. The couple then begins to stagnate, meaning they operate on a nonintimate basis with many areas of communication closed off. The couple then begins to avoid the company of one another. Messages often convey antagonism and unfriendliness and excuses for inaccessibility. When one or both members of the couple wish to terminate the relationship, divorce or some other specific message expressing the relationship's end is communicated. Finally, partners return to individual status, changed by the experience of having been in a relationship.

THE CHANGING FACE OF MARRIAGE

A number of variables affect marriage. Among them are that the average age of marrying has risen, the longevity of marriage has decreased, chances of divorce have increased, long-distance relationships (marriages) have increased, sex role expectations have shifted from more to less traditional, dual-career and dual-earner relationships have increased, and fluctuating economic factors have influenced the face of marriage. Role reversals with men staying home as child care providers and women playing the role of wage earner reflect changes from the marital relationship of the past. Otto

(1988) reports that in 1955 Ward and June Cleaver, with working father, housewife mother, and two or more school-aged children, represented 60 percent of all families; in 1988 they represented only 7 percent. In 1950, only 28 percent of married women with children worked outside the home, but by 1986, 68 percent of the same group worked. Alternative life-style arrangements, such as communal living and same-sex households, have also changed the nature of relational partnerships.

These shifts in the profile of men and women in relation to one another and the impact of these shifts on communication represent the greatest social changes of the last three decades. Although they do affect the face of marriage, the primary responsibility of breadwinner still falls on men, but women do assist, and the primary responsibility of housework and child care provider still falls on women, but men assist. However, Hochschild (1989) reports 80 percent of husbands did not share in housework or child care as late as 1989. Over the past few years, participation in household and child care responsibilities has increased (Seward et al., 1993), but the majority of that participation takes the form of activities such as reading to children, playing with them, or teaching them (Thompson & Walker, 1989). Women's responsibility for child care was illustrated by Zoe Baird's and Kimba Wood's withdrawing from the selection process for attorney general over child care issues; questions of child care have never come up in Senate confirmation hearings for men. Problems exist for men who play the role of primary housekeeper and child care provider, as well. Men who take on these responsibilities, rather than full-time employment outside the home, often complain of low self-esteem and subtle rejection by society. The small numbers of men who decide to play this role does not appear to be the subject of much research at this time. As this tendency increases we'll probably hear more about it from researchers.

Thirty years ago, a strong social norm prohibited divorce, making it difficult to obtain and stigmatizing those who divorced. This clearly has changed. At a recent wedding the minister performing the ceremony changed the vow to "as long as you both shall love" rather than "live." But divorce isn't working either, because people are remarrying. Marital satisfaction seems to be correlated to a number of variables. A significant percentage of both husbands and wives report more satisfaction if the husband is seen as more intelligent, more competent, and of higher professional status than the wife. People who indicate marital satisfaction report the importance of listening rather than talking, the ability to meet and exceed the role expectations of their spouses, reciprocal trust, equal sharing of home and child-rearing responsibilities, sharing of tasks, pleasant and positive everyday interactions, high mutual level of self-disclosure, assurances of worth and love, and sharing of time and space.

GENDER ROLE CONFLICT

When women carry the burden of full-time work outside the home, as well as the responsibility for housework and child care, this situation produces a double work load, often referred to as the *second shift*. If the role involves leadership or management at work a sense of commitment in both places creates enormous pressures that often result in gender role conflict. The sense of commitment required of managers often involves long hours when necessary, relocation when the organization requires, and loyalty to the organization over the family when the two conflict. Whereas the commitment of working men does not appear to conflict with family considerations, that of working women does.

Pressure from others through comments like "You should be home with your children" or "If you'd taken better care of your husband he wouldn't be flirting with me" increase gender role conflict for women managers who are already burdened. Women also may experience pressure from people who discriminate against them at work by sexually harassing them, isolating them, sabotaging their work, writing anonymous letters, or even making death threats. But the degree of sex role conflict felt by women managers may be determined by their level of commitment to family or job. For example, women with nontraditional attitudes toward sex roles will likely experience lesser sex role conflict than women with traditional attitudes. If a woman rises to the level of management by assuming a leadership role she may already have rejected traditional attitudes, or the intellectual stimulation of her job may create a sense of commitment overriding sex role conflict (Nelson & Quick, 1985). Negotiating roles within close relationships has been the focus of a number of researchers.

FITZPATRICK MODELS

A gendered biosocial issue in marriage is how each member of a couple interprets the concept of masculinity and femininity. In a thorough study of marital partners, Fitzpatrick (1988) describes couple types. Placing them along a continuum, she describes Traditionals, at one end, holding fairly conventional values, whereas Independents, at the extreme other end, hold nonconventional values and Separates fall in the middle. Additionally, Fitzpatrick describes "Mixed" couple types, for example, a Separate/Independent or Traditional/Separate marital combination. In what ways do these couples vary with regard to gender role differentiation, communication, egalitarianism, and self-disclosure?

"Traditional" couple types hold conventional ideological values about gender role specialization in their relationships (Fitzpatrick, 1988). Conventional orientations toward marriage suggest a wife should take the last name of her husband and infidelity constitutes inexcusable disloyalty. Fitzpatrick (1988) claims Traditionals exhibit interdependence in their marriage with a high degree of sharing and companionship. This companionship reinforces a certain level of daily routine and shared physical space. Additionally, Traditionals say that although they may not communicate assertively, they tend not to avoid conflict with their spouses. Couples who define themselves as Traditional assign wage earning roles to the husband and child care to the wife, and Whyte (1951) agrees these roles do define the Traditional couple.

Fitzpatrick (1988) describes Independents as holding fairly nonconventional values about gender roles, relational life, and family life. At the opposite end of the ideological continuum from the Traditionals, an Independent believes relationships should not constrain an individual's freedom in any way. The Independent couple enjoys a high level of companionship and sharing in their marriage, but they are qualitatively different from the companionship and sharing in a Traditional marriage. The Independent tries to stay psychologically close to a spouse but maintains separate physical space, may even live in a different city, and has difficulty maintaining a regular daily time schedule. Independent couple types report some assertiveness in their relationship with their spouse and tend not to avoid conflicts.

Separate couple types seem to hold two opposing ideological views on relationships at the same time. Although a Separate believes in traditional conventions about gender roles and marital issues, he or she at the same time supports the values upheld by Independents, stressing personal freedom over relationship maintenance. Supporting two opposing sets of values suggests the Separates feel somewhat ambivalent about their relational values. They experience significantly less companionship and sharing in their marriage. They attempt to keep a psychological distance in their relationship and try to maintain some autonomy through their use of space. Interdependence is expressed by keeping a regular daily schedule. Separates report some attempts at persuasion and assertiveness toward their spouses. They also indicate they tend to *avoid* open marital conflict.

In addition to these pure couple types, spouses who disagree on the major aspects of these basic dimensions end up in different clusters; Fitzpatrick (1988) refers to them as *Mixed* types. In other words, both members of the couple describe the marriage differently. A Mixed marriage may include a Separate husband married to a Traditional wife, for example. In the Fitzpatrick (1988) work, 60 percent of the couples categorized themselves as pure couple types and 40 percent as Mixed types. Confusion over gender role stereotypes may consume the marriage of a Mixed couple type.

In this work, Fitzpatrick claims the marital system appears to be evolving toward egalitarianism, becoming more similar to the Independent couple type than to any other on the continuum. In speculating about the future of marital couple types, Fitzpatrick argues the Independent couple type represents an advanced evolutionary form of marriage. Further, Fitzpatrick believes couples work out their own definitions of satisfaction, with some preferring varying degrees of communication, differing understandings of egalitarianism, and creative ways of experiencing intimacy. Curiously, however, Fitzpatrick unambiguously proclaims that Traditional couple types report the highest levels of dyadic adjustment and marital satisfaction.

TRANSITION TO ADAPTIVE/INDEPENDENT

Peplau (1983) also describes marriages along a continuum with two basic dimensions: gender role specialization between the spouses and power between the sexes, or the amount of control the husband holds over the wife. At one end of the continuum, Peplau (1983) claims, in the Traditional marriage the husband dominates the wife and the couple exhibit considerable male–female gender role specialization. In the center of the continuum, the Modern marriage, described by Peplau, shows male dominance as muted and role specialization as less extensive. Peplau's third couple type, at the other extreme end of the continuum, Egalitarian, rejects the basic tenets of male dominance and gender role specialization.

Payne (1988) describes wives as moving along the traditional–modernity continuum, using the descriptors of *Traditional, Transitional*, and *Adaptive*. This more detailed description of wife roles gives us a sharper focus as to how the women in these couple types work out their lives. This research claims Traditional wives support, nurture, make a home, raise the children, act as good listeners and stabilizers: "the keeper of the retreat, the one who rests and rejuvenates the man for the next day's battle" (Whyte, 1951, p. 89). The Payne (1988) work describes the Traditional wife as one whose stabilizing involves more than good homemaking; she also trains the children not to bother Dad. As a stabilizer between her husband's work and home life, she acts as a "sounding board," "refueling station," and "wailing wall" (Whyte, 1951) and as a form of therapist, made increasingly necessary by the corporate way of life consuming her husband. Her "career" often involves the role of social "operator" (one who manipulates through social interaction). She needs to be well read so she can be a good conversationalist. She needs to know how to put people at ease and remember names. So as not to call attention to herself, she needs to be attractive and dress in clothes understating her grace. Accordingly, Whyte (1951) has identified a number of rules for guiding the behavior of wives: Don't talk shop gossip with other wives; don't invite superiors in rank, and let them invite first; don't get too chummy with the wives of associates your husband might pass on the way up; don't be disagreeable to any company people you may meet; be attractive; never get drunk at a company party; blend in; and don't buck the system.

Over time, the Traditional wife begins to notice her skills as a listener are becoming less valuable. As her husband comes home to discuss the details of his work life, she finds herself less curious about those details and becomes progressively more passive. As the corporation provides more and more growth opportunities for him, and as she digs in at home with the children, she gradually begins to realize she has not the faintest idea of what he is talking about when discussing work problems, and begins to see herself as a member of a "muted group" (Kramarae, 1981). Since she has become increasingly less knowledgeable about the technical aspects of her husband's work life, she cannot give him good advice. As she becomes excluded from her husband's life, she begins to listen to feminist rhetoric invalidating her role.

She hears feminists saying all of society works toward the same end, the self-actualization of the male (Janeway, 1971). Power and weakness in the marriage relationship tend to flow into each other, creating dignity and status for only one member of the relationship. Society then forces women to play public roles not matching their private feelings. The outer false self, or social role, contradicts the inner true self, causing it to collapse. A role then seems a haven, a mask for no identity at all. If the reward for working at home involves receiving the affection of the husband and the success of the family and the wife fails to receive her reward, she often turns away from her old role, reverses it in a total looking-glass shift to its opposite, thinking if the old way did not work she will get as far from it as possible. An alternative to changing roles involves changing partners. Janeway (1971) recommends society avoid freezing behavior into old roles without much utility and inviting misunderstanding when the roles do not suit the members of a relationship.

Parsons's (1953) analysis of marriage provides the most influential work for feminist rhetoric to combat. In his view, the roles of husband and wife encompass mutually exclusive functions. The husband's role comprises those activities tying the couple to the larger social system, and the wife's role centers around expressive functions maintaining a favorable emotional climate for the family when they need to retreat from the world. Parsons's ideas stem from an era when traditional ideals of marriage were rarely challenged. Today, however, feminists claim the tasks most highly valued in any culture are those performed by males (Barnett & Baruch, 1978), and in the American culture if women want to improve their status they need to go to work. Further, Sheehy (1974) says a viable alternative to the housewife role involves getting wives into the world of work, if they want to avoid the "empty nest syndrome" when children leave home.

The second-generation wife, in the Payne (1988) research, finds herself in the midst of great social and family upheaval. While the feminist rhetoric tells her to buck the system and find new ways for fulfillment outside the marriage relationship, she has already unquestioningly assumed the Traditional role of subordinate person (Papanek, 1973). She struggles with the expectations for her role that are advocated by the woman's movement, while her husband struggles with changes at work. He may go home hoping to find a warm and loving "mother-type" woman waiting for him but cannot be sure what he will find on the other side of the door because not even she knows who she is.

The apparent confusion and anxiety produced by her gender role make the second-generation Traditional wife restive. Dransfield (1984) says without a career outside the home, this transitional woman may be slightly defensive. She wants to make her own contribution, to be taken seriously for her own accomplishments. So, in addition to the role of homemaker, good listener, and nurturer of the family, she decides to pursue a paying job, volunteer work, or a graduate degree. She also wants to correct the outgrown wife syndrome talked about by Whyte (1951) and experienced by her predecessors. Transitional (Payne, 1988) women find it necessary to attend college to avoid feeling inferior and to ensure they will be able to take care of themselves if something happens in the marriage. With increasing corporate pressures on the husband to travel (Renshaw, 1976), creating absentee husbands, wives find it necessary to pick up more and more of the slack at home. Consequently, Transitional wives experience disconnected marital relationships (Culbert & Renshaw, 1972). The literature describes how many Transitional wives experience psychological problems associated with their role (Adkins, 1984; Allen, 1981; Chasler, 1985; Culbert & Renshaw, 1972; Jacobs, 1980; Katz, 1982; Mlachak, 1984; Mollay, 1981; Papanek, 1973; Price, 1979; Renshaw, 1974). But women who break out of the Traditional role and go to work, whom Parr (1977) describes as superwives, experience exhaustion and psychological anxieties in trying to fulfill both career and wife/mother roles.

Shedding the traditional image of wife has confused not only women but men. In spite of it all, in the 80's and 90's both mothers and fathers encouraged their daughters to prepare for the work world and their sons to prepare to help out more at home. The twenty-first century woman has grown up with the expectation of having her own substantial career, and the twenty-first-century man has grown up with the expectation of having a wife who works outside the home and of helping out at home. Within the framework of this couple, glimpses of their life together begin to come into focus. The couple rarely sees one another or the people with whom their partner works. The wife cooks an evening meal less often; the couple has little time to share work concerns, and little time together exists except to accomplish important daily life routines (Norwood, 1985). When the husband receives an opportunity to relocate, the corporation often helps his wife find employment, as well. Often, when both careers are paramount to both members of the couple they may even live in separate cities. With both halves of a couple serious about their career, one may have to spend more time at work than the other. Although both work full time, one might be constantly waiting for the other to finish up. The resulting interpersonal conflict often has the potential for poisoning a relationship (Moore, 1984), creating a whole new set of tensions for couples already burdened with the challenges of being social pioneers. The problems associated with new roles often contribute to communication problems as these couples may resort to anger and sabotage, or ambivalence and guilt. When children enter the picture the complicated scheme becomes more difficult. Even when wives choose not to pursue a career they appear much more self-directed than couple-directed. They expect their husbands to share equally with the child care and housework (Dobson, 1982), despite job pressures. The goal of these self-directed women is to create a balance between their husband's career and their own self-interest, hoping to become more complete persons (Friedman, 1983; Kolbenschlag, 1979; Norwood, 1985; Vandervelde, 1978).

The traditionalist-modern/independent continuum reflects roles whereby men and women may be at different points. As many men and women have understood their roles, they have followed the traditional idea of male as dominant and female as submissive with highly specialized sex roles (Schmidt, 1994). But more modern views of marital gender roles align themselves away from male dominance, encouraging images of husbands that portray strength and power as nonviolent, noncompetitive (Schmidt, 1994), nondominant values. Schmidt says the relationships between the two members of a couple and the idea of leading their partners rather than dominating reflect a more desirable understanding of the role of husband. Weaver (1995) defines this kind of power as energy, effective interaction, and empowerment. Bate (1992) describes it as becoming powerful to accomplish your own goals and spreading the power you possess to enable the partner to accomplish his or her goals. Finally, the concept of power can be compared to love by suggesting that the more of it you give away, the more you get.

CONCLUSION

This chapter has discussed the hierarchical and partnership models of marital relationships, courtship, the changing face of marriage, and gender role conflict. The models are reflected in the Fitzpatrick, Peplau, and Payne marital partnership relationships. The "traditional wife" has experienced an environment influenced and affected by feminist rhetoric, as well as a general desire among women to experience more independence. Consequently, women are moving along a continuum ranging from the traditional, through a transition, toward a more adapted/independent role. Men are also moving as they adapt to the changes in women. The change in roles affects communication between husbands and wives, with some resulting confusion. Many men recognize they have lost power in the relationship, but they enjoy the benefits of having a more independent wife. Consequently, both members of the couple share in the work and home responsibilities. It is unlikely the shift in roles will at any time soon be reversed.

6

Gendered Issues in Communication about Sex

> If you wish to destroy a nation, destroy its morality and it will fall into your lap like a ripe apple from a tree.
>
> V. I. Lenin

INTRODUCTION

The sexual revolution of the 60's and 70's advocated a goal of liberating both men and women from prior restraints, allowing them to become impervious to public judgment and anesthetizing them from feelings of guilt. The average normal person, in whatever society we find him or her, when attracted to the opposite sex experiences passionate and sentimental episodes he or she often describes as the most significant events of his or her existence. Since the sexual revolution the language describing these sexual episodes reflects increasing approval of sex outside the sanctions of marriage. For example, in the early 50's the word *adulterer* was applied to a person who "fooled around" outside marriage. In the 60's *unfaithful, indiscreet*, and *loose* described such a person; and in the 70's the terms *extramarital, playing the field*, and *swinging*, described his or her actions. In the 80's *sexually active* characterized a person who had sex outside marriage, and in the 90's we heard terms like *responsible sex* and *safe sex*. In the new century people simply refer to it as *having sex*. It becomes apparent from the language used that sexual episodes outside the sanctions of marriage have become increasingly socially acceptable.

Historically, the United States government advocated the values that originated in the Holy Bible of the Christian church. In nearly every state in the nineteenth century, sexual intercourse of unmarried partners was against the law (Hunt, 1974), often resulting in action against the offender. Over time those laws gradually have not been enforced or have been removed from the books. The most recent outcry for change of the law has involved abolition of sodomy laws in a special effort to remove restraints for sexual activity among homosexual males. Although the goal of the sexual revolution may have been to anesthetize guilt associated with sex outside marriage between a man and woman, another effort promoted a change in the idea of sexual activity for the purpose of procreation to sex exclusively for pleasure. Levine (1988), for example, claims society should not fear sex, despite acquired immune deficiency syndrome (AIDS) and other sexually transmitted diseases, but should welcome it as a pleasurable and healthy part of life. Murdy and Hayse (1995) advocate unapologetically prosex, prolesbian, progay, prowoman, and prochoice positions in the sexual revolution of the new century. Canavan (1995), however, says the sexual revolution may have emancipated men and women from former moral norms but has tended to unravel the cultural fabric of society, playing an important role in removing God's blessings from the land.

This chapter describes gender issues in communication about sex as it relates to men and women. Sexual language describing intercourse and genitalia as used by men and women is discussed, including euphemisms and derogatory words. Gender differences in communication about value perceptions of morality and homosexuality are included. A discussion of the gender differences in attitudes toward pornography and its effect on violence is presented, and gender issues relating to sex education are discussed. An underlying premise of this discussion is that gender differences in communication affect relationships and distort meaning.

LANGUAGE

Sexual language profoundly affects the perceptions of men and women, and it affects the way they communicate with one another. Maslow (1970) describes sex as a basic lower-level need in the same category with other physical needs such as those for water, air, and food. Varying beliefs about how men and women differ in their perceptions of sexuality exist, but generally perceptions of men as active or dominant and women as passive permeate the sexuality lexicon. The language used to describe sexual intercourse and sexual partners often portrays women negatively and men positively. Along with dominant/passive, positive/negative differences in language describing sex and sexual partners, another controversial issue surfaces. Characterization of behavior as appropriate for men but inappropriate for women rankles feminists, who refer to it as a double standard. Haas (1979) believes the double standard has been replaced by the humanist standard of the "individual ethic," which assumes individuals should behave in ways that make them feel comfortable.

One reason men and women experience sexual behavior differently is that they have different vocabularies for intercourse and body parts. Men view sex as a physical activity; women see it as relational. Consequently, men use graphic, active terms to describe sexual intercourse and body parts. On the other hand, women, who are viewed as more polite, use vague terms, euphemisms, and clinical terms in efforts to keep the subject in the abstract (Wells, 1990). Baker (1981) surveyed students and found language differences depicting men as active and women as passive partners. Male students who use active language report the following words to describe intercourse: *screwed, laid, had, banged, humped, jumped, poked* (Cameron, 1985), and *made love to*. Female students, in efforts to remain abstract, use words such as *did the wild thing, did it, he made me feel good, we had some fun*. Male students use power slang evoking strength and dominance in describing male genitalia or sexual activity: *dick, cock, male member, tool, weapon, soldier*, and *stud*. Some males even name their penis and blame it for their mischief. Male students describe female genitalia or sexual activity with what women view as negative terminology such as *twat, snatch, hole, pussy, beaver, cherry, box, slut, cunt, whore, screw*, or *lay*. Female students describe male genitalia with euphemisms such as *his thing, riding the balony pony, it*, and *you know*. Female descriptions of female genitalia included *hm hm, down there, my place, you know, my whatsit*, and *my stuff*. These differences affect the way partners think about each other and how they communicate; the differences reflect the society's view of human sexuality as dominated by men. Blumstein and Schwartz (1983) argue that when it comes to sexuality men and women behave differently. Men feel pressure to perform but express more latitude in their sexual behavior, whereas women feel constricted and report having a lack of control over the experience. Paludi (1992) says culture shapes and limits the sexual experience for women. Women resist challenging men's sexual dominance because many still depend on men for their economic security (Hite, 1981). Further, women use less direct, more vague terms for describing sexual intercourse or genitalia because they are expected to use more polite speech (Lakoff, 1975; Crosby & Nyquist, 1977).

Kaats and Davis (1970) report men engage in more nonmarital sexual activity than women and tend to talk openly about it. Further, Peplau, Rubin, and Hill (1977) report males continue to initiate sexual activity, even though the attitude of the female determines whether or not it will happen. In the same study, men overestimate their partner's desire for sex and have a greater desire for sex than women, so women need to be clear about their desires. Males also report more sexually permissive behavior than females. In other words, males accept more nonmarital sexual intercourse for themselves or other males and like to talk about it but do not accept such behavior among females (Gray et al., 1978). Kirkendall and Sibley (1966) describe women as preferring permanent relationships: when seeking out a man they look for someone who seems stable, ready to settle down. Men, on the other hand, want diversity and more casual sexual partners, but when wanting to settle down look for women who appear healthy and able to reproduce so as to continue the family name. In the 70's women reported more tolerance for marrying a nonvirgin than did men. Men also reported a higher sexual urge than women (Mercer & Kohn, 1979).

Despite the demands by the feminist movement that the female body not be objectified, as late as the mid-90's research still found such objectification (Johnson & Gilmore, 1993). Females report perceiving sex as a competition between women reflecting their own attractiveness and ability to gain a man's attention. Males report interpreting sexual acts in violent ways, to demonstrate dominance, to show hatred for another, to demonstrate a grudge, and to cause humiliation. They also report using humor, inside jokes, and teasing about sexual activity with one another.

A widely quoted research study by Koss (1988) claims that one out of every twelve men admits to forcing a woman to have sexual intercourse. On the basis of her survey of 6,159 students at thirty-two colleges, 27 percent of females reported being victims of rape (15 percent) or attempted rape (12 percent) an average of two times between the ages of fourteen and twenty-one. The majority of offenders were acquaintances, often dates. The findings of her study have been reported in several professional journals and quoted in newspapers, on television, and during the 1991 and 1993 Senate hearings on the Violence against Women Act. Gilbert (1995) claims Koss misinterpreted her research to promote a particular agenda. He says almost three-quarters of the students whom Koss categorized as victims of rape do not think they have been raped. Second, he says in support of the students' own accounts of their experiences, 42 percent of them had sex again with the man Koss (but not the students) claim raped them. Finally, he says that two of the five items used to define rape and attempted rape were the vaguely worded questions "Have you had a man attempt sexual intercourse (get on top of you, attempt to insert his penis) when you did not want it by giving you alcohol or drugs, even though intercourse did not occur?" Further, Gilbert (1995) claims Koss never cited miscommunication as a result of perceptions of rape. Society teaches men to be aggressive and competitive, and their hormones reinforce this behavior. Women learn submissiveness and cooperativeness, and their hormones reinforce this behavior. Consequently, men need to be careful not to let their own desires color their interpretation of a woman's nonconsent to sexual activity. Women need to be sure to communicate clearly with both verbal and nonverbal cues (Abbey, 1982). Men need to unlearn the game of trying to turn a woman's no into a yes. Women need to avoid sending mixed messages about sexual activity, feigning resistance to sexual overtures, or teasing men who want to have sex (Muehlenhard & Hollabaugh, 1988).

VALUES

The sexual revolution of the 60's and 70's ushered in rhetoric about sex promoting sexual conduct between consenting adults as an activity to be enjoyed without guilt. The rhetoric emerged largely from feminist groups who wanted the freedoms previously associated with male sexuality, including unrestrained sexual activity without social disapproval. Historically, males made sexual advances and females determined whether the advances would be accepted, and the sexual revolution did not substantially alter this arrangement. It did, however, generate sexual decision making dilemmas for women. In the past, women who said no were pursued by males as a challenge, they received respect for saying no, and the no stimulated more sexual energy from both men and women who were attracted to one another. Since the sexual revolution, society has attributed much more power to the sexual *urge* than to *restraint* (Goodman, 1979). Some males report not dating a woman twice if she does not "come across" on the first date; others say that if they spend a certain amount of money on a woman, they expect her to "put out." For males who fall into this category, the goal of the date is sex, whereas the goals of dating for females are making a connection, establishing a relationship, and getting a commitment. Abbey (1982) looks at perceptions of sexual interest and finds male observers more often perceive female friendliness as seduction, make more judgments about female interactants' being promiscuous, and frequently report being sexually attracted to female interactants. Male observers also rate male interactants' behavior as sexual in nature; female observers see less sexuality in male subjects' behavior. Abbey (1982) concludes, "Men are more likely to perceive the world in sexual terms and to make sexual judgments than women are" (p. 830).

Canavan (1995) claims the cultural changes ushered in by the Industrial Revolution have only within the last few decades come out into the open as a rejection of and attack on the sexual morality of major religious groups. Sobran (1995) says the pursuit of the orgasm is assumed to be an end in itself, limited only by the inconvenient health hazards associated with it, and the phrase *safe sex* has reduced the most intimate human experience to the level of fast food. Levine (1988), on the other hand, considers pleasure a revolutionary goal. She believes in destabilizing traditional sexual arrangements and removing the guilt accompanying such a cultural upheaval. She wants women to be more like men, suggesting they stop seeing sexual engagements as relationship commitments. She believes in challenging the sexual hegemony of the nuclear family and resisting its enforcement of adult heterosexual monogamy and its policing of all other forms of sexuality within it and outside it. Today, as a result of the sexual revolution, women and men find it increasingly difficult to commit to relationships.

Many researchers (Leigh, 1989; Bascow, 1992; Bell & Weinberg, 1978; Peplau, 1981; Peplau & Gordon, 1983; Carroll et al., 1985; Whitley, 1988) explore the reasons why people engage in sexual activity. Male subjects place more emphasis on having pleasure, pleasing one's partner, and relieving tension than do female subjects. Females rate the expression of emotional closeness as a more important reason for having sex than do male subjects. These findings are consistent across sexual orientations. Gay male subjects engage in sexual activity for the same reasons as heterosexual males. Lesbian females engage in sexual activity to promote closeness, love, and emotional involvement much the same as do heterosexual women. In providing reasons for not engaging in sex, males rate the fear of AIDS and a fear of rejection more highly than do female subjects, but males report "never passing up an opportunity" more frequently than any other answer in the Carroll et al. (1985) study. Females give reasons such as fear of pregnancy, lack of interest in the partner, insufficient love/commitment, and a general lack of enjoyment of sexual acts. The biological sex rather than the psychological gender role acts most often as the predictor of reasons for engaging in sexual activity. In other words, an androgynous subject conforms to the patterns of his or her biological sex. In this regard, the sexual revolution has changed nothing, except that sexual activity appears to be more overt and to provoke less social disapproval.

To early Christians, the body was a beast to be tamed, not a master to be served, and men had more of a problem with this than women. St. Paul gave a scant amount of attention to sex; his primary focus was the second coming of Christ. Since Christ would dissolve the old world and usher in a new one, Paul viewed sexual problems as of secondary concern. In the sense that all humankind still awaits the second coming of Christ, or the Day of Judgment, and society has succumbed to the Freudian gospel anesthetizing religious abhorrence for fornication, sex itself has disordered society. Religious prohibitions against sex outside marriage strike the modern liberal as outrageous and ridiculous. The promotion of masturbation, contraception, homosexuality, and sodomy has replaced the emphasis on institutions such as marriage and male headship of the family. Canavan (1995) claims the sexual revolution negatively affected all of us, and as it continues and grows, we may expect a further unraveling of society. Increasing numbers of women and men alike seem to be opting not to marry, postponing marriage, or having multiple marriages. Men and women even turn to homosexual relationships to fulfill their basic relational goals. For men the goal might be pleasure; for women it might be love and closeness. Since someone of the same sex theoretically has the same goal, the miscommunication that occurs between people with differing goals is reduced in same-sex relationships.

The Church of Jesus Christ of Latter-Day Saints (Quinn, 1997) proclaims marriage between man and woman central to the Creator's plan, the means for creating a family. The sacred powers of procreation, by lawfully wedded husband and wife, affirm the sanctity of life and its importance in God's eternal plan. By divine design, fathers preside over their families in love and righteousness, responsible for providing the necessities of life and protection. Mothers primarily have authority over the nurturance of their children. Fathers and mothers help one another as equal partners. Those violating the covenants of chastity, or abusing children, or failing in their fulfillment of family responsibilities will be reminded of their accountability before God. Disintegration of the family causes individuals, communities, and nations to suffer the calamities foretold by ancient prophets.

As society moves away from the notion of exclusive sex within the holy bonds of heterosexual marriage, those who wish to push the boundaries of guiltless sex assert that nothing is unnatural about any shared love, including that of people of the same sex. Nugent and Spong (1995) claim a significant portion of people want to engage in homosexuality and do not believe God views homosexuality as a "sin." The rhetoric of articulate homosexuals claims for all people "sin" means freely acting contrary to one's deeply held moral or ethical convictions, whether they originate in organized religion or a personally developed value system. Grant and Horne (1993) assert that regarding homosexuality as a genetic condition rather than a sin obstructs the homosexual from renouncing his or her sexual orientation and becoming free of its sinful burden. Although God prohibits all forms of extramarital sex and states it in Scripture, premarital heterosexual offenses are adjudicated (settled) within the option of covenantal marriage (Exodus 22:16–17; Deuteronomy 22:28–29). No such options for homosexual relationships exist because God does not recognize covenantal marriages between people of the same sex. Contrary to the rhetoric of those who charge that Christians fear homosexuals, Christians in fact feel love and concern for reconciliation to God for all humankind. Reconciliation to God requires repentance of sin and turning away from it. If homosexuals believe they do not sin, they will never feel the need to repent; consequently, in their strategies to promote acceptance of their lifestyle, they resist the notion of homosexuality as sin. At the same time, Christian zealots do not glorify God by using rhetorical strategies bludgeoning homosexuals with scriptural law, but would do better to convince them with the gospel. Often homosexual life-styles and other non-covenant sexual life-styles, begin when young people view pornography.

PORNOGRAPHY

Selle (1995) interviewed two members of the Los Angeles Police Department, who described pornography as a moral plague contributing to many of the nation's social ills, such as organized crime, exploitation of and violence toward women, as well as unhealthy male sexual attitudes and sexual dysfunction. Further, they believe Los Angeles distributes pornography to the entire world. Denmark and Sweden produce child porn and Japan has increased their production of pornography, but none compares to the distribution system of the United States. Opposing perspectives on the effects of pornography clarify the rhetorical strategies used by both sides. Although many Americans do not approve of pornography, they do believe government should not censor it. Harvey (1995) argues prevention of production, distribution, and viewing of pornography interferes with the rights and freedoms of Americans and imposes a public morality. He contends pornography causes no harm and has legitimate functions. Harvey says when violence enters into pornography some viewers tend to harden in ways we may not like, but the violence, not the sex, produces the negative results. Katz (1995), a feminist who opposes censorship, supports the freedom to produce pornography and refuses to accept the protection offered to women against pornography in exchange for censorship. She disagrees with the idea that pornography degrades women; further, she says, sex therapists view nonviolent pornography as a useful means to improve sexual relationships.

Wyre (1995) argues a direct relationship exists between pornography and sexual violence against women and children in some men. Pornography creates a climate of thought and belief impacting and influencing attitudes. Wyre (1995) reports about Gary Bishop, a convicted homosexual pedophile who murdered five boys in Utah to conceal his sexual abuse of them. Bishop says procuring increasingly more sexually arousing materials became an obsession for him, fueling his sexual fantasies. His conscience became desensitized and his sexual appetite entirely controlled his actions. In an interview with James Dobson just hours before his execution, the serial killer Ted Bundy told stories about a number of his fellow inmates who had been involved in violent sex crimes. He said hard-core pornography had influenced and motivated them to commit increasingly heinous acts. Christensen (1990), however, maintains no substantial evidence of a connection between pornography and crimes of sexual violence exists. He says that statistical findings do not prove a causal relationship; rather, they suggest that sexual materials play only a minor role in the thinking of sex offenders, whose lives are already disordered and violent for other reasons. In fact, he says, pornography may actually reduce violence among sex offenders by providing them a safety valve for antisocial impulses through imagination or fantasy. Bundy, however, said that after a while, imagination and fantasy no longer satisfy the hunger and increased desire, so the sex offender who crosses the line needs more and more stimulation to satisfy his impulses. Pictures and stories, therefore, increasingly anesthetize the sex offender toward increasingly harder-core pornography until finally he must act it out.

On a far less extreme level, pornography affects relationships between normal men and women. At a college in the Northeast, both male and female students talked candidly about the effects of pornography. Males frequently agreed they had experienced their first sexual pleasure with a centerfold magazine as their imagined partner or their first sexual experience resulted from reading pornographic literature. As they continued to read and look at pornographic material, they claimed, they began to expect their dates to behave in the way depicted by pornographic materials. When their dates acted reluctant, they would persuade, or even force them to comply. In several instances, the male students claimed they could not even reach orgasm unless they imagined their partner was someone they had seen in pornographic materials. Females reported feeling reluctant to comply with their partners requests, saying their partners kept saying things like "You like this, don't you? I know you like this," although they did not like it and on occasion said so. In any case, such relationships developed into unhealthy ones the couples finally realized needed to be discussed openly, a motive for their attending the meeting. Learning about sex by reading pornographic literature and viewing pornographic pictures does not constitute adequate sex education.

SEX EDUCATION

Many families want schools to teach comprehensive sex education because they feel inadequate and embarrassed about providing the right information to their children. Such education encompasses teaching about subjects such as abstinence, contraception, homosexuality/life-style options, and sexually transmitted diseases. Some educators believe it takes a long time to teach children to respect themselves and others, make responsible decisions under pressure, and clarify their personal and family values. Opponents of sex education in the schools (Ankerberg & Weldon, 1993; Limbaugh, 1992) do not want educators to teach sex education because they believe educators take a neutral stand on morality while attempting to teach students techniques for putting on a condom and having "safe sex," such as oral sex, masturbation, and other forms of petting. Opponents of sex education in the schools believe teaching children to be accepting, rather than discriminating, about sexual behavior transmits the wrong message about sex, because, they say, sex education taught by a "values-neutral" method opposes traditional major world religious teachings, moral absolutes, and parental values and supports secular humanism. Ankerberg and Weldon (1993) say everyone must advocate a morality of some kind; the question is whether the one chosen is good or bad. Character and personality are inextricably bound up with sexual behavior and can therefore not be values-neutral. Consequently, when children receive sex education they learn about contraception; Dr. Robert Kistner of Harvard Medical School (codeveloper of the birth control pill) said in 1977 that he had thought "that the pill would not lead to promiscuity, but I was wrong." Dr. Min Chueh Chang (codeveloper of the pill) said in 1981, "I personally feel the Pill has rather spoiled young people. It has made them more permissive" (reported in Ankerberg & Weldon, 1993).

On the other hand, one of the most far-reaching social movements of our times has brought about the revolt of women against sexual servitude to men. Formerly, women knew little about their own reproductive nature and less about the consequences of excessive childbearing. Today, however, millions of women assert their right to voluntary motherhood, determined to decide for themselves whether they shall become mothers, under what conditions and when. Sanger (1920) believes women should control and be responsible for their own reproduction. She sees health problems experienced by women with too many children and wants motherhood elevated to a plane of voluntary, intelligent choice. In contrast, Martin and Martin (1916) say the woman's movement has moved society toward progressive national degeneration and ultimate national suicide. They argue that only women can bear children, which perpetuates the best part of a nation, the regeneration of the species, and women should accept this way of serving society. Thompson (1917) believes that society should revere women for their ability to bear children, should protect babies, and should not try to control the number of babies born.

CONCLUSION

Men and women describe sex differently, and these differences have a profound effect on the way they relate to one another. Both men and women describe sex in ways that provoke images of dominance for men, with men still claiming macho images for men who frequently change partners. Women and men describe sex in ways that provoke images of passivity for women, with negative images of women who frequently change partners. What is perceived as appropriate behavior for men and women often produces some confusion over what feminists have described as a double standard. Feminists, instead of advocating that men change the way they talk and behave about sex, have encouraged women to become more like men. Consequently, society's view of appropriate sexual conduct has encouraged more rather than less sex "outside of marriage" as permissible and even desirable for both men and women.

The cultural shift in the way men and women communicate about sex and engage in sexual episodes has generated a drift between traditional and liberated views. Yet, even with these changes males still make the sexual advances and women still determine whether the advances will be accepted. The cultural shift has caused considerable confusion, however, since men now perceive women as more willing to be promiscuous. Consequently, men often perceive female friendliness as desire, while females do not understand why they see it that way. And despite the changes in the sexual culture, males still see sexual intercourse as a way to achieve pleasure and please their partner, while females still view it as a way to achieve emotional closeness.

On the two sides of the pornography issue, one side argues that violence, not sex, produces behavior society does not like. Others maintain that no evidence connects pornography with crimes of violence and, in fact, pornography might even act as a safety value for antisocial impulses through the use of imagination and fantasy. On the other side of the issue, sex criminals claim pornography influences and motivates them to commit increasingly heinous acts, as they need more and more stimulation to fulfill their sexual impulses until they have to act them out. Some researchers assert that pornography also affects relationships between normal men and women and often leads to violence against women.

When educators attempt to teach sex education in the schools, they often include information about contraception, homosexuality/life-style options, and sexually transmitted diseases, with little persuasion for abstinence. People who oppose sex education in the schools often do so because of this "values-neutral" method, which tends to undermine the traditional values of people of faith. To combat this "values-neutral" approach, people of faith have started their own church-sponsored schools where traditional values relating to moral absolutes are taught.

7

Gendered Differences in Language and Aggressive/Argumentative Communication

If you want to get the world by the tail, you must take the bull by the horns.

Anonymous

After listening to a speech calling for the use of more "ladylike" language by women and a less masculine communication style, the next speaker launched into a discussion of her role as a law student, in which she used excessive profanity—particularly "the *F* word"—and a demanding, direct, loud, fist pounding, masculine communication style. Apparently, this law student had adapted a communication style consistent with the profession she had chosen, stereotypically a male-dominated field. Fighting stereotypes about females on a continual basis, she had no desire to hear how much more effective females might be if they fulfilled the expectations of their listeners or, at the very least, prepared their audiences for more intense language and style. Clearly the communication style used by men and women reflects and shapes their perceptions and experiences of the world. We form lasting impressions of people that are based on the way they communicate, and as individuals perceive others, they often adjust their communication to fit the exigencies of a situation.

This chapter describes the differences in language use by males and females and aggressive/argumentative communication styles. We stereotypically expect men to use more intense language, often describing them as argumentative. We stereotypically expect women to use less intense language, often describing them as passive or assertive. When males use an intense aggressive style of speech that entails greater use of curse words, people may call them "bastards." When females use more intense language and an argumentative style they are often called "bitches." Most people prefer not to be characterized by labels such as these and may go to great lengths to avoid them.

LANGUAGE

Our use of language reflects our communication competence, including the knowledge of communication rules, such as when to speak or be silent, how to speak appropriately for specific occasions, and how to transmit respect, seriousness, politeness, intimacy, or humor (Milroy, 1980). Coates (1988) and Lakoff (1975) indicate men and women use language differently, and these differences raise conflicting views about why they do. Lakoff (1975) has been criticized not for noting these differences, but for implying that a deviation from the male standard is a deficiency for women who want to be successful. Wood (1994) explains one view, that women experience life as an oppressed, marginalized group and their communication reflects this life experience. Another view Wood (1994) describes is that women and men are different creatures, with consequently different communication competence. In a third view, Bradley (1981) claims women use linguistic devices that are devalued not because the devices themselves are weak, but because women have lower status in society.

Female Language Style

Societal expectations and stereotypical beliefs about communication behavior do, in part, become prescriptive in nature, often determining sex-role-related behavior (Berryman & Wilcox, 1980). Barron (1970) describes the oral speech of women as compared to that of men as reflecting a greater concern with internal psychological states. Historically, women's language indicated a greater interest in the female role, clothes, buildings, interior decorations, the opposite sex, and appearances and exhibited greater shyness (Moore, 1922). Balswick and Avertt (1977) describe certain emotions as feminine: tenderness, compassion, sentimentality, gentleness, and soft-heartedness. In their study, they find females more expressive of love, happiness, and sadness than males. Gottschalk and Hambidge (1955) also find females using a higher percentage of words connoting feeling, emotion, or motivation; making more references to self; and using more auxiliary words and negations than males. Women use fewer words connoting time, space, or quantity and fewer words referring to destructive action than males. Chafetz (1974) claims females want affection, explaining, in part, why they use language expressing tenderness. This poses a problem for women once the completion of the courtship stage of a relationship occurs because males express these feelings less often after courtship than females. Bardwick (1973, p. 16) suggests stereotypes about men prevent them from "expressing their feelings," and stereotypes about women prevent them from expressing anger.

Lakoff (1973) argues women use language forms suggesting uncertainty, reflecting their socialization. As evidence of this phenomenon, researchers observe females using more of the following: tag questions, a statement plus a type of confirmative phrase such as *right* (Gleason & Weintraub, 1978; Hartman, 1976; McMillan et al., 1977); qualifiers, words that modify, soften, or weaken other phrases such as "Perhaps he should go with you" (Hartman, 1976; Martin & Craig, 1983; Mulac & Lundell, 1986); intensifiers, words intending to create greater impact such as *really, so much, such, quite,* and *awfully*; evaluative adjectival phrases, words intended to modify a noun, such as *a definite decision*; diminutives, words indicating small size such as the "tiniest"; color vocabulary, including a wide variety of shades of a color such as baby pink, hot pink, rosy pink, rusty pink; and civilities, words indicating politeness or courtesy (Brouwer et al., 1979; Hartman, 1976; McMillan et al., 1977; Mulac & Lundell, 1986; Rich, 1977), as indicators of their tentativeness. Lakoff (1975) describes these indicators of tentativeness as reflectors indicating women lack full confidence in the truth of their claims. Further, females tend to ask more questions (Tannen, 1994) and use compound requests, such as "If it wouldn't be too inconvenient for you, would you please come over here?" more frequently than do men (Thorne & Henley, 1975; Zimmerman & West, 1975). When they use these linguistic devices, women are perceived less positively and are less persuasive than women who use more direct approaches (Bradley, 1981). Curiously, perceptions of language use can be influenced by gender, as well. When men use these same linguistic devices they receive higher ratings than women on intelligence and credibility (Bradley, 1981).

Kramer (1977, 1978) describes the speaking traits identified as characteristic of women's speech, including clear enunciation, wide range of pitch and rate, excessive talking, inclusion of large amounts of detail, good grammar, polite speech, and gibberish. In children's television programs certain language choices actually enable people to identify female characters accurately. Female characters tend to use longer sentences, more verbs indicating a lack of certainty, more concrete (rather than abstract) nouns, more polite words or phrases (such as *please*), more verbs, more adverbial phrases at the beginning of sentences ("In the summer, it rains a lot" [Mulac et al., 1985, p. 500]), and more judgment adjectives (like *silly* or *beautiful*). Females tend to use modal auxiliaries, words of predication (preachy) such as *can, should, must, might, may* (Goodwin, 1988) rather than direct requests ("Could we leave now?" as opposed to "We will leave now!").

The expectation that women act as the preserver of the cultural value of politeness manifests itself in the way men and women speak in Japan (Kawaguchi, 1990). Women use language depicting a higher level of politeness than men, as evidenced by the use of honorific forms in Japanese sentences. In a study (Ide et al., 1985) concerning the use of Japanese terms of politeness, more honorific linguistic forms, such as *da* and *dai*, characterize female speech. In fact, if a woman and a man use the same form in the Japanese culture, the woman is viewed as less polite (Kawaguchi, 1990) because of differences in stereotypical expectations. Although these gender differences do exist, both sexes are expected to be polite in conversation, though the sanctity of the value ultimately appears to rest with the female. In the American culture, more polite language expectations for women also appear to be the norm. Balswick and Averett (1977) find females use more courtesy words, such as *please, thank you,* and *excuse me*. Girls are more likely to take turns and to observe the unstated rules of conversation (Rategan, 1993). Conversational maintenance through the asking of questions engages others in interaction, a task Fishman (1978) ascribes to women.

Hiatt (1977, pp. 225, 226) finds the female writing style is conservative, structurally sound, and logical in its own way but uses the word *really* two and a half times more than the male style. Lynch and Strauss-Noll (1987) found differences in tone in a letter-writing assignment designed to persuade a reluctant landlord to return a security deposit. Among ten forceful letters, six were written by females. This finding contradicted what the researchers had heard about male aggression and female diffidence. Differences in writing style varied according to the subject's understanding of what might be effective with a landlord rather than according to gender. This study also found females used more precise descriptors of color such as *lilac, lavender, violet, mauve,* and *orchid* to describe a swatch of purplish-blue cloth.

Male Language Style

Sause (1976) describes boys' oral language as having more references to aggression, time, space, quantity, and acts of physical movement than the language of females. It appears to be more inquisitive, displays a greater interest in self, and indicates more willingness to make value judgments. Masculine emotions include aggressive feelings, such as anger and hostility, but discourage open displays of affection. Male characters on television use more vocalized pauses (such as *ah, um*), action verbs, justifications for behavior, present tense verbs, subordinating conjunctions, and grammatical errors (Mulac et al., 1985b). Men's language is characterized as using more profanity, dominating speech, straight-to-the-point wording, forcefulness, aggressiveness, bluntness, and ideas represented by a sense of humor. Key in the difference attributed to males is a greater use of instrumental states, or things being acted upon. Boys use speech to initiate activity, direct others, and assert themselves more than girls (Cook, 1985). Males are more likely to provide physical assistance (Zeldin et al., 1982) as an act of giving direction. When males use tag questions and hedges (tentative language), they are viewed as polite and other-directed; however, when they are used by women, women are seen as powerless. Some researchers argue that because women have lower status, the use of these language forms becomes an indicator of their lower status (Bradley, 1981) rather than the other way around.

Hiatt (1977, pp. 225–226) finds that the male writing style includes longer complex sentences, fewer logical sequence indicators (such as illustratives *for example*; illatives, *therefore*; adversatives, *however*; causatives, *because*; and additives, *and*). Males also use fewer adverbs of emotion but more adverbs of pace (*gradually, hastily, slowly*). Gilley and Summers (1970) find a significant sex difference in the use of hostile verbs in composing a series of one hundred sentences. Males consistently use hostile verbs and appear less inhibited about expressing hostility in their writing.

In later studies, Bischoping (1993) finds little difference in the most popular topics for men and women, including the subjects of work and money. Leisure activity, or "amusement," ranks second in importance, and appearances are the least popular topic for both sexes. Thus, in contrast to the Moore (1922) study (referred to earlier), men and women in the Bischoping (1993) study prefer to talk about similar topics in same-sex, as well as in opposite-sex conversations. Zeldin et al. (1982) says boys expect girls to listen to them, and fewer girls expect boys to do the listening. Boys ask questions because they want information, whereas girls ask questions to display interest in other people. When males listen to problems they provide solutions, rather than sympathy; however, the reverse is true when females listen to problems (Tannen, 1991).

GENDER-LINKED LANGUAGE EFFECTS

With these differences in language usage, would it be possible to determine sex by reading transcripts of oral language? Mulac and Lundell (1980) wanted to determine receiver perceptions and found clearly demonstrated differences between perceptions on two of three dimensions. On *aesthetic quality*, female speakers received substantially higher scores than male speakers. The female speakers were perceived as more "pleasant," "attractive," and "beautiful" and as "sweeter" than the male speakers. On *sociointellectual status*, male and female speakers were perceived as comparable in terms of "high social status/low social status" and "literate/illiterate." On *dynamism*, males received higher ratings. The language of male speakers led to perceptions of them as "stronger," "more active," "more aggressive," and "louder" than the female speakers. On *verbosity*, men talked more than women (James & Drakich, 1993). When describing a dialogue between a man and woman, both men and women attributed more talk time to the man (Konsky, 1978).

Mulac, Bradac, and Mann (1985) studied the gender-linked language effect in children's television programming as well. The dialogue of female television characters rated higher on *sociointellectual status* and *aesthetic quality*, and that of male characters rated higher on *dynamism*. These ratings showed a gender-linked difference on the average about 200 percent higher than in real world conversations. Wanting to test the gender-linked language phenomenon further, Mulac et al. (1986) examined perceptions during public speaking situations. They found male public speakers used more first-person-singular pronouns, indicating a relatively egocentric orientation. They also found males focused on the present rather than the past or future. They used active voice, had a low level of concern with formal linguistic standards, and showed a high level of concern with holding the floor. They used a relatively large number of syllables per word, suggesting high intensity and a willingness to state evaluations in the form of judgmental adjectives ("the best way," p. 124). Finally, they more often used noun phrases but vague references to people. The linguistic features distinguishing female public speakers suggest a relatively complex literate and formal style, with longer sentences and a greater number of prepositional phrases.

In summary, females demonstrate the frequent use of fillers (or hedges), a relatively high degree of tentativeness or uncertainty, greater politeness and interpersonal sensitivity, frequent use of negations (what something is not, rather than what it is), more references to emotion, frequent uses of intensive adverbs, and less assertiveness: all connotative of lower social power. Female language uses are reported to be comparatively complex, literate, tentative, and attentive to emotional concerns, again suggesting a relatively powerless condition, depending on one's point of view. In summary, males, on the other hand, are egocentric, nonstandard, active, controlling, and intense, focusing on the here and now and using a direct, more aggressive language style.

Testing the gender-linked language effect and sex role stereotypes, Mulac, Incontro, and James (1985) checked perceptions from spontaneous conversations. They say female speakers rate higher on *sociointellectual status* and *aesthetic quality*, and male speakers rate higher on *dynamism*. Because subjects were unable to guess the sex of the speakers, it was highly unlikely the raters were influenced by sex role stereotypes while reading the transcripts; therefore, the differences in perceptions were probably due to the differences in the language used. Checking whether differences would be greater or lesser depending on same-sex or mixed-sex dyads, Mulac et al. (1988) again checked for gender-linked language effect. Greater differences were found in same-sex dyads than in mixed-sex dyads. In same-sex dyads, females were rated higher on *sociointellectual status* and *aesthetic* quality, but no gender difference was found on *dynamism*. In mixed-sex dyads, men were rated higher on *aesthetic quality*, whereas women were rated higher on *dynamism*. Male/female language differences decreased in mixed-sex, as compared to same-sex dyads, indicating a reduction in gender-indicative language use. This contradicts the idea that people display more stereotypical roles when interacting with partners of the opposite sex.

Ferber (1995) claims there is a significant tendency to identify a speaker's gender on the basis of the language used. In Zahn's (1989) effort to disprove this gender-linked language effect, he at least partially supported it within-sex-of-speaker situations. Evaluations of stereotypical language usage in naturally occurring conversation produce no effect on ability of subjects to identify the sex of the speaker. A number of other studies (Kanter, 1977; Mischel, 1974; Peterson et al., 1971; Shinar, 1978) imply women are evaluated less favorably than men, but only when they are identified as engaged in out-of-role occupations, when unsuccessful at a task, or when unempowered, such as in organizations with highly domineering management. Successful women who work in traditional female or neutral occupations or who have acquired power through successful performance and occupational prestige are less likely to be evaluated differently than men. In fact, speech styles depend in great part on the power relations between speaker and listener. Women who have access to networks, contacts, and mentors may use communication styles not unlike those men use in similar positions.

VERBAL AGGRESSIVENESS AND ARGUMENTATIVENESS

Infante (1986) described aggressiveness in interpersonal communication along a continuum as either constructive or destructive. Constructive types included assertiveness and argumentativeness, leading to satisfaction and enhancing interpersonal relationships. Destructive types included hostility and verbal aggressiveness, leading to dissatisfaction and relationship deterioration. On the positive side, assertiveness consisted of an individual's "general tendency to be interpersonally dominant, ascendant, and forceful" (Infante, 1987, p. 165). Assertive individuals stated their points and respected the right of others to express their position. Argumentativeness was a generally stable trait predisposing an individual to advocate positions on controversial issues and verbally attack the positions other people take on these issues (Infante & Rancer, 1982). Inherently interesting, verbal conflict leads to advocacy and refutation. On the negative side, hostility includes irritability, negativism, resentment, and suspicion (Infante, 1987). Hostility is usually aroused by frustration; otherwise, it might remain latent. Verbally aggressive individuals attack the self-concepts of individuals in order to make them experience psychological pain. Examples include character attacks, competence attacks, insults, maledictions, teasing, ridicule, profanity, and nonverbal emblems (Infante & Wigley, 1986). Even some nonverbal actions have become functionally equivalent to aggressive words (Ekman & Friesen, 1967), for example, "giving the finger," "long duration of eye contact using squinting eyes," and "sticking out the lower jaw" while "getting in someone's face."

The effect of verbally aggressive talk is self-concept damage (Infante et al., 1984), sometimes escalating into violence (Patterson & Cobb, 1973). Among the reasons for verbal aggression are frustration, social learning, psychopathology, and argumentative skill deficiency. Verbally aggressive individuals may also attack their opponent's position on controversial issues (Infante & Wigley, 1986). This is similar to the behavior of argumentative individuals, but the difference occurs when they want to win so much they cross the psychological boundary and actually wound their victim. The negative consequences of verbal aggressiveness include lower relational satisfaction (Rancer et al., 1986); greater likelihood of violence (Infante et al., 1989; Infante et al., 1990; Sabourin et al., 1993); depression—especially among husbands of wives who are verbally aggressive (Burleson & Denton, 1997; Segrin & Fitzpatrick, 1992; Millar & Rogers, 1987); and unfavorable organizational interactions (Infante & Gorden, 1991). On the other hand, research on argumentativeness reveals a number of benefits.

Arguing acts to stimulate curiosity and learning. People learn more about positions on controversial issues that disagree with their own, thereby reducing egocentric thinking while increasing multiple perspectives on issues (Johnson & Johnson, 1979). People who enjoy arguing communicate with more dynamism, seem more interested and more verbose, exert a greater effort to win, are more task oriented, and are more inflexible than people who prefer to argue less (Infante, 1981). In terms of credibility, people who enjoy arguing appear more enthusiastic, persuasive, confident, and certain; they reflect energy and boldness of presentation (Berlo et al., 1969–1970).

Males score higher on scales measuring both argumentativeness (Infante, 1985; Schultz & Anderson, 1982) and verbal aggressiveness (Burgoon et al., 1983; Infante et al., 1984; Roloff & Greenberg, 1979; Whaley, 1982). However, Canary, Cunningham, and Cody (1988) suggest females may be more aggressive than males in familiar contexts, using tactics to seek personal gain through coercion, criticism, and intimidation. Interestingly, Rancer and Dierks-Stewart (1985) explored biological (sex) and psychological (gender) differences in argumentativeness and found no biological sex differences but significant differences when subjects were classified according to psychological gender. Subjects classified as masculine (instrumental) rate higher in argumentativeness than those classified as feminine (expressive), androgynous, or undifferentiated. In other words, people "with a traditional masculine psychological sex-role orientation exceeded all others in argumentativeness" (Nicotera & Rancer, 1994, p. 287). When adversaries use verbal aggression to provoke them, males respond with verbal aggression, whereas females respond by increased argumentativeness and rationality (Infante, 1989). In the same study, Infante (1989) found a highly argumentative individual able to influence whether he or she was the recipient of argument or verbal aggression. People who like to argue indicate that they consider it enjoyable, believe it yields pragmatic outcomes, and feel it has a positive impact on self-concept, functional outcomes, and high ego involvement. People who do not like to argue indicate they believe arguing acts to produce a negative impact on self-concept, dysfunctional outcomes, little ego involvement, and little enjoyment or few pragmatic outcomes (Rancer et al., 1992).

Stereotypical sex role expectations for females discourage them from both argumentative and verbally aggressive behavior, and they often view arguments as stressful events. People with a low desire to argue are more socially oriented, prefer to shift the focus of interaction from a controversial issue to a social emotional matter (Infante, 1981), or concede with premature agreement, correlating with stereotypical feminine communication expectations. When females violate these expectations, communication outcomes (Burgoon, 1983) are often affected. For example, if a woman acts more aggressive than expected, she might experience social disapproval and be called a *bitch*; if a man acts less aggressive than expected, he might experience the same social disapproval but be called a *wimp*. Even so, males who act more aggressive than socially expected often receive the label *bastard*. The gender stereotyping of individuals attributes more power to men and less to women even when differences in communication depend more on status and role rather than gender. If women in organizations see argumentativeness as negative, they probably will not argue and will therefore be seen as less competent (Onyekwere et al., 1991).

Putnam (1988) describes three other tactical choices for resolving conflict: (1) nonconfrontation (avoiding, withdrawing), (2) control (assuming a controlling attitude in the interaction), and (3) solution orientation (integrating behavior). The decision to engage someone in the process of arguing begins with developing a positive self-concept so an individual will choose to confront another person in an effort to resolve the conflict. Putnam and Wilson (1982) say the choice of either nonconfrontation or control tactics perpetuates a negative self-concept; therefore, unlearning these tactics becomes important and necessary. The second step in developing the decision to engage someone in the process of arguing involves skill development techniques in the solution-oriented planning of arguments. Despite stereotypical views of many women that associate negative connotations with arguing, Infante (1985) says when reluctant women are induced to argue more, female observers rate them more favorably on issues of credibility. Men more favorably perceive women who are high in the trait of argumentativeness than women who are low in argumentativeness, suggesting males do not derogate an argumentative female. However, speculation in the Infante (1985) study suggests men with more rigid, traditional views of sex role behavior might react more negatively to an argumentative woman. Also, a negative reaction might occur in men who are themselves low in argumentativeness. Perhaps, then, a more concentrated effort should be made to motivate feminine females to be more argumentative, after analyzing their audience. Competitive academic forensics offers a unique educational opportunity for teaching students to conduct extensive research, develop critical thinking abilities, and refine communication skills (Colbert & Biggers, 1986). The process, although beneficial in some ways, can damage interpersonal relations. Knowing when argumentativeness is appropriate may enhance credibility, but it may not always be in the best interest of the individual to argue.

SEXIST LANGUAGE

Sexist language is that which discriminates against someone because of sex. In the past few decades educators, feminists, and other groups have determined our perception of the world mirrors our language, and language serves to shape the way we perceive reality; this perspective has become known as the *Sapir-Worph hypothesis*. Consequently, sexist language may describe the world in ways directly impacting women and men. Examples of sexist language may include man-linked words, generic pronouns, married names, religious language, and profanity. A thorough discussion of sexual terms and euphemisms for men and women appears in Chapter 6.

Man-linked words include the suffix-*man*, as in *mailman, fireman*, and *milkman*. After extensive and thorough research (Todd-Mancillas, 1981; Bem & Bem, 1973; Shimanoff, 1975; Gottfredson, 1976), it was determined that in various situations when individuals used man-linked words women felt excluded. Over time success has been achieved in ridding much English usage of man-linked terminology. New, more inclusive words have developed to replace the old sexist terms, for example, *chairperson, mail carrier*, and *salesperson*. As is always the case with social change, when people feel uncomfortable with that change they tend to use humor to help them overcome their discomfort. A famous joke told about man-linked language describes a mailman in the most politically hypercorrect way as a "person-person."

Generic pronouns are pronouns such as *he, him, his*, and *himself*. Historically these pronouns were supposed to represent women and men. Densmore (1970), Murray (1973), Farwell (1973), and Strainchamps (1971) claim generic pronouns are confusing, ambiguous, and exclusive and reflect outdated sexism. These researchers determined that when generic pronouns are used women believe they are not included. Over the last few decades nonsexist pronoun usage has not been found to affect the comprehensibility or pleasantness of written or spoken work. Such nonsexist pronoun use includes phrases such as *he or she, him or her, his or her*, and *himself or herself*. To avoid the encumbered nature of the multiple generic pronouns many people simply use the plural form: *they, them,* or *their.*

For many years women changed their last name when they married and assumed their husband's. Both linguistically and literally women became a member of the husband's family and changed their identity. Periodically women have rejected this custom. One alternative is to hyphenate the wife's name with the husband's; another is to retain the maiden name. Other women continue to take the name of their husband. Deciding how to name their children often produces complications usually negotiated by the couple.

In addition to changing of the name at marriage, society still refers to a married woman as *Mrs.* whereas no indication of marital state identifies men with *Mr.* The term *Ms.* arose from the controversy about identifying marital status as a substitute for all women, married or not. Atkinson (1987) found in a survey of 325 people, considerable confusion existed over the term *Ms.* The notion led Atkinson to conclude women were identified by three categories: "available (Miss), taken (Mrs.), and used but available again (Ms.)" (Atkinson, 1987, p. 37).

Religious language originated in patriarchal societies many authors describe as overwhelmingly male-oriented. Masculine pronouns refer to God and to humanity, a usage many feminist groups have sought to change. Most egregious to particular feminist groups is reference to maintaining the position of males as the head of the family and the church. (This subject is discussed further in Chapter 3.) But Miller and Swift (1976) describe God as being one single spirit with a dual nature, describing him with one neutral pronoun, as is found in most religious writings. In most world religions, God is described by a male pronoun but is known as a spirit with either no sex or qualities of both sexes.

Media, particularly movies and rap music, depict individuals who use excessive profanity. Many people indicate the frequency of media use of "the F word" has caused them to become so desensitized to it they do not even hear it anymore. In studies (Staley, 1978) in the use of profanity, both males and females used about the same number of expletives; however, males predicted women would use fewer expletives, and women predicted men would use more expletives than they actually did. Stereotypes of men and women often cause people to experience different perceptions of behavior for men and women. In other words, though they engage in similar behavior, people judge them differently. In more recent research about the use of expletives, Selnow (1985) confirms the social expectation that women use less profanity than men.

CONCLUSION

This chapter has described the differences in language use by males and females and aggressive/argumentative communication styles. Masculine individuals use more intensive, aggressive, task-oriented, argumentative language forms. Feminine individuals use less intense language, show more concern with internal psychological states, and are more gentle and compassionate. When males move deeper into the masculine style, they become aggressive communicators. In familiar situations, females use aggressive communication as well. Generally, when faced with an aggressive opponent, females resort to argumentativeness and rational discourse. In terms of sexist language, the use of man-linked words, generic pronouns, married names, and religious language often ignores or pigeonholes women but not men. Much restructuring of language alternatives has been occurring over the past few decades.

After considering the research and reflecting on the law student speech in Washington, D.C., referred to in the opening paragraph of this chapter, one might speculate she intentionally used intensive language to provoke argument, an ingredient of her profession. She did not provoke argument, because the audience attending this formal public forum, successful professional women, did not have the opportunity to argue with her as a result of time constraints. They did, however, openly express a measure of lost respect for the speaker because of her profanity. For example, after her presentation individuals made the following comments: "I know a number of intelligent law students who do not resort to such base language." "She insulted me with her repeated use of the 'F word.' " "I'm sure she's probably a good law student, but I would never hire her to represent me because of the way she expresses herself." These comments reflect attitudes consistent with the research findings in this chapter.

8

Gender and Power

K. Payne, H. E. Fuqua, Jr., and J. Cangemi

He or she who dies with the most toys wins!

Anonymous

This chapter describes power through the lens of gender. It discusses (1) the sources and types of power; (2) the currencies, strategies, and tactics for gaining power; (3) the advantages and disadvantages for men and women; and (4) the perceived sense of powerlessness. The lens of gender acts to delineate some of the misunderstandings in the power style traditionally used by males and females and the way those styles affect workplace productivity and interpersonal competence. Many women have negative feelings about power, expressing discomfort with the idea of using it. Many men assume they will be expected to wield power in many of their life capacities and consequently tend to be comfortable with the idea and may feel threatened as women assert themselves in the power arena. In any case, men and women traditionally have used power differently and have accessed it with differing degrees of expertise. Among those who fail to access power, perceived powerlessness causes them to react in unique ways. This chapter discusses these ideas.

INTRODUCTION

Power requires the ability to produce an effect; it is described by Dubin (1951) as exclusive to membership in organizations. Given this, we carry our strengths with us but leave our power behind when we exit an organizational system. If the sources of power operate within organizations, and if it's true women and men operate differently, then confusion about power has the potential to create enormous conflict in organizations.

Female Power

Historically, feminists have defined power as possession of control, authority, or influence over others, involving dominance in relationships. Among communicators, interaction acted as the way of identifying this idea of power. The early feminists gained recognition and momentum for a growing group of women by naming an enemy (the chauvinistic patriarchy) and rallying around to fight that enemy, who seemingly had all the control, authority, and influence. To advance the notion that women must break out of this oppressive relationship, feminists encouraged women who want power to enter the work force and politics and to compete for power. In the process they often used a masculine communication style, which often included a "bravado" that did not suit them and sometimes caused them to be disliked. The twenty-first-century woman softened her communication style and claimed ambition and competition as qualities consistent with a new kind of femininity. Concomitantly, many men noticed something else happening: a loss of control, authority, and influence over women in society and at home. This social shift produced the loss of power for men and gain of power for women. As many men have come to terms with their loss of power, they have made way for women by changing their own roles and discovering how dual-career relationships and women's working in general benefit men as well as women. Many women, mainly feminists, still point out that the patriarchy continues to oppress women, claim they must never forget that, and assert that they must never give up the fight for fear of losing what ground they have gained. Since the media historically looked to these groups to get the pulse of women, they often failed to recognize that they were advocating an increasingly radical view; one not always held by the majority of women in America (Hoff-Sommers, 2000).

Nonradical feminists used a communication style often differing from that used by radicals. Addington (1968) claims the traditional feminine voice, or the way women talk, is associated with qualities of breathiness, softness, and sometimes stridentness. Such a voice rates low in maturity, intelligence, and depth, but high in beauty and femininity, reinforcing stereotypes about females. The reasons women talk also differ from those of men. For women, talk tends to be the center of relationships. They use it to equalize status through the matching of experiences, a communication style Tannen (1994) calls "troubles talk." Women use conversation to support others as they focus on the relationship level of communication (Tannen, 1994) and to include others, sharing conversational turn taking

(Helgesen, 1990). By using hedges, qualifiers, and tag questions more frequently than men, women often sound powerless as communicators (Giles et al., 1979). Another interpretation of women's apparent tentativeness is that it is inclusive and affiliative, rather than powerless. Hedges, qualifiers, and tag questions may be a woman's way of establishing a nonthreatening atmosphere, whereby the power advantage held by men is not directly confronted. As little girls, women learn not to criticize or put others down, but to be sensitive and responsive to others. Historically, women used self-disclosure to solicit trust, as well as to equalize status and control.

Male Power

In traditional organizational life men were in positions of power and used masculine forms of communication. Logically, the masculine style became the norm for organizational styles of communicating (Eakins & Eakins, 1978). Expectations in organizational life are for qualities of independence, competitiveness, self-confidence, assertiveness, and sometimes even aggressiveness. Masculine forms usually exhibited directive and unilateral communication. Masculine men use talk to establish and maintain their status: to dominate the "talk stage" (Wood, 1994). They more typically use the communication experience to solve problems than to listen or match experiences (Tannen, 1994). When compared with women, men tend to assert themselves by using greater volume, lower pitch, and greater inflection to add passion to their ideas and to give force to their positions (Eakins & Eakins, 1978; Payne, 1996). Some researchers say men also discourage others from talking by interrupting or giving minimum responses (Giles et al., 1982). Addington (1968) says masculine voices rate higher in maturity, intelligence, and sophistication. Men tend to express themselves in a more linear fashion, getting to the bottom line, using more abstract, less concrete ways of communicating.

As researchers (Korda, 1975; Ringer, 1973) study the use of space (proxemics), they accord power and status to various groups. Privilege and importance often correlate with size of an office, a person's home or car, even a chair. Executives occupy larger offices; their secretaries occupy smaller spaces crowded with computers and filing cabinets (Korda, 1975). Men often defend their own space at home: a workout room, a workshop, an office. They sit at the head of the dinner table, the place reserved for the head of the household, a place symbolizing their leadership in the family. Men continue to take up more space in standing and use more expansive postures in sitting, commanding more attention than women (Henley, 1977; LaFrance & Mayo, 1979; Merabian, 1971). When one is looking through the lens of dominance and control, these communication variables of power generally indicate more patterns of control among men in mixed-sex conversations.

More frequently, those in power tend to invade the spaces of those with less power (Henley, 1977). Men tend to indicate and reinforce status differences in more aggressive, nonaffiliative ways through touch (Deaux, 1976; Henley, 1977; LaFrance & Mayo, 1979; Leathers, 1986; Major, 1980). Men more often use touch to assert power, direct others, and express sexual interest (Deaux, 1976; Leathers, 1986). Afraid to use forceful speech, women use humor to discourage unwanted touch, an indirect use of power. Over time, women have seen these methods failed to work, so they have redressed the power imbalance through the law by sexual harassment claims. The problem of sexual harassment affects the power dynamics of touch and space in the workplace, as men now behave in ways exhibiting reluctance to touch or enter the space of women, or even to exhibit any form of dominance. These ideas of power, expressed through voice, space, and touch, act to reiterate society's traditional view of masculinity and femininity (Berryman-Fink, 1993). Further, it would be incorrect to say the masculine form of communication in the workplace is in any way unvarying.

SOURCES AND TYPES OF POWER

The currency of leadership, essential to influencing others, comprises a wide variety of factors. Various authors (French & Raven, 1959; Baldridge, 1971; Kanter, 1977; Hackman & Johnson, 1991; King, 1987) have described sources, types, and uses of power essential to effective leadership. Eight primary sources of power are support systems, information, credibility, visibility, legitimacy, persuasiveness, charisma, and agenda setting. *Support systems* include both formal and informal opportunities for networking. Historically, males enjoyed this source of power almost exclusively. Families provided home support, and mentors helped men find their way through the political maze at work. Often families and society discouraged females from branching out into traditionally nonfeminine activities. When women first entered the workplace, few mentors were available, so they at first experienced a disadvantage in accessing this power source. *Information*, the second source of power, includes not what you know, but how fast you find it out, encouraging power players to be good listeners. Power flows to those who have the information and know-how to accomplish organizational tasks. Knowing how to tap into informal organizational power acts as the key to gaining information fast. Those who have been in organizations longest understand better how this works. *Credibility*, the third power source, resides in the respect you attain. We rely on highly credible people who have established a history of experience and expertise. People who flounder in a new position may appear unprepared and lose their potential for gaining power. When this happens they may have to go underground. If they do, their strategies of power may appear under-handed, and they may never regain the trust of others.

Visibility, the fourth source of power, means taking on tough jobs so people notice you. For women this has been an especially useful way of gaining power. Assuming they entered the work force well prepared, women often focus on spending long hours at tasks in an effort to produce something of value to the organization. Often this results in the loss of family life, interpersonal relationships, and health, but the long-term contribution produced by all their hard work results in high visibility. Those contributions provide a rhetorical platform for the next generation of women. Ambitious men also did this as a means of gaining power when entering a new workplace environment, as a way of communicating seriousness about career development. *Legitimacy* the fifth source of power, works in concert with visibility as respected power players commend you publicly, thereby creating acceptance among potential skeptics. Some sort of public reward usually follows after a person takes on a tough job and works hard to achieve success. This sort of an accomplishment benefits bosses as well because they can claim departmental credit, making them look good too. Theoretically, someone who does a good job gains legitimate power when highly respected, powerful people publicly acknowledge and reward his or her success. Both men and women enjoy this access to power, especially when working with bosses who treat employees fairly.

Persuasiveness, the sixth source of power, determines how successfully a person uses rational or emotional appeals. One's ability to persuade depends on personality, content of a task, motivation, and confidence. Among these, Andrews (1987) argues, females express less confidence than males in their ability to communicate their arguments persuasively. Montgomery and Burgoon (1980) claim once trained in the use of critical methods (analysis of fallacies in argument), females become more confident and males become better listeners. *Charisma*, the seventh source of power, inspires trust and entails magnetism for leading a group. One attribute of charisma is physical appearance. Taller, physically fit, attractive people who take up a lot of psychic space tend to have charisma. Powerful eye contact, dynamic energy, a smiling mouth full of clean white teeth add to dimensions of charisma. We tend to think of men as charismatic, whereas we think of women as poised, possessing strength, courage, or beauty. *Agenda setting*, the last source of power, rests in knowing when meetings will be held and accessing the group leader to put items on the agenda at just the right time. Two of the by-products of networks and alliances are access to decision-making arenas and ability to influence the agendas in those arenas. People or groups who have access to agenda setting frequently represent their positions, whereas the interests and concerns of those not present may be distorted or ignored (Lukes, 1974; Brown, 1986).

While operating in a system, knowing how to identify power makes it easier to access the most effective type for a specific situation. The five most commonly identified types of power are *coercive, reward, legitimate, expert,* and *referent* (French & Raven, 1959). *Coercive* power bases its effectiveness on the ability to administer punishment or give negative reinforcement. Harper and Hirokawa (1988) discover male managers rely more often on punishment-based power strategies, such as "warning ultimatums." Female managers rely more often on altruism and rationale-based strategies, indicating a preference for counsel, "Is there anything I can do to help?," or explanation "You need to do this because," when attempting to gain compliance from subordinates.

Reward, the second type of power, rests on the ability to deliver something valued by the receiver. People who can deliver money, jobs, or political support have something other people want and therefore become extremely powerful in organizations. *Legitimate* power, the third type, resides in a person's position rather than in the person. This type of formal power relies on status in an authority hierarchy. Occasionally, people with legitimate power fail to recognize it, and then they may began to notice others' going around them to accomplish their goals. Early socialization for women encourages them to establish connection, to nurture, and to provide support for others. Having power over, rather than power with, may be confusing to women (Helgesen, 1990).

The fourth type, *expert* power, relies on a person's special knowledge and expertise in a given area. Experts influence because they supply needed information and skills. In our culture, those with expertise demonstrate more power than those without credentials. However, practical knowledge and skill can sometimes substitute for credentials. Anyone can have it who formally and informally prepares. The last type, *referent* power, activates our admiration of someone into an acceptance of his or her influence (French & Raven, 1959). Referent power is a little like role model power; it depends on respecting, liking, and holding another individual in esteem. It is an asset developed over a long period. Males enjoyed referent power for a long time, but females, as a result of their recent advent on the scene, will gain referent power over time.

Among these five sources of power, creating a positive operating climate implies choosing the most appropriate compliance-gaining tactics, which tends to lead to greater "life" or job satisfaction (Plax et al., 1986). McCroskey et al. (1985) claim relying on expert, reward, and referent power appears to produce the greatest satisfaction; reliance on coercive and legitimate power has the opposite effect (McCroskey et al., 1985). Rahim (1989) finds that legitimate power is useful in gaining compliance, but that it causes satisfaction of supervisees to decrease. Expert and referent power bases correlate with both compliance and satisfaction. Masculine individuals stereotypically use more aggressive power strategies; feminine individuals chose power strategies more closely linked to relational maintenance. Androgynous individuals would likely choose compliance-gaining strategies that are situationally appropriate, rather than selecting those consistent with gender role identity.

CURRENCIES, STRATEGIES, AND TACTICS

Among the types of power, three styles of relational currency operate in organizations as men and women attempt to gain power. First, *legitimate* (or personal) power uses the currency of trust where the action evidences collaboration (all those on the winning team win). Men and women understand trust differently (Reisman, 1990; Crawford, 1977; Tavris, 1992) so researchers conclude some confusion emerges as men and women attempt to establish trust. Researchers (Paul & White, 1990; Tavris, 1992; Wright, 1982) say women prefer to establish trust through higher levels of self-disclosure, whereas men prefer more instrumental methods. *Clout*, the second style of relational currency, uses the currency of force where the action indicates coercion (someone has to lose). Stereotypical males tend to use more competitive, aggressive forms of communication more closely aligned with the use of coercion. Stereotypical females tend to use more accommodating styles (Giles et al., 1982); consequently, if females hold true to their gender role stereotypes they will likely lose when the currency of clout is imposed. *Chit exchange*, the last style of relational exchange, uses the currency of obligation where the action means exchange (both people admit they have power and they exchange it). Of the three relational currencies operating in organizations, chit exchange will likely be the least confusing in a gender role diverse (both masculine and feminine) situation. But no one should make the mistake of thinking the goal among power players is to reduce confusion; in fact, quite the reverse holds true, explaining in part why references to power often include the idea of "game playing."

Game playing acts as one of the strategies of power; the other two involve *negotiation* and *coalition formation*. When using the strategy of *game playing*, people depend on confusing, frightening, and/or even violating their opponents' expectations. It takes an experienced "gamesperson" to know how to work this strategy, and males should not make the mistake of thinking females do not get it just because they are relatively new to the scene. Often in the realm of game playing, ethics and values suffer because they play a distinctly subordinate role to the facts of human behavior and the strong motive to win. For example, people have often speculated about incompetent women with power, describing them as "sleeping their way to the top."

In an interesting study by Fiske et al. (1993), two groups of men involved in task-oriented supervisory situations were asked to judge the competence of subordinate women. Half the men expected to date the women; therefore, their romantic fate depended on them. The other half expected only a task-oriented interaction with the women. The men who expected to date the women were unable to distinguish competence from incompetence in the women's performance. The same kind of bias was found among women supervising men they expected to date. In both cases, a romantic goal clouded judgment. So if women or men were sleeping with their bosses, blatant incompetence could be undetected, but nonetheless power would have been established. Predictable, as well as unpredictable, strategies for gaining power both intrigue and mystify those who enjoy the game. To accomplish goals, power becomes both necessary and inevitable; it must be sought to be acquired, as was the case with the power player who slept his or her way to the top.

Winning usually acts as reward enough for game players, but on occasion, a destructive achiever, as described by Kelly (1987), may enter the scene. The destructive achiever has the energy of a leader but lacks operational values, supplanting them with strongly held beliefs in his or her own absolute value system. Without the ability to analyze problems objectively, the destructive achiever may willfully deconstruct a vibrant organization into a classic systems-bound survival-oriented bureaucracy. Hoff-Sommers (1994) points to groups of antimale and anti-Christian radical "gender feminists" rallying around political correctness often misrepresenting research findings to accomplish their own agenda as an example of destructive achievers.

The second power strategy specifies using *negotiation*. When people negotiate, they expect to ask for more than they think they can get. Consequently, good negotiators start bidding high, expecting to get about half of what they want. Whenever people disagree about what they inherently value, those who want to win will appeal to a sense of fairness and decency and in so doing will seek to gain a slight edge at the moment, with the intention of getting more later. When this happens, the organization's value base becomes diminished and the way opens to faster deterioration or change, depending on perspective. New players often seek to change the organizational values once they have established a power base.

People use negotiation when they do not have the power to achieve their goals unilaterally. Negotiation requires a positive setting, with fair-minded people who have an intention of reaching an agreement. Everyone gets something, but everyone also pays. No rules or judges exist in the initial stages of negotiation; negotiators decide what is fair. People who use the strategy of negotiation should prepare to negotiate from strength. Start with all you know they know. Get them thinking *yes*. You can always bargain better if you know all the facts. When you make concessions make them progressively smaller, do not antagonize your opponent, and don't bring a gun. Negotiators do not have to be reasonable or rational.

The third power strategy depends on gaining leverage over the power holders. This strategy seizes the chance for *coalition formation*. Most power strategies operate simultaneously, but the ultimate goal of this type of change agent is achieved once he or she has established enough support to overthrow the reigning establishment. Power players constantly seek out people who might agree with them and negatively stereotype those who disagree. Stereotypes act as shortcuts overburdened people use when their cognitive capacity is limited (Fiske, 1993). People with highly dominant personalities pay less attention to the potential information contradicting and undermining their stereotypes, preferring instead the information confirming them. Choosing coalition formation as a strategy to overthrow power holders appropriately completes the picture. These strategists play hardball and may resort to cutthroat tactics, but their goal always figures on overthrowing the establishment. Cutthroat power players are usually assumed to be men, but women also use the tactics.

The most effective power players recognize the need to access the energy of people by tapping into their self-interest. Using the currencies and strategies of power may either encourage people or prohibit them from accomplishing their personal and organizational goals. As one considers the measurement of power, he or she should look at results, not effort; productivity, not control. In efforts to move people toward change, it may be useful to realize conflict will emerge and the trick is to gain the leverage needed to move people to change behavior (Simon, 1951).

Three useful power/conflict tactics require both skill and risk. The first tactic, *win–lose*, entails the risk of losing, but the prize of winning. Socializing males to win, not lose, encourages them to use the win–lose style. Socializing females to appreciate the importance of relationships may cause them to avoid using this style because someone has to lose. In using the second tactic, *negotiation* (also a strategy), the risk is that the other person might not honor his or her part of the bargain. Women may be more sensitive to verbal and nonverbal cue conflicts in the perception of sincerity but may be naive about the strength of the desire to win of some people and the lengths they might go to for a satisfying win. The tactic of negotiation relies almost completely on chance. The third tactic, *win–win*, includes the risk of trust, but has the highest positive results. The threat to both players is the fear that the other person does not value his or her self-interest. When entering into an exchange with another person, knowledge of his or her reputation is one of the most valuable pieces of information involved in the process. In using any of these conflict tactics or any other power currency or strategy, self-respect must be an overriding factor determining participation. Additionally, a player must remember not to enter the power arena until he or she is strong enough to become a target of those whose power is threatened. Men established the rules for power and understand them well; women, therefore, often appear reluctant to enter the game without first donning a "bulletproof vest."

ADVANTAGES AND DISADVANTAGES FOR MEN AND WOMEN

Competition operates at the core of power with some people enjoying the game of hardball and others preferring a less intense approach. Competitive cultures train their members to compete, but everyone does not receive the same training. Attitudes and behavior about competition differ between traditional men and women. These differences emerge in the way males and females talk. American males learn early in life the importance of winning, with the objective of being envied; not to be part of a group but to distinguish themselves to be number one. Males use speaking as an opportunity to establish who is best, strongest, smartest, toughest, and ultimately most powerful. American females learn early in life the importance of relationships, with the objective of being liked, being part of a group, blending in, being inclusive. Females use speaking as an opportunity to include others, to establish and maintain relationships. These are two different approaches to accessing power, yet both are effective in their own way. Paradoxically, not all effective strategies involve getting and maintaining power because sometimes a leader may want to distribute it among members of the group.

Curiously, we often associate dominance with males and domineeringness with females. Dominant communication strategies are characterized by directness, assertiveness, task orientation, independence, competitiveness, and self-confidence, followed by affirmation or acquiescence from the listener. Domineeringness, or counterdominance, attempts to control interactions and relationships through "one-up" comments. McClelland (1970) maintains power has two faces. One face seeks dominance and control over others (personal power); the other looks toward the betterment of humankind through strong interest in exercising power for the greater good of others (social power). The first face McClelland terms "personal power," the other face "social power." McClelland (1985) claims men and women express the power motivation differently at various stages of development. Freeman and Lanning (1989) find feminine females have a strong desire for dominance over individuals and a low desire for organizational power. They have a desire to achieve independently, while holding personal power over others. In masculine males, Freeman and Lanning (1989) find a desire to achieve for the purpose of the good of the organization, with a dislike of personal domination over other people. In other words, females tend to prefer personal power (connection), and males tend to prefer social power (status).

The idea of making connections with others can become confusing when people compete for power and status. Tannen (1994) describes what happens when competing for status becomes part of the process for establishing connections. For males, avoiding a one-down position operates at a high level of importance in a relationship. This may explain why males enjoy frequent "jocular sparring" with one another. It may also contribute to the negotiation that occurs when males compete to pay the check. The desire to dominate, common among male animals, means influence, control, or rule by power or authority. On the other hand, acting domineering means ruling arbitrarily.

When males dominate females, connection usually remains intact, but when females dominate males, connection suffers. Interestingly, when females dominate other females, connection also breaks down. Females, accustomed to avoiding open displays of competitiveness, operate by agreeing, supporting, and making suggestions, wanting to maintain relational connections, while holding contradictory opinions privately. When these connections break down, fierce backbiting, gossip, personal attacks, snubs, and avoidance between women occur. Women have trouble with the idea of competing for connection, often making it the most difficult area of power to deal with in an organization. When operating in this arena, women often feel their self-interest has been devalued. When males compete for social power, they also compete for dominance as a measure of their self-esteem and masculinity. When males dominate other males, connection does not usually suffer; instead, the other males see themselves as "giving way" and offer their respect.

PERCEIVED POWERLESSNESS

Two major players in any social system are authorities and partisans (Gamson, 1968). Authorities act as targets of influence and agents of social control. In this capacity they have the power to make binding decisions about the lives of partisans. Partisans, on the other hand, have the opposite role. They initiate influence but are targets of social control. Authorities cannot produce social control if partisans refuse to comply. So even though we often think of partisans as having perceived powerlessness, they do in fact hold the key to giving authorities power. It all depends on how much partisans trust authorities. Partisans will trust authorities when they expect them to make good decisions; they probably will not mobilize against authorities if trust is high. When trust is low, partisan groups will probably make an effort to grasp power from authorities. Consequently, it becomes paramount for authorities to keep partisans happy. Further, it is incredibly important for all members of an organization to recognize they all have power or capacity to access power through some source. Partisans do not have authority, but they do have a number of other sources of important power, most notably coalition formation and the threat of violence.

The existence of multiple forms of power means the capacity for authorities to make arbitrary decisions, which can be constraining. They must weigh the possibility of generating resistance and may even find themselves outflanked. Curiously, authorities often seem more powerful to their subordinates than to themselves. They often see subordinates as having more power than the subordinates actually realize. We often hear about employees at some company sabotaging the product, shooting up the place, pilfering supplies, or embezzling large sums of money. Yet, the traditional view of organizations incorporates a political perspective suggesting partisans receive control and authorities impose it. When women first appeared on the corporate scene they saw men as authorities and themselves as relatively powerless.

It no longer seems unusual to find women in jobs of heavy responsibility where they will be held responsible for the results of subordinates. A sense of perceived powerlessness appears to be diminishing for women. Pioneers in the realm of power often experience power dilemmas. Frequently, women find themselves without the informal power their formal roles demand. Reasons for this are lack of powerful mentors or sponsors, inability to gain access to resources, little input or influence in the planning and decision-making process, bosses who sometimes undercut their authority; or on occasion women may convey a sense of insecurity or a reluctance to take risks. When operating with a sense of powerlessness, male or female members of organizations tend to concentrate their power needs on their subordinates. This manifests itself in controlling behavior and close supervision, as they become overly concerned with rules and procedures and focus on turf rights. These powerless types of behavior prove especially damaging to women because they often reinforce negative stereotypes of women as domineering.

Second, both men and women should be careful not to demonstrate behavior that makes them look powerless even when they are convinced they have no power. Curiously, researchers (Kipnis, 1972; Berger, 1973) find the more power holders believe they control (strong influence) a target person's behavior, the lower their evaluation of the target person's worth. The point is, if you think you have no power, fake it. Researchers have confirmed the widespread observation that those in positions of power actually move away from social contacts with the less powerful (Jackson, 1964; Kipnis, 1972; Sorokin & Lundin, 1959; Zander et al., 1959). Reasons for doing so involve distrust of the less powerful person's motives, as well as a sense that they have nothing of great interest to offer the more powerful. Power holders who believe they control a compliant target person's behavior evaluate themselves more favorably than they evaluate the target person (Kipnis et al., 1976). Imagine the occurrence of gender communication breakdowns if males used strong influence on females to get compliance, and females complied because their primary goal was to maintain relationships. Males would think they caused the compliance, think less of females, distance themselves from females, and think more highly of themselves. The same thing could happen if females used strong influence to gain compliance from men. Imagine if males refused to comply because they needed to maintain status and females upped the ante by threatening to fire them just to get them to comply. Would females think less of males, distance themselves from them, and think more highly of themselves? The action of distancing and the arrogance of thinking one's self superior reduce the likelihood of establishing trust, a necessary component of any authority/ partisan relationship.

The alternative view of power, as the ability to act or produce an effect, encouraging partnership, preferring persuasion to control and dominance, and incorporating a reconnection with men, reinforces positive relationships. This view of power provides new opportunities for both men and women to practice more gender-neutral communication styles. If the goals of powerful communication no longer are dominance and control, but rather persuasion, cooperation, and partnership, new schemas for revealing power might need examination. This alternative definition of power indicates another way of comprehending the communication variables used by men and women in mixed-sex conversations. Feminine forms of communication, such as collaboration, deference, and inclusion, formerly associated with subordinate roles, now actually advance the communication styles most useful in team building and participative management.

Reducing power differences often enhances group effectiveness and often is the key to organizational survival. Yet there has been a tendency among some to reject the terms *power* and *authority* as being inconsistent with democracy. Arguably, in fact, power acts as the cement holding societies together. In a democracy this power should be held by a large number of individuals subject to the will of the people. Keeping a balance in power differences among authorities and partisans helps social systems develop relationships that give leaders "power with" the group. This participative type of leadership decreases the possibility of group chaos (Wiles, 1955) and increases the possibility of group decision-making acceptance. A skill women stereotypically use in gaining compliance is reducing power differences by empowering others. This skill frequently causes people who use it to gain more power (Tannen, 1994). Several reasons for giving power away are increased job satisfaction, increased production, and reduced feelings of powerlessness. Kanter (1977) says this style of power dispersion reduces the likelihood of sabotage by disgruntled employees. Giving power away also fosters cooperation, generating increased group accomplishment. Another reason for decentralizing power is to keep groups competitive by putting the decision-making authority in the hands of those whom it will most directly affect. The last reason for giving power away is to enable people to become more mature and productive. Maturity and productivity engender satisfaction and enable people to tap into their own self-motivating interests (Hackman & Johnson, 1991), all agreeable organizational dynamics. These compliance-gaining skills of empowering others reflect early childhood socialization for women, giving them an advantage in leading organizations in the twenty-first century. This socialization encourages women to use conversation to equalize status, support others, invite and include others, and be responsive to the needs of others—all identifying the relationship level of meaning defining connections between individuals as a basis of empowerment (Helgesen, 1990).

CONCLUSION

Despite the many advances feminist groups have achieved on the power continuum for all women in America, more recently radical feminists have been criticized for their extreme sexual agenda, biased research, and anger against those who disagree with their philosophical underpinnings. In some academic departments, for example, if you do not agree with the radical, liberal philosophy of feminism, the most common characterization of you is that you are "unenlightened." A surprising number of powerful feminists still believe men collectively want to keep women down. They vent their anger and rage and advocate using it to forward their agenda. Hoff-Sommers (1994) refers to these women as "gender feminists." These "radical and socialist feminists have shown us the old ideals of freedom, equality and democracy are insufficient" (Jaggar, 1988, p. 148). Instead, the "feminist ideology has taken a divisive, gynocentric turn, and the emphasis now is on women as a political class whose interests are at odds with the interests of men" (Hoff-Sommers, 1994, p. 24). Consequently, many women today disdain the *radical feminist* label, while claiming to accept many of the core beliefs of equal rights for women. The outcome of this chilling relationship has been to introduce a new voice, whom Hoff-Sommers (1994) has referred to as that of the "equity feminist." This twenty-first-century feminist ideology redefines power as the ability to act or produce an effect and encourages partnership involving persuasion and a reconnection with men as friends rather than foes.

The concept of power both fascinates and challenges us. Who has it? In what forms does it become manifest? How and when should we use it? All have become intriguing questions to those who may be novices in the game. Many women do not understand the power game as played in organizations; therefore, realizing how traditional power players use it enables them to gain leadership positions. Women have attempted a variety of compliance-gaining strategies defining effective short-term successes, but relatively ineffective long-term strategies. Among the least successful strategies is the "bulldozer" technique. This technique incorporates aggressive communication, causing opponents to scatter and later plot against them.

Another strategy used by women has been the "victim" technique, which employs the legal establishment in opposition to sexual harassment, changing the workplace atmosphere. Women gained some credibility from this technique but were often privately ridiculed. These strategies may have been necessary for women just to break down the establishment door, but with the door now open, both women and men need to comprehend the changing strategies of power for accomplishing their goals in the twenty-first century.

How do we enhance our power base effectively? Yukl (1981, pp. 43–58) suggests these guidelines to build and exercise our power bases: Subordinates will more likely comply with a leader's instructions if he or she provides them clearly and confidently, making sure they are legitimate, explaining reasons for them, following the chain of command, insisting on compliance, and verifying compliance. Further, power players might seek appropriate education and training to overcome deficiencies in their expert power base. They may seek human relations training to enhance their referent power base. If people want to be admired and therefore be more able to influence others, it becomes paramount for them to understand the importance of being considerate of other people's needs and feelings, treating them fairly, and defending their interests when acting as their representative.

In this chapter we have discussed power through the lens of gender. We have considered the sources and types of power; the currencies, strategies, and tactics for gaining power; the advantages and disadvantages for men and women; and the perceived sense of powerlessness. The lens of gender acts to delineate some of the misunderstandings generated by the differences in the power styles traditionally used by males and females and how those styles affect workplace productivity and interpersonal competence. For people eager to enjoy power, giving it away actually produces more, just as giving away love does.

A variation of this chapter also appeared in Fuqua, H. E., Jr., Payne, K., and Cangemi, J. (1998). Leadership and the effective use of power. *National Forum for Educational Administration and Supervision Journal, 15E* (4), 36–41.

9

Nonverbal Gender Communication

Men walk from the knee, women from the hip. Men strike matches toward themselves, women away. Men dress to look like other men, women to look unique within the current fashion. Men look at their fingernails by cupping their palms and bending their fingers toward themselves, women extend their fingers palms outward. Men nag their wives for what they do, women nag their husbands for what they don't do.

Kenneth Colby

Many researchers suggest that differences exist in the nonverbal communication behavior of males and females (Knapp, 1978, 1980; Dittmann, 1972; Burgoon & Saine, 1978; Malandro & Barker, 1983; LaFrance & Mayo, 1978). Birdwhistell (1983) classifies these differences by three categories: primary, relating to hereditary characteristics of male and femaleness; secondary, relating to modeling or observation of same-sex role models; and tertiary, relating to popular explanations of reinforcement or conditioning for male or female behavior, such as rough-and-tumble play for boys and cuddling and nurturing for girls. With regard to primary nonverbal characteristic differences, males and females develop different bone structures determining their walk, gestures, and other nonverbal behavior. The shapes of male and female bodies also help to determine some of our nonverbal presentations. For example, larger breasts in women may influence their posture, and a larger shoulder span for men may influence theirs. With regard to secondary nonverbal characteristic differences, children learn to follow the patterns of same-sex role models: little boys grow up to use nonverbal movements similar to their fathers' and little girls act like their mothers. With regard to tertiary nonverbal characteristic differences, when behavior by others provides positive reinforcement of appropriateness, a child increases the behavior, whereas negative reinforcement decreases it. The culture in which we live helps to define appropriate behavior for boys and girls.

Differences between men and women often develop along lines of the sex role expectations of society (LaFrance & Mayo, 1979). These socialized sex role differences manifest themselves in communication behavior of men and women. Although men and women learn specific gender role nonverbal communicative behavior, they also learn to cross gender lines for practical purposes. Nevertheless, in this chapter the focus is on stereotypical gender role manifestations of nonverbal communication behavior. Men learn proactive, dominant behavior; women learn reactive, affiliative behavior. Socializing women as reactive and affiliative motivates them to learn nonverbal behavior that enables them to interpret the moods and feelings of others. Since women often occupy subordinate positions, learning to interpret important information about the moods and feelings of those in power provides an important survival skill (Bettelheim, 1943). Further, since society socializes women as helpmates, nurturers, those who please, and caretakers, using passive, submissive, expressive, and accommodating communication skills, women also learn perceptive skills that help them to read nonverbal cues and ensure their ability to act responsive, useful, and socially acceptable (Berman & Smith, 1984). The social rules for women help them establish a nonthreatening persona when in the company of others. Mehrabian (1981) describes nonverbal cues such as touching, holding eye contact, standing close to others, having vocal warmth, and engaging face-to-face to signal trust and liking: assets women use to establish relationships and reduce power threats.

Socializing men as proactive and dominant motivates them to display communication behavior that empowers them to control interactions. That control often entails "not tipping your hand," meaning men learn not to reveal their emotions overtly. Paralinguistic cues such as a deeper, louder voice often are factors that influence to whom the group will listen. Physical characteristics such as broader shoulders, greater height, and higher weight also contribute to nonverbal aspects of dominance by simply taking up more space. Men manifest dominance through other nonverbal cues such as unresponsiveness to questions asked by subordinates or dismissiveness of ideas of subordinates. When these communication actions accompany nonverbal gestures designed to control interactions, they increase dominance.

How people say something may be more important than what they say (Hegstrom, 1979). Mehrabian (1981) estimates 93 percent and Birdwhistell

(1970) estimates 65 percent of the social meaning in face-to-face interactions arises from nonverbal communication. Because of the importance of nonverbal communication, this chapter considers the major gender differences between men and women, including the use of proxemics, kinesics, haptics, paralinguistics, and artifactual communication. The implications of gendered nonverbal communication are also explained.

PROXEMICS

Proxemics is the way people use space (Hall, 1968). Hall (1959) explains early in the study of proxemics how different cultures use space differently. For example, in Latin American, Southern European, and Arab cultures, people interact at closer distances than in other countries, such as the United States (Watson, 1970), where people feel more comfortable interacting at greater distances. In the United States, how one uses space acts as a primary means of designating who has status and privilege. Larger homes, bigger (or more expensive) cars, larger offices (with windows and plants), larger chairs often denote who has the power and where it originates (Korda, 1975). People with power tend to invade the spaces of those with less power (Henley, 1977). Gender differences in the use of space correlate with socialized gender role oral communication patterns.

Women tend to use less space than men, keep their elbows closer to their bodies, hold their knees closer together, take smaller steps, and use smaller gestures while speaking (Evans & Howard, 1973). Female dyads tend to sit closer than male dyads (Sussman & Rosenfeld, 1982), and women tolerate closer approaches by other communicators than men do (Hartnett et al., 1970; Shafer & Sadowski, 1975). Women will more likely yield space to men when passing on a sidewalk (Silveira, 1972). Under conditions of high density, women curl their body with arms closer to the trunk, look down, and behave in nonaggressive ways (Freedman et al., 1972).

Territoriality is a person's need to establish and maintain certain spaces of his or her own. It often comprises staking out territory and claiming it to prevent encroachment. Staking out territory entails the use of markers, such as personal belongings that lay claim to the space—coats, umbrellas, purses, hats, briefcases, and so on—that identify a space as taken. Markers act as signs indicating others must keep out or specifying a place has been reserved or taken (Knapp, 1980). Another method of staking out territory involves looking aggressive and formidable in efforts to ward off anyone who might want your place; females will likely use markers of personal belongings; males will more likely use aggressive looks.

When our territory is encroached upon by others we become physically aroused as a result of their encroachment (Knapp, 1980). Encroachment may be either positive or negative. If it is positive, a person might produce a reciprocal response. For example, if a man steps into a woman's space and she likes it, she may lay her head on his chest or take his hand. If it is negative, a person may engage in a reaction of compensation. Negative encroachment may take the form of invasion, violation, and contamination (Lyman & Scott, 1967). *Invasion* is the imposition of physical presence upon the territory of someone. For example, when women move into the physical space of men, as in all-male military academies, they invade their traditional space. Men often respond by sexually harassing women who invade their turf. *Violation* is the unwarranted use of someone's sacred space without permission. For example, someone who enters your office and uses your phone, computer, and desk in your absence has violated your sacred space. *Contamination* is rendering the territory of another impure with respect to its general usage. For example, when you use someone's territory and change it or leave something behind that does not belong there, you contaminate the space. When someone's territory has been encroached upon through invasion, violation, or contamination and he or she interprets it negatively, that person may compensate in several different ways. People may withdraw, by moving away and allowing the encroacher to take over (Malandro & Barker, 1983). They may insulate themselves by erecting visible boundaries or engage in turf defense by repelling the invader from the territory. Or, they may simply say, "Don't touch me."

Since women tend to occupy lower-status positions in society, they often become the subjects of invasion, violation, and contamination. Feminine markers do not work as well as male markers at discouraging encroachment. Schaffer and Sadowski (1975) find that tables in barrooms marked with feminine sweaters, purses, and female jackets are taken over more frequently and quickly by arriving customers than those marked with masculine objects. Further, women allow others to approach them more closely than men do (Hartnett et al., 1970; Willis, 1966). Men invade women's spaces more than women invade men's spaces and more often than men invade other men's spaces (Evans & Howard, 1973).

KINESICS

The term *kinesics* refers to all forms of body movement, excluding physical contact with another's body. It is most commonly recognized as "body language," a term coined by Fast (1970), who titled his book on nonverbal communication with this name. Birdwhistell (1970) claims preschool children acquire and use body movements and gestures appropriate for their gender. Peterson (1976), Eakins and Eakins (1978), and Henley (1977) all suggest males use more dominating gestures than females when communicating in mixed-sex dyads. Females tend to use more submissive gestures when communicating with males: using less body space, pulling in their body, tilting their head while talking or listening, putting their hands in their laps more often, crossing their legs, yielding space, sitting forward in a chair, and lowering their eyes. Males tend to stare more, point more, take up more space, keep their head straight, stretch their hands, stand with their legs apart, sit in more outstretched positions, spread their knees while sitting, stroke their chin more often, use larger and more sweeping gestures, sit back in their chair, and hold their arms away from their body.

Studies show men tend to hide their emotions more than women. However, women have been socialized to signal friendliness, approachability, and an air of unassumingness. Consequently, Caucasian women smile more frequently than do men, even when not genuinely happy or pleased. This smiling behavior has not been found, however, in studies of African-American women (Halberstadt et al., 1988). Since society conditions women to smile more often, society expects them to do so. When they fail to do so, they receive more harsh evaluations than men or African-American women. Deutsch, LeBaron, and Fryer (1987) find nonsmiling women are perceived as less carefree, less happy, and less relaxed than nonsmiling men. For women, the smile appears to act as an interactional device (Burgoon et al., 1988). Since women smile more, their smiles become more difficult to interpret than those of men. Women may be trying to convey happiness or social approval, or they may even smile because they feel nervous and want to cover their feelings. Because men smile less frequently, the interpretation of their smiles becomes easier, usually an assumption that they feel positive about something.

Another area of kinesics is the study of eye contact. Most commonly, eye contact signals interest or attention; it can also signal positive affect and liking, or anger and threat, depending on the movement of the eyebrows. Eye contact may also reveal status or dominance within interactions. Weitz (1976) claims more dominant individuals receive more eye contact than less dominant people. Women look at another person during a conversation more than men do, and they hold eye contact longer with other women and men than men do with one another or with other women. This behavior may establish and maintain interpersonal relationships, something society expects women to do. One other explanation for this phenomenon may relate to lower status, requiring the subordinate person to give the superior person more attentive behavior. Since women often play the role of listener more often than men in male/female interactions, they often watch the other more, while collecting other nonverbal cues (Richmond et al., 1987). In the acquaintance stage of a relationship men usually establish eye contact with women first, but this tendency may be changing. Women and men differ in their use of eye contact, in part because of cultural stereotypes of how men and women should behave.

In U.S. society, the person who appears attractive may receive higher ratings on credibility, persuasiveness, power, charisma, and so on, than the one who appears unattractive. People perceive attractive people as more sociable, more outgoing, more likable, more intelligent, and more happy, whereas unattractive people may be seen as less sociable, less extroverted, less likable, less intelligent, and not happy (Richmond et al., 1987). Even such inborn features as a square jaw (Arnold Schwarzenegger), a broad face, height, and thick hair convey dominance, whereas rounded jaws, a small head, and narrow eyes convey weakness (Keating, 1985; Wilson, 1968). Because men are larger than women they receive higher ratings of dominance, as a result of sheer size. Women, on the other hand, who want to increase their power might consider more formal attire, because that denotes higher status (Sybers & Roach, 1962). Knowles (1973) claims people who set out to purchase a car have noticed the deference and attention given them as a direct result of the formality and expensiveness of their clothing. Although physical appearance is not supposed to affect status in a democracy, people do react to the way people look.

HAPTICS

Haptics is tactile or touching behavior in nonverbal communication. Touching enhances the emotional health of people. Adler and Towne (1978) discovered that it actually related to health. Observations of infants made during World War II found when babies' other needs were met, but not their need to be held or touched, they contracted illnesses and died (Bowlby, 1952; Montague, 1971). Condry and Condry (1976) discovered in parent–child relationships parents tend to touch their sons less often and more roughly than they do their daughters. Daughters receive gentle, more protective touch from parents. Goldberg and Lewis (1969) say early tactile messages teach boys not to associate touch with affiliation, whereas girls expect it and associate it with affiliation. People react positively when touch occurs within an intimate context; it may denote sexual interest (Jourard & Rubin, 1968) or social intimacy (Burgoon et al., 1982). When such touch occurs and denotes reciprocity, it indicates solidarity among equals (Henley, 1973). Women initiate hugs and touches expressing support, affection, and comfort; men use touch to direct others, assert power, and express sexual interest (Deaux, 1976; Leathers, 1986).

Touch may be viewed as feminine-appropriate and masculine-inappropriate role behavior. Jones (1984) describes greater total touch and reciprocation of touch among women; women receive encouragement to touch and be touched as part of their feminine nurturing role. Males, on the other hand, recognize touch as feminine-appropriate behavior, thus indicating why they touch less often. Also, when touch acts as an indicator of status rather than solidarity, then it may not be returned by the lower-status person. Because early socialization encourages men to enter the private spaces of others and to use touch to establish power, they may engage in touching behavior women coworkers may perceive as harassing (Poire et al., 1992). Because society trains women to act nice to others, when they experience unwanted touch they may be reluctant to stop it. Often women use humor or avoidance tactics to sidestep unwanted touch rather than using confrontive strategies with individuals who hold higher status. Gendered patterns of nonverbal communication often lead to miscommunication between men and women with regard to sexual harassment episodes.

Some controversy exists about who touches more and in what context. For example, researchers (Jones, 1984; Stier & Hall, 1984) have found women equal or exceed men in their initiation of touch. Henley (1977), however, claims women receive more touch than men, and men touch women about twice as often as women touch men. Not only do women receive more touch, but they make more specific distinctions concerning its meaning. The type of touch (patting, stroking, squeezing) and the place touched (hands, face, arms, genitals) help women distinguish among love, friendliness, and sexual desire. For men, the place touched does not act as a distinguishing factor in meaning, but type of touch does (Nguyen et al., 1975). Research findings are somewhat confusing about who touches whom more often, but when considering the sex role script of dominance alone, men initiate more touch and women receive more. With regard to nurturing, women initiate more touch than men. Sex role scripts of affiliation may also determine why women make more distinctions in meanings of touch.

Sexual harassment problems in the workplace reoriented touch among professionals. Previously, two perceptions of problems existed in the workplace for women who worked for male bosses. Some male bosses fail to recognize the significance of touch but when enlightened change the way they nonverbally interact with female employees. On the other hand, other male bosses or colleagues may have wanted to exercise their power over women as a part of a macho self-image. Enlightening such men failed to cause them to change their ways; laws about touch in the workplace were the result. Today, most men recognize the importance of the perceptual interpretations or misinterpretations of touch by women with whom they interact. It may no longer be true that men touch women more often as a result of dominance, as some previous studies demonstrated. New studies in this area need to be conducted to determine whether sexual harassment laws have actually changed the way male and female colleagues touch one another.

PARALINGUISTICS

Paralinguistics refer to all vocal cues accompanying verbal communication, most notably habitual pitch, pitch variety, inflectional patterns, vocal quality, and articulation. Male voices sound deeper, louder, and more rotund as a result of shorter, thicker vocal folds; larger chests; and larger larynxes and pharynxes. On the other hand, female voices sound higher, smaller, and more strident as a result of longer, thinner vocal folds; smaller chests; and smaller larynxes and pharynxes. But the logical explanation of physiological differences between male and female vocal organs does not account for all of the differences in the quality of voice. When a particular timbre of the voice receives criticism, a person may attempt to modify it through delicate changes in use of the laryngeal structure. As a result of social pressure actual physical changes may result. Society does teach us, however, to limit ourselves to a certain range of intonation appropriate to our sex. Although voices reflect individuality, which is often affected by hereditary endowment (Sapir, 1949), they also have a social quality. Each of us, it seems, received many vocal attributes as a result of who we are and the society where we grew up.

Pitch variety may be accompanied by variation in rate and loudness. Personality often influences the way an individual chooses to vary his or her pitch, but it may also be influenced by culture. Male speakers use a fairly limited pitch range compared to female speakers. On the average, females tend to use more of their upper range, with as many as four distinctive intonational levels, whereas males use only three (Brend, 1975). The perception of women as emotional and excitable and men as stable and invulnerable may be impacted by these pitch variances (Edelsky, 1979). Arnovitch (1976) concludes when a man uses pitch variation it tends to distinguish him as exceptional and he receives positive evaluations. Since society expects women to sound emotional, variability is expected, so for female speakers the absence of variability is more harshly criticized. Variability, however, is a positive characteristic for both women and men.

Inflectional patterns are voice melodies, which should not become predictable, so as not to distract a listener from the message. (A sing-songy pitch pattern would be an example of a distracting inflectional change.) Inflectional patterns may be specific to culture, a means of becoming part of the process of learning how to speak. Females use more distinctive inflectional patterns, whereas males learn to camouflage emotion by *not* using distinctive inflectional patterns in efforts to avoid sounding feminine. For example, if a man creates a double pitch change, starting high, then dropping low, when he says, "Really," or if he uses a sharp upward glide at the end of a question, he is using a female inflectional pattern (Arliss, 1991). These inflectional patterns are used by males when they impersonate females and become obvious female characteristics when males use them (McConnell-Ginet, 1983).

A listener's perception affects the sound production known as *vocal quality*. A speaker may be nasal, denasal, hoarse, breathy, strained, throaty, thin and weak, falsetto, or rotund. Sometimes listeners hear quality affected by a glottal click (a vocal deviation experienced when the vocal folds become hypertense and "explode" the initial release of breath) or a vocal fry (when puffs of air get caught in the glottis during phonation), which tend to distract the listener and distort tone production. Addington (1968) speculates about how male and female voices shed light on the cultural aspect of vocal quality. Women with breathy, small, tense voices are judged as pretty, feminine, petite, shallow, immature, and unintelligent. Men with throaty, tense voices (also undesirable) are judged as mature, masculine, intelligent, and sophisticated. Addington says feminine women often are assigned flighty, immature, and unintelligent attributes when rated even when not using breathy, small, tense voices. Masculine men often are judged intelligent and mature when rated, despite their vocal quality. Studies (Sherer & Giles, 1979) describing habitual pitch levels as an enculturated aspect of vocalization, chosen, not physically determined, motivate men to use even lower pitch levels than may be healthy (Lieberman, 1977). Sherer and Giles (1979) claim feminism promotes masculine speech styles even for women, to help them combat stereotypical impressions of them as the weaker sex, with emotional, weak sounding voices. As a consequence of wanting to sound more authoritative, women's voices have lowered slightly over the last several decades. In either case, both men and women may be damaging their vocal mechanisms by using habitual pitches not matching their vocal mechanisms as a result of cultural pressures.

Articulation refers to the precision individuals effect while uttering standard phonemes. American speakers all use some substandard varieties of misarticulation when with friends or when relaxed. Often, however, these substandard varieties become habits of misarticulation that lead to "sloppy speech." An example of substandard articulation would be *jeetyet* for "Did you eat yet?" or *comin'* for "coming" or the use of double negatives. Labov (1972) claims males across ages and geographical locations use more nonstandard forms than women. Women may use them less often when in public, comparably to putting on their best behavior in formal settings (Trudgill, 1975). Arliss (1991) describes the nonstandard speech of males as "cowboy" speech used in efforts to sound rough and more masculine, perhaps even desirable. Formal speech may be seen by some men as effeminate, and therefore to be avoided. In any case, nonstandard speech forms may be deliberately selected by those who know standard speech but decide not to use it in some situations. Female speakers use more formal articulation than males in all social groups.

ARTIFACTS

Artifactual communication comprises the exchange of messages by means of objects, clothing, jewelry, cosmetics, and color or any other material things. Individuals can determine age, status, role, values, life-style, occupation, nationality, socioeconomic class, group memberships, personality, as well as gender by artifactual communication (Rosenfeld & Plax, 1977). Personal objects influence how people express the identity they want to create for themselves. These objects often depict gendered identities for individuals.

When babies lie in the hospital nursery, nurses often wrap them in white blankets with blue or pink stripes. These stripes indicate sex, defining the child as male or female. As children grow, their parents often give them toys that coincide with cultural perceptions of their sex. Male children often play with toys that invite more rough-and-tumble play, whereas girls play with toys that encourage them to develop nurturing, domestic activities (Caldera et al., 1989; Lawson, 1989; Pomerleau et al., 1990). These beginnings often cultivate gendered cognitive and social skills. After childhood, artifactual communication continues to manifest itself in masculine and feminine stereotypes.

Clothing serves our need for creative self-expression (Fisher, 1975). Perry et al. (1983) identify an interest in clothing as evidence of a high level of self-actualization. Procter (1978) and Hillestad (1974) claim clothes allow us to identify with a particular social class. Rosencranz (1972) indicates clothing enables individuals to display their economic resources and status. Over time, clothing fashion for women evolved (Brain, 1979; Polhemus & Procter, 1978) from restrictiveness and restraints to comfortableness and utility. Modesty, a characteristic of women's clothing, may be associated with taboos related to feminine attributes such as breasts, menstruation, or pelvic bones. Covering and constraining such areas call attention to the physical assets of women but often hamper their movements and activities. During earlier times, the clothing of men did not vary much in design or color (usually dark), intending to depict seriousness and strength and allowing for more activity than the clothing worn by women. Over time, clothing for men has remained relatively unchanged in style and color.

More comfortable, practical styles of clothing and shoes for women originated when women went outside the home to work. Today unisex clothing often makes gender indistinguishable. After the Heaven's Gate suicides of 1997, depictions of victims appeared on television through videotaped representations of the people while they had been alive. These people portrayed androgynous gender types whereby sex became indistinguishable except in some cases by voice. Males claimed they had elected castration as a means of purification, and females had cropped their hair. In each case, these people adopted gender neutral nonverbal depictions that caused them to appear nonsexual. Some of the broadcasters who described this mass suicide described the inability to define the sex of these people as somewhat disconcerting.

We often associate artifacts of men and women with their sex. Advertisements reinforce cultural stereotypes of men and women by associating homemaking products with females and those associated with physical labor (such as cars, garage cleaning, lawn mowing, bug killing) with males. Women through advertising learn to condition and curl their hair and find out how much value society places on jewelry and cosmetics. For example, the type of watch a person wears tells much about him or her (Rolex versus a cheaper brand). Advertising often reinforces attitudes about credit cards, banking, investments, and business oriented products for men. Advertising changes are occurring, however, with more emphasis on cross-gendered ideologies.

A most curious development of the 90's, the cap, expresses new information about a person. You cannot enter a school without seeing a wide variety of caps or hats on student heads: some to cover their unwashed hair, others to signify their loyalty to a movement or a sports team, others to indicate a visit to a fashionable place. Cowboy hats and baseball caps, to name just two, appear every day. These caps or hats identify individuals as display artifacts, giving personal information about the wearer. Formerly, only men wore these hats, but in the 90's this phenomenon reached across gender lines.

IMPACT OF NONVERBAL COMMUNICATION ON GENDER

Most of the literature indicates women assess various emotional states of associates more accurately (Rosenthal et al., 1979). It also claims women look at others more, give up space to others, allow others to touch them more, and interpret facial expressions more easily than men. Women also appear to demonstrate more open emotional responsiveness, but what they display may not represent what they really feel. Men do not express their emotions openly; therefore when they do, their emotions appear to be more genuine. At the same time, women exhibit greater affiliative behavior, often making them more approachable than men. Men display more dominating behavior, even in their nonverbal communication, making them appear less approachable.

We should recognize different approaches to nonverbal communication in efforts to encourage respect even though some of our language choices may encourage polar thinking. Respecting differences enables individuals to suspend judgment and reduce egocentric thinking. Drawing out individuals who may be both verbally and nonverbally deferential may help to encourage assertiveness in shy individuals. Recognizing nonverbal differences in communication allows personal effectiveness to increase with a new range of alternative options for communicating with different people in diverse contexts for different reasons. By becoming aware of how nonverbal communication speaks, people can become conscious of a style reflecting the identity they may or may not wish to project.

Androgynous people adjust to others by using masculine and/or feminine nonverbal communication styles, depending on the exigencies of the situation. If a person wants to be responsive and assertive at the same time, an androgynous role is suitable. The androgynous person exhibits warmth, compassion, sincerity, helpfulness, sympathy, submissiveness, competitiveness, risk taking, assertiveness, independence, and dominance—all at different times depending on the situation. The androgynous person will more likely respond appropriately across contexts, be able to assess situations, and relate to more different types of people with ease.

CONCLUSION

The research presented in this chapter contrasts the nonverbal communication of men and women. Consistent with oral communication, nonverbal communication depicts men as acting more territorial and women as tending to use smaller personal space zones. Men use more expansiveness in their movements; women keep their gestures closer to the body. Women engage in more reciprocal touch, whereas men, in response to sexual harassment rules, may touch less frequently than past research indicated. Masculine paralanguage projects logical, cool, and aloof images of men, whereas feminine paralanguage depicts women as more emotional, warm, and caring. Finally, this chapter has described artifactual communication, especially clothing, reflecting stereotypes of men and women. Modifications of nonverbal communication for either sex can create images of men and women less bound by sex-related norms.

PART III

10

Gender Differences in Leadership

K. Payne and J. Cangemi

Give a person integrity, common sense, and a sense of humor, and he
or she has within the main essentials necessary for leadership.

Charles Reynolds Brown

Institutions such as religious, commercial, medical, and service organizations operate in ways reflecting and sustaining traditional beliefs about gender. These beliefs established gender stereotypes in the structures, human relations, political policies, and symbolic artifacts of organizations. Both men and women have operated, at some time, under these highly restrictive stereotypes in institutions. The communication climates emerging from these stereotypes often provide different opportunities for women and men in organizations. Norms for communication practices in institutions were established by using male patterns, and since women have entered the workplace, some discussion about differing styles between men and women has raised many questions. This chapter talks about what the experts now describe as effective leadership, including differences in the way males and females lead. Variables of effective leaders include being able to control anger, competing for status, dealing with stress, and being persuasive. These aspects of leadership, as they impact gender communication, are discussed in this chapter.

INTRODUCTION

Without training, leaders may operate by simply trying to guess what strategy will outdo their opponents so they can accomplish their goals, be in control, and dominate others. To a certain extent, having power and using it to accomplish an organizational vision often involve goals of domination. The desire to be in a dominant position, or to have power, emanates from a variety of sources. To project power a person must establish hierarchical authority, accomplish difficult tasks, be competitive, generate respect, facilitate high control, be capable of unemotional analytic problem solving, and, when necessary, exhibit a tough attitude. Some of the most famous and wealthy business persons of our time have manifested these power assets. In fact, norms for leadership practices in institutions were established with these patterns, and people who do not use them often are dominated by others. If, for example, a leader has as his or her central goal the desire "to be liked," that goal will become a major obstacle to obtaining or maintaining power. In a study by Schein (1973) both female and male executives believed successful middle managers possessed an abundance of characteristics associated with masculinity, which were most associated with men in general than with women. *Leadership for the twenty-first century, however, requires people to use a style of leadership incorporating both task and consideration.* If individuals had to guess whether a task or relationship style would achieve their vision and enable them to grasp control of an organization, however, task would always accomplish it, even in the absence of consideration, though organizational gurus advocate incorporating consideration as a strategy for generating higher productivity and subordinate satisfaction.

EFFECTIVE LEADERSHIP

The way leaders behave, the assumptions and values they hold, the practices they employ in great measure determine their effectiveness. Donnell and Hall (1980) identify five dimensions of effective leadership: (1) leadership philosophy, (2) motivational dynamics, (3) participative practices, (4) interpersonal competence, and (5) leadership style. *Leadership philosophy* constitutes the beliefs and values shaping the attitudes and behavior of leaders toward subordinates. *Motivational dynamics* include the leader's own motivational needs and how those needs affect surbordinates' motivation. *Participative practices* refer to the extent to which a leader empowers subordinates in the decision making process. *Interpersonal competence* refers to a leader's ability to solicit trust from subordinates and be approachable. *Leadership style* refers to the ongoing attention to people and production.

Leaders demonstrate their *philosophy* every day as they live out their basic beliefs and values toward subordinates. McGregor (1960) first identified attitudes about power and control held by managers, portraying them as either pessimistic (Theory X) or optimistic (Theory Y) about employees. Among others, Theory X assumptions indicate that a subordinate requires direction and control and has little desire for responsibility; Theory Y assumptions promote trust of and empowerment of employees. McGregor advocates Theory Y assumptions to facilitate the achievement of organizational objectives and employee growth and development.

Maslow (1970) and Hertzberg (1966) similarly identify *motivational* needs as arranged in levels, with organizational members experiencing those needs at different levels. A widely accepted belief among motivational theorists is that leaders cannot inject motivation into an employee. They can, however, identify subordinate needs and channel activities toward organizational goals. Consequently, generating job satisfaction by providing an atmosphere whereby people can creatively demonstrate their competence signals effective leadership.

Participative practices entail the extent to which a leader empowers subordinates in the decision making process. Highly motivated employees who share in decision making and experience supportive leadership characterize a healthy organizational climate. Communication flows upward, downward, and horizontally when leadership practices empower others. Teamwork, cooperation, sharing, group loyalty, responsibility for one's actions, extremely high performance goals, trust, and confidence typify the participative system (Hoy & Miskel, 1982), and successful leaders employ them.

Interpersonal competence is a leader's ability to solicit trust from subordinates and to be approachable. Argyris (1962) studied bureaucratic organizational structures and found poor, shallow, and mistrustful relationships between authorities and partisans. He says that such relationships do not permit free expression of truth, and the result is decreased interpersonal competence. Without a safe environment of "free expression" the organization becomes a breeding ground for mistrust, intergroup conflict, rigidity, and a decrease in organizational success in problem solving (Bennis, 1969). Argyris (1962) claims using humanistic or democratic values promotes trusting, authentic relationships and generates increased interpersonal competence, intergroup cooperation, and flexibility. These qualities identify effective leadership.

Leadership style is the ongoing attention to people and production. The Ohio State leadership studies (Stodgill & Coons, 1957) identified effective leader behavior along two dimensions: initiating structure and consideration. *Initiating structure* delineates the relationship between the leader and subordinates by establishing well-defined patterns of organization, channels of communication, and methods of procedure. *Consideration* refers to behavior indicative of friendship, mutual trust, respect, and warmth in the relationship between leader and subordinates. Blake and Mouton (1964) popularized the terms *task* and *relationships* to identify these same variables. By plotting scores for each variable on a separate axis they identified effective leadership as characterized by high scores on both task and relationship concerns.

According to Barnard (1938) potential for conflict exists in attempting to satisfy both task and relationship concerns at the same time. Stereotypical female patterns used high task workplace leadership styles. Stereotypical female patterns utilized a stronger orientation toward relationship leadership styles. Since women and minorities have entered the workplace, and since the international environment has demanded changes in organizations in order to remain competitive, leadership style has also changed. Revisionists, concerned with economic factors and productivity, observe the pendulum swinging to the middle from its once extreme task position (Bennis, 1969), but not to the other (relationship) extreme. Consequently, we find effective leaders maintain a strong concern for task and relationship.

MALE LEADERSHIP

The existence of different expectations for men's and women's leadership styles has been documented in extensive research on gender (Broverman et al., 1972; Deaux & Lewis, 1983; Eagly & Steffen, 1984; Ruble, 1983). In summary, their findings indicate we expect men to act independent, masterful, assertive, and competent. Loden (1985) claims a masculine style of leadership manifests competitiveness, hierarchical authority, high control by the leader, and unemotional and analytic problem solving. Males become involved in economy and business. Stereotypical roles for men lead them to task-oriented activities. Eagly and Karau (1991) predicted men would excel more frequently than women on measures of general leadership, as well as task leadership. They based their hypothesis on the notion that gender role expectations would produce behavior consistent with those expectations. They found that when task accomplishment becomes a group's primary goal, males do emerge as leaders, as they are slightly more task oriented than females. Further, they argue, this should not be interpreted as a tendency to choose men over women, but rather as a definition of leadership in terms of task-oriented contributions. Eagly and Johnson (1990) agree, asserting that gender role expectations contaminate organizational roles to some extent. Consequently, when male leaders behave in ways that violate gender role expectations, they often lose the respect and trust of subordinates.

Donnell and Hall (1980) claim that high-achieving males score low on Theory X assumptions and are motivated by concern with work environment, pay, and strain avoidance and by opportunities for growth, autonomy, and challenge. Subordinates of male managers express higher basic needs, such as esteem and actualization, than those of females. With regard to participative climate, males and females employ similar participative styles. Along dimensions of interpersonal competence, males are more willing to share relevant data with their colleagues than females. Also, males solicit more feedback from subordinates, and subordinates relate differently to male leaders. On scales measuring task/relationship, subordinates rate male leaders high on the autocratic (9/1) scale and low on the relationship (1/9) scale (Blake & Mouton, 1964).

Anger

No man who harbors deeply felt anger toward women should occupy a position of leadership. In other words, males who experience known or denied anger toward women will not work well with women, particularly those women who refuse to acknowledge males as authorities. One of the most widely accepted findings in the field of sex differences claims males act more aggressive than females. Aggression in males has been not only permitted, but encouraged (Kagan & Moss, 1983). Curiously, researchers generally claim males are emotionally inexpressive, with the exception of the emotion of anger. However, males and masculine gender types express more anger outwardly. As a result, researchers (Averill, 1982; Biaggio, 1980; Thomas, 1989) report masculine individuals need help with controlling anger. Male leaders typically use direct methods to discipline their subordinates and express that anger: yelling, stomping their feet, pounding their fists, and even swearing without much inhibition. This may be physically healthy for males, but it may be psychologically stressful for their subordinates. When directed at a subordinate, anger acts as a policing function (Tavris, 1982), expressing messages about how one ought to behave. In fact, the use of anger displays can be a legitimate part of a supervisory role. Non-work-related factors that can provoke anger in males include physical (hitting) aggression and assertions that they are sexually inadequate, worthless, or cowardly. Society expects men to protect women and children and defend the social order; consequently, aggression in males, when properly directed, achieves those goals (Kagan & Moss, 1983).

The extent to which a person identifies with the masculine gender role affects his or her expression of aggressive and dominant behavior (Condry & Condry, 1976; Kogut et al., 1992; Shields, 1987; Tavris, 1982). Tavris (1982) argues that expressions of anger may be status-related. High group status produces feelings of power and expectations of competence for oneself (Webster & Foschi, 1988). Russel and Mehrabian (1974, p. 79) conceptualize dominance as "the degree to which a person feels powerful or in control of a situation" and asserts that it entitles individuals to the expression of anger (Novaco, 1976). Smith and Ellsworth (1985), however, claim the perception of being in control should diminish rather than enhance the experience and expression of anger.

Social Influence/Status

Leader effectiveness depends to a large extent on the competition for social influence. Eagly (1978) claims men typically influence more and appear more difficult to influence than women. One reason for this perception may be that men engage in greater amounts of disagreement (Piliavin & Martin, 1978) and task behavior such as giving opinions, suggestions, and directions (Aries, 1982; Carli, 1989; Heiss, 1962; Piliavin & Martin, 1978; Strodbeck & Mann, 1956; Zelditch, 1955) just to gain status. Desire for status can be explained by social expectations of men's having higher status than women, which would motivate men to maintain that status, acknowledging that society rewards masculine traits more than feminine traits (Broverman et al., 1972). Consequently, higher-status group members operate with greater confidence and appear more competent; they receive more opportunities to make task contributions and rally more support for their contributions (Berger et al., 1972; Berger & Fisek, 1974; Berger et al., 1977; Berger et al., 1980).

Competing for status, a legitimate activity for high-status group members, but not for low-status members, acts to keep low-status members down. Vying for status produces competition between two people for the same position or object. Dominance, on the other hand, indicates control through superior power or influence (McCarrick et al., 1981). Most studies agree men act more competitive than women, and society considers dominance, like competitiveness, a stereotypically appropriate male trait (Bem, 1974; Broverman et al., 1972; Megargee, 1969). Dominance strongly relates to a role relationship of interactants, defining who's in charge, whereas competition relates to the context of the interaction (McCarrick et al., 1981). Interrupting, interrupting back, talking over, topic control, one-down or one-up comments, overlaps, all constitute communication strategies of dominance. McCarrick et al. (1981) find men enjoy competing with other men but do not like competing with women. Even sports studies (Gill, 1988) demonstrate that males score higher than females on competitiveness and win orientation and prefer competing with men.

Kohn (1986) claims debate exemplifies competitiveness with the goal of scoring points and winning, a strategy used by men. In competition, the enhancement of one's own power and the minimization of the legitimacy of the other side's interests in a situation become the objectives. When listening in on a conversation, it is readily apparent when someone is engaging in a lively exchange of ideas and when someone is trying to win or score points. The cost of competing for success is that it creates a sense of loss by alienating all those who fail. So, when men win, they become isolated from those who lose. Maccoby (1976) describes men of the corporate scene as emotionally inaccessible and detached as a result of their style. *Competition rather than cooperation epitomizes capitalist organizations* (Maccoby, 1976; Slater, 1970).

Stress

Large numbers of workers in the United States report high enough levels of stress at work to request stress-related compensation. In men high blood pressure and high cholesterol levels develop and smoking increases with increased levels of stress (LaCroix & Haynes, 1987), all enhancing the risk of coronary heart disease. Role demands, interpersonal conflict, overload, and extraorganizational problems contribute to male stress (Nelson & Quick, 1985; Powell, 1988). Society still expects men to play the bread-winner role and as large numbers of women and minorities enter the work force and "reverse discrimination" occurs, good jobs for men are becoming harder to find. The fear of layoffs, low pay, and menial labor all contribute to stress for men in their efforts to fulfill the expectations of society. White men now face challenges not seen before in the United States: increased international competition, adjustment to jockeying for positions in the workplace by women and minorities, as well as cutbacks and downsizing. Among whites and minorities, when men are laid off, relational problems often develop at home as self-esteem goes down and stress goes up.

Early studies of stress in managers used male subjects. "These studies found that men who held more taxing jobs, such as that of manager, were particularly prone to Type A behavior" (Powell, 1993, p. 169). Type A behavior consists of extreme levels of competitiveness, aggressiveness, achievement orientation, impatience, and haste, putting individuals under pressure of time and responsibility. This behavior increases the risk of coronary heart disease and often contributes to high consumption of alcohol, tranquilizers, or sleeping pills; exhaustion; overweight; lack of exercise; high blood pressure; and family problems. Although these symptoms also affect Type A women, currently more managerial positions are still held by men.

Persuasion

Exerting influence over one's employees is a crucial and pervasive aspect of the daily activities of leadership, motivation, and satisfaction in organizations. Although there is little evidence of differences in persuasion among males and females, when they are classified according to psychological gender orientation, significant differences are found. Masculine individuals, who experience higher self-esteem, who use more aggressive persuasive strategies, will be more likely to produce arguments that support their positions, thereby making them more persuasive than feminine or androgynous individuals (Montgomery & Burgoon, 1980). Further, traditionally sex-typed males (masculine males) are less likely to change their positions or attitudes and are more likely to produce counterarguments to protect their position than any other type.

Harper and Hirokawa (1988) find male managers rely more often on punishment-based strategies, such as "warning ultimatums" when attempting to convince a subordinate to comply. For an organizationally sanctioned request, both male and female managers use reward or punishment about equally but use nonauthoritarian influence strategies when the action is not organizationally sanctioned. Consequently, when problems arise, male and female leaders attempt to influence the organization to sanction a punishment or reward for the next time something similar occurs. Brown (1979) claims that findings of research conducted with "real" managers in actual organizations (rather than students) tend to contradict stereotypes. Also, *the more recent the study, the more likely it will show fewer competence-based differences between male and female leaders.*

Burgoon et al. (1983) suggest we have expectations about appropriateness of communication behavior that differ for males and females. Consequently, these expectations affect our acceptance or rejection of persuasive messages. Use of strategies that contradict those expectations inhibits persuasiveness, whereas strategies more closely conforming to expected behavior facilitate it. Consistent with this theory, Burgoon, Jones, and Stewart (1974) find males are expected to use highly intense language in persuasive attempts and are more effective when they use that strategy. Similar findings correlate high source credibility with the use of intense language. The two strategies considered to be most masculine are threat and aversive stimulation; when they are not used, persuasive appeal decreases. When masculine females use these strategies, people react negatively because their expectations have been violated.

FEMALE LEADERSHIP

The existence of different expectations for women's leadership styles also has been documented in research on gender (Broverman et al., 1972; Deaux & Lewis, 1983; Eagly & Steffen, 1984; Ruble, 1983). In summary, findings indicate that women prefer and tend to behave in ways characterized by cooperativeness, using collaboration, minimizing their status, and using a problem solving style based on intuition and empathy, as well as rationality. We expect women to act friendly, unselfish, other-centered, and emotionally expressive. The stereotypical leadership role for women leads them to relationship-oriented activities, even in occupational roles. Eagly and Karau (1991) find on measures of relational versus task leadership style that women emerge more frequently than men as relational, or social, leaders. They also find that men and women not only behave differently in groups, but also are treated differently. L'Heureux-Barrett and Barnes-Farrell (1991) report that lower expectations for task-oriented contributions significantly affect female managers in terms of reward allocation. Contributions to group morale and harmony enhance the effectiveness of task-oriented groups but may not be recognized as constituting leadership by members of such a group. Interestingly, as task-relevant competence diminishes over time, and as skills increase and group members become aware of each other's competencies, or as social interactions became more complex, Eagly and Karau (1991) find the tendency for women to emerge as leaders strengthens. Because of gender role expectations, *feminine* female leaders using a task-oriented leadership style often experience conflict between their gender and their leadership role. Also, as female leaders move away from relationship-oriented roles, they often experience resistance and conflict from many group members. This conflict arises because the normal expectation for leadership still includes more masculine than feminine qualities. Curiously, L'Heureux-Barrett and Barnes-Farrell (1991) found that *bias against female managers arose predominantly from other females.*

Women who plan careers in male-dominated occupations have higher career aspirations than those who desire careers in female-dominated occupations and also encounter more traditional attitudes toward the tensions between work and home/children. Donnell and Hall (1980) found high-achieving females score higher than low-achieving females on McGregor's (1960) Theory X assumptions (autocratic behavioral style). We can speculate about the reasons why high-achieving women often have believed their success depended on acting in ways that made them appear to be "more like men." Compensating for the attitude that women are the weaker sex may, in part, explain why some women leaders have adopted this style. Some say high-achieving females achieve, but pay the price interpersonally because they believe maintaining personal relationships might jeopardize their success. Regarding motivational needs, women report lower basic needs and higher needs for self-actualization than men. Female leaders were more concerned with opportunities for growth, autonomy, and challenge and less concerned with work environment, pay, and strain avoidance. Further, Donnell and Hall (1980) found subordinates of females had lower basic needs than did subordinates of males. This might be explained, in part, by the lower "breadwinner" pressure on females. Also, it may be that for females work is more closely tied to ego and self-actualization. Along the participative continuum, female and male leaders operate in about the same way. With regard to interpersonal competence, females express a lower willingness to share relevant data with their colleagues. Further, their subordinates report soliciting less feedback from their female managers. Finally, when subordinates appraise their female managers, they see them as using a hands-off approach to both task and a relationship, a 1/1 style of leadership according to Blake and Mouton (1964).

The dominance and control style of leadership may have contributed to the glass ceiling effect experienced by many high-achieving women. Because acting masculine violates stereotypical expectations for women, those women may have breached interpersonal alliances by acting masculine. Also, acting masculine opposes what we now know about the stereotypical leadership style of women. Kanter (1977) says that what comes "naturally" to women is the use of strategies that involve consideration such as nurturing, helping, and encouraging, all of which enable others to achieve their goals. Even so, no one ideal kind of leadership behavior achieves optimal performance under all conditions, and women can certainly use other, more task-oriented strategies with great success.

Anger

No woman who harbors a deeply felt anger toward men should occupy a position of leadership, particularly one who has acknowledged or unacknowledged anger toward men who do not consider females as equals. Aside from this neurotic condition, women who lead in organizations often experience and express normal everyday anger in unique ways. In popular as well as professional literature, the expression of anger is described as socially prohibited for women. Kopper (1993) reports feminine sex role types denote a high level of anger directed inward and a high level of control against the expression of anger. As a result, feminine individuals need more help with controlling depression and anxiety (Averill, 1982; Biaggio, 1980; Thomas, 1989). In the last thirty years, however, feminists have encouraged women to acknowledge and express anger, even though anger often is thought of as a masculine emotion (Shields, 1987; Sharkin, 1993). Fisher et al. (1993) report women of the 90's appeared to be experiencing and expressing about the same amount of anger and depression as men. One reason females become angry is that others treat them with a condescending and insensitive attitude. Also, they do not like being referred to as promiscuous or being treated dismissively. Further, women become angry when others treat them with a patronizing attitude or do not listen to them and accept their ideas as worthwhile. These anger producing phenomena frustrate women and cause anxiety, because the direct expression of anger is considered socially prohibited for women (Kagan & Moss, 1983).

Current research on the role of appropriate emotional expression in the work environment suggests gender plays an important part in the assessment and interpretation of anger displays (Blier & Blier-Wilson, 1989; Chiauzzi et al., 1982; Hochschild, 1983; Tavris, 1982). In the case of Ann Hopkins versus Price Waterhouse (Seligman, 1988), Hopkins was denied full partnership in the firm because of her overbearing and abrasive personality. Women as leaders receive higher evaluations when they work out their anger through consideration (relational communication) rather than through structuring behavior (ordering more formal rules) (Bartol & Butterfield, 1976) because expressions of anger in women go against social expectation. Tannen (1994) reports when women get angry, they typically just walk away, shed a few tears alone, then return to a conversation and pretend nothing happened. Acting angry undermines the desire "to be liked." Consequently, women as leaders often act extra nice, attempting to assure others they will not throw their weight around. Their unexpressed anger may build up to be later expelled in the form of "gunnysacking," whereby grievances are so extensive they overwhelm both parties.

Research on communication behavior (Blier & Blier-Wilson, 1989; Chiauzzi et al., 1982) argues that females express negative feelings with great difficulty. They experience anxiety about aggression and disagreement with others during discussions involving collaboration (Frodi et al., 1977). Women judge their own angry displays to be costly to their interpersonal relationships. If angry displays act as a policing function (Travis, 1982), helping to regulate social relations, helping express messages of how one ought to behave, and acting as a legitimate part of a supervisory role, then women who have trouble expressing anger may be at a disadvantage in a leadership role.

The extent of identification with aggressive and dominant behavior (Condry & Condry, 1976; Shields, 1987; Tavris, 1982) may be closely aligned with the masculine gender role and the degree to which an individual identifies with that role (Kogut et al., 1992). Kogut et al. (1992) claims women higher in masculinity are more aggressive than those in the low-masculinity group. In an unpublished research project in which the Bem Sex Role Inventory was administered to university students, Payne and Payne-Houchen (1999) found that more females self-scored as masculine than feminine or androgynous in gender role. This finding suggests women are moving from a dependent, submissive, feminine role in the workplace to one of more independence, assertiveness, and competitiveness in efforts to achieve higher status.

Curiously, we generally view females as emotionally expressive, except in relation to anger, whereas we view males as emotionally inexpressive, except with respect to anger. Consequently, the presence of males in an organization creates an awareness of the possibility of violence. Women know some men will resort to violence against women. However vaguely and in the background the threat of violence lurks, women recognize it could happen, though it probably never will. Intimidation characterizes the feeling best, even among women who recognize their own dominance and strength. Given this intimidation, *expressions of legitimate anger and protest from women produce the risk of reprisal*, or at the least the risk of standing alone, experiencing disapproval and loss of the love of others. For women as leaders, this tendency requires a particular degree of courage and autonomy. Women leaders who recognize this take responsibility for their own choices, determine their own risks, and assume the challenge for their own growth and development.

Social Influence/Status

The major focus of participative management is a reciprocal system of trust and influence. It implies joint participation in the making of work-related decisions. When one seeks to resolve conflict by arriving at consensus, the objective is to create a collaborative process of searching for a solution and responding to the needs of others. This style of resolving conflict prevails in group discussion, the hallmark of participative management. Consideration of other people's needs, characteristic of women's style of leading, enhances the collaborative process in participative management. In fact, Sassen (1980) claims women actually experience anxiety within a climate of competition. McCarrick et al. (1981) state that women do not typically like to compete with other women but do not mind competing with men. Sassen (1980) advocates not teaching women to compete, but rather restructuring institutions so competition will be only one avenue to success. Reducing the win orientation and replacing it with an achievement orientation, she says, will cause people to reach inside to compete with themselves rather than others. Weaver (1995) claims women leaders already tend to share information and power by inspiring good work through interacting with others, encouraging member participation, and showing how member goals relate to group goals.

Rather than thinking of competition for status and a reciprocal system of trust and influence as at opposite ends of a continuum, women may see them as intertwined. Tannen (1994) claims women see status and connection as helpful in accomplishing individual and group goals. She states that women may view competing for status as a way of establishing connection, as in the case of sports and popularity contests. Establishing relationships with people helps identify whom to call on when it is necessary to get around rules or when support on a salient issue is important.

Eagly and Carli (1981) say women may not always display their real opinions, in part because of their strong emphasis on maintaining at least an appearance of a "relationship orientation." In efforts to maintain that orientation, women often exhibit more positive social behavior, such as relieving group tension and showing group solidarity, just to be polite. For example, women often avoid disagreeing publicly and prefer to operate behind the scenes before or after a meeting to rally support for a project or to oppose an issue. Consequently, women may be perceived as acting in contradictory ways, or as sneaky, backstabbing, unpredictable, two-faced, vengeful and as plotters and schemers. This apparent contradiction can work against women as leaders, because subordinates may not understand why they seem reluctant to speak up or to speak more directly. People who understand this phenomenon will recognize and provide support for female leaders who may be experiencing a conflict between their private opinions and social rules. Another strategy women leaders may employ is making greater use of referent power, relying on their similarity to others and being likable (Raven et al., 1975).

Challenging the notion that task behavior generates more status, Carli (1989) finds that agreement and disagreement directly predict influence and that agreements between partners increase their influence with each other, whereas disagreements decrease it. This finding opposes findings of earlier studies that claim that more disagreement elicits influence. Further, the partner's gender rather than one's own gender influences the use of agreement rather than disagreement. When interacting with females, both males and females tend to be more agreeable. When people agree with one another, they tend to think of each other as supportive and want to support them in return, thus generating a reciprocal system of influence.

Stress

Both women and men report job stress, but for women some unique aspects of stress contribute to health problems. *Stress* is a combination of two or more of the following: an environmental stimulus, a psychological or physical response, or an interaction of the two (Ivancevich et al., 1990). Common stressors experienced by women and men are role demands, work overload, interpersonal relationships, and extraorganizational problems (Nelson & Quick, 1985; Powell, 1988). However, women may experience additional on-the-job stresses because they are women and because they may interpret and cope differently than men. Three unique sources of stress affect women managers: social and organizational stresses and stresses that result from unique attributes of women (Fagenson, 1993).

Social sources of stress may be grounded in highly resistant attitudes about women and work. For example, the career-family interface may present role conflict between the career and family roles played by women, conflict that does not affect men in the same way. Since women still assume primary responsibility for home and child care activities (Googins & Burden, 1987; Jick & Mitz, 1985; Zappert & Weinstein, 1985) they often spend more time working than resting. Among married couples with children fathers report a combined weekly work/home job load of sixty-eight hours, whereas mothers report eight-three hours (Googins & Burden, 1987). Physiological reactions of men managers include a quicker winding down time after work, whereas women managers' blood pressure remains high and their level of the stress hormone norepinephrine actually increases after a stressful event (Frankenhaeuser et al., 1989). Social support provided by family and friends positively correlates with psychological well-being for employed women and men (Pugliesi, 1988). Both women and men who have off-the-job support show better psychological adjustment to stressful events and faster recovery from illness (House et al., 1988).

Organizational sources of stress often include both formal and informal policies and practices, as well as on-the-job support, sex differences in access to power, sexual harassment, and sex discrimination. Women managers report less on-the-job support than men managers. Women managers who report low perceived supervisor support assert that they experience high job anxiety, depression, psychosomatic symptoms, irritation, anger, drug use, and frequent job turnover (Greenglass, 1987). Morrison and Von Glinow (1990) report women managers occupy lower-level positions with less authority and less pay. They often have less access to the main power holders in the organization (Brass, 1985), and less upward and downward influence as a result. Sexual harassment also produces stress for women. Even though men also report sexual harassment from women, they generally experience it differently than women do. Women who experience blatant sexual harassment by a superior or a nonsuperior report symptoms of psychological stress such as nervousness or depression, headaches, stomachaches, changes in weight and blood pressure, and even mild strokes. Once hired, women managers more likely experience pay inequity, which also causes stress.

Women themselves may contribute to their own stress. A person who has a Type A personality experiences chronic feelings of time pressure or urgency, a competitive achievement orientation, and more characteristic traits of hostility and aggression (Glass, 1977). Type B behavior seems less harried and angry. Women managers report scores higher on Type A behavior, with 90 percent scoring at or above the sixty-fifth percentile (Lawler et al., 1983). Type A behavior in women is twice as likely to produce coronary heart disease as it is in their male Type A counterparts (Davidson & Cooper, 1986). Type A behavior in either men or women deserves more attention, particularly the hostility component described by many researchers as the most predictive of coronary heart disease (Taylor, 1990).

Persuasion

In a study by Andrews (1987) females express low confidence in their ability to communicate their arguments persuasively. When successful at persuasion, women tend to attribute their success to circumstance (Henning & Jardim, 1976) but attribute their failure to themselves. The kinds of arguments used to persuade reveal something of a person's values, and women tend to use persuasive strategies based on more equitable or humane decisions. Their arguments focus on contributions to society and the theme of maintaining relationships. Burgoon et al. (1983) suggest people develop expectations about appropriateness of communication behavior, and when speakers do not meet those expectations, their influence strategies are weakened. Consequently, female leaders are most persuasive when they use persuasive strategies, and tactics as well as language choices they are expected to use. The strategies considered most feminine include promises, positive moral appeal, altruism, and liking. When women do not use these strategies their persuasive appeal decreases. Burgoon et al. (1983) claim females use more prosocial message strategies, use less verbal aggressiveness, and are penalized for deviations from the expected strategies. Harper and Hirokawa (1988) find female managers rely on direct requests, altruism, and rationale-based strategies, indicating a preference for counsel ("Is there anything I can do to help?") or explanation ("You need to do this because") when attempting to persuade a subordinate to comply with requests. This does not mean women cannot be effective using more task-oriented persuasive strategies; it merely means they have to work up to those strategies by slowly preparing their audience to expect them.

To become more influential, women can elect to participate in projects intended to help them make a name for themselves, gain respect, and receive recognition. To be noticed, people have to do more than what their job description specifies. Initiative, rather than conformity, causes people to promote women into leadership positions. An individual who is a reliable source of information, one who knows how to anticipate the reactions of others, one who can warn superiors about "land mines" and calls potential problems to the boss's attention will likely become a valued and trusted worker. Defending and supporting the boss's decisions to organizational peers put a worker in a position to be noticed and promoted. It does a woman no good to work hard and suffer in silence while those around her are completely oblivious to her efforts and her expectation of reciprocity; at the very least she should initiate a conversation, asking bluntly but politely whether that expectation matches theirs.

Women leaders are often complimented for being "approachable," perhaps because of the widely held belief that women are highly persuadable (Scheidel, 1963). Kanter (1977) says women typically employ communication strategies connoting open-mindedness and nurturance. Another reason for this perception might be women's freely being self-disclosing, reducing psychological distance between them and others. In any case, Sistrunk and McDavid (1971) find that in certain circumstances females are susceptible to social pressures and therefore act more persuadable. Further, they argue, control of other factors, such as personality, content of the task, sex of the influencer, and motivation, influences susceptibility to persuasion more than sex. Researchers (Montgomery & Burgoon, 1980; Rosenfeld & Fowler, 1976; Nord, 1969) suggest feminine females, especially those with lower levels of self-esteem and aggressiveness, react to persuasion with less motivation to produce counterarguments to defend their own position. Nord (1969) explains this, in part, by suggesting women have a high need for affiliation and achievement. But Donnell and Hall (1980) claim that *women report lower basic needs and higher needs for self-actualization,* especially women who are leaders. Interestingly, all other females, including masculine and androgynous females, in the Montgomery and Burgoon (1980) study demonstrate resistance to persuasion. Especially when trained in critical methods such as analysis of fallacies in an argument, female listeners become less open to persuasion, but not so when untrained, probably as a result of needing to learn to create their own refutational arguments (Rosenfeld & Fowler, 1976). Goal achievement appears to persuade women leaders more than any other variable (Gill, 1988). Contrary to popular belief, Donnell and Hall (1980) claim, females do not have the great need to belong that previous research suggested. Beh (1994) argues these findings indicate a change in performance and represent a significant shift in attitudes toward the acceptance of equality of roles for women leaders.

CONCLUSION

Development of organizational leaders has long been the subject of inquiry. Professional socialization has recently become an area of extensive research. Interest in this inquiry stems from examining the changing climate of organizations, which is creating a uniquely positive situation for women leaders in the twenty-first century. This chapter has discussed effective leadership in general, male and female leadership specifically, with specific consideration of displaying anger, competing for status, dealing with stress, and being persuasive as variables in male and female leadership styles. The philosophical underpinnings that prompt this inquiry include the belief that women and men do not differ in leadership style when they have been trained but differ along stereotypical lines when untrained. Leaders can be trained to incorporate both task and consideration in their leadership style, but masculine individuals will use task as a backup style, and feminine individuals will use consideration as a backup style.

Once trained, managers differ not so much along gender lines as in terms of high and low achievement. Women who plan careers in male-dominated occupations have higher career aspirations than those who desire careers in female-dominated occupations. Women in female-dominated occupations tend to have more traditional attitudes toward the tensions between work and home/children. The existence of different expectations for women and men as leaders appears to be a bigger problem for women, as has been documented in extensive research on gender (Broverman et al., 1972; Deaux & Lewis, 1983; Eagly & Karau, 1991; Ruble, 1983). In summary, these researchers believe gender role expectations will cause behavior consistent with those expectations. These beliefs cause gender stereotypes to emerge in the structures, human relations, political policies, and symbolic artifacts of organizations. Both men and women have operated, at some time, under these highly restrictive stereotypes in institutions. The research indicates we expect men to act independent, masterful, assertive, and competent; we expect women to act friendly, unselfish, other-centered, and emotionally expressive. Consequently, men and women have been thought to be well suited to roles they traditionally occupy. The stereotypical roles for men lead them to task-oriented activities, whereas the stereotypical roles for women lead them to relationship-oriented activities, even in occupational roles. Relying on stereotypical gender leadership styles, however, restricts both men and women who want to establish leader roles in the twenty-first century. Fortunately, through training male leaders can break out of stereotypes and learn to utilize more supportive communication styles, and females can break out of stereotypes to utilize more task-oriented styles.

A variation of this chapter also appeared in Payne, K., & Cangemi, J. (1997). Gender differences in leadership. *IFE PSYCHOLOGIA: An International Journal,* 5 (1), 22–43.

11

Cultural Expectations of Attractiveness: Presentations of Men and Women in the Media

You can tell the ideals of a nation by its advertisements.
Norman Douglas

The media provide images of men and women that influence the lives of people. Those images reflect the cultural Values and expectations associated with the shaping of gender roles. By defining what is newsworthy and controlling what society hears and sees, the media act as a gatekeeper. Media depictions of women and men contribute to the creation, maintenance, or change in widely shared gender social definitions. They often show how women and men should be, rather than portraying the realities of their lives. Traditional gendered social definitions constitute a fundamental bulwark for maintaining and reproducing a system of gender satisfaction. The media guide the engenderment process of new generations, serving to legitimate, and thereby strengthen, the traditional gender divisions of labor and the apparent inequities within them. The rejection of traditional gender definitions and the creation of new, more equitable ones marshaled feminist, gay, and lesbian activists to act (Chafetz et al., 1993). With new gender definitions, the inequitable system based on gender is becoming delegitimized. Accomplishing the transmission of this type of information depended on the willingness of the communication media to participate by changing gender depictions. Because of the vast capacity to stereotype views of women and men, formerly limited and distorted images have been slow to change. For example, the media often reinforce stereotypical images of men as tough, independent, aggressive, and in control of their emotions and present women as younger and thinner than the general population, with expectations of dependence, deference, and decorativeness. Changing these images to more androgynous forms has occurred as the general population has received these new messages and images. The impetus for change has originated largely among feminist groups and advocates of homosexuality in efforts to gain social power.

Throughout history concepts of attractiveness have reflected the aesthetic standards of each period. From the Rubenesque women of the seventeenth century to contemporary symbols of fashion, different body shapes have reflected desirable social status. Historically, the majority of societies preferred plumpness in females, and some cultures even admired obesity (Rudofsky, 1972). Western culture, however, within the last twenty years has demonstrated more positive attitudes toward slenderness, leanness, and angular body shapes for women, with the exception of large breasts (Calden et al., 1959). In North America, higher social status has been strongly related to thinness (Stunkard, 1975). Clearly, as women deviate from the social stereotype, self-satisfaction decreases (Calden et al., 1959; Nylander, 1971). In 1966, Heunemann et al. (1966) found as many as 70 percent of high school girls wanted to lose weight. Sociocultural pressures for thinness apparently also increase the incidence of eating disorders (Bruch, 1973; Palazzoli, 1974; Boskind-Lodahl, 1976).

Historically, physical standards for males were less specific. More important qualities of men were the ability to earn a good living, kindness, good manners, and unobjectionable looks. Since 1980 Western culture has demonstrated a changing standard for men, too, with pressure for them to develop chest and shoulders muscles, a diamond upper body shape ending in a small buttocks, angular leanness, neatness, clear eyes, clean teeth, and clean hair, plus the ability to earn a good living. Within the last couple of decades standards for young men have shifted yet again. Lord (1993) claims women prefer men who mosey rather than strut, amble rather than swagger, shuffle rather than saunter. She calls it the school of lean not mean, of androgynous not virile, of fearful not fierce. She claims women want good lovemaking from men, men not all hopped up on hormones but maybe even a few "quarts low on the stuff" (Lord, 1993, p. 122). Most recent looks for young men appearing in ads and movies depict a neurasthenic, just crawled out of bed look, with tousled hair, unshaven face, bare chest, or T-shirt, unclear as to whether they are straight, gay, or bisexual.

This chapter describes the aesthetic qualities of male and female portrayals reflected in the media. Images of men and women in magazines, newspapers, movies, television, and music are described. Although much of the literature on the images of men and women focuses on the negative impact of the sexual images of women in the media, this research attempts to look at both male and female images in an effort to give a balanced report of cultural pressure to achieve a "certain look, or ideal role." The underlying assumption is that the source of pressure on men and women to conform to media images is neither sex, but rather the persuasive images that induce all of us toward "what sells."

Since the years following World War II, the media grew quickly, and so did the study of the media. In the earlier years of studying women in the media, academics looked first at a few women in ads, as columnists, as editors, on television, and in the movies. Second, they looked at the perception of women in the media and found symbolically subservient women, victims of bad guys, who were domestically oriented "elbow jewelry" for men and corresponded to sexist stereotypes. The standards depicted in the media represented women as an underclass of victims, dependent on men for just about everything. Feminists, armed with earlier studies of women in the media, generated a media blitz against these portrayals (Busby, 1975). All of these activities assumed these images of women impacted women detrimentally not only in terms of individual consciousness but in the collective social life, as well. The content of the complaint involved the following: (1) Few women held positions of power in media organizations, and so (2) the content of the media often distorted women's status in the social world, not presenting them as viable role models, and therefore (3) the media's deleterious role models often prevented and impeded female accomplishments (Tuchman, 1979). The complaints effected a significant but gradual change not only in the numbers of women represented in the media, but in their characterization as well.

WOMEN IN MAGAZINES

Magazine advertising portrays women with perfect female faces and forms. The Victoria's Secret catalogue, for example, presents women with fantasy faces and figures that only a plastic surgeon could produce. The persuasive objective of the catalogue, accomplished through sexy lingerie and form fitting clothes, is to entice women to imagine themselves looking as sexy as the models. The stereotypes targeted at females, especially in women's magazines, depend upon their advertising to make money, making editors careful not to offend their sponsors. In one situation, a gray-haired editor showed a gray-haired woman in an ad in her magazine and lost the Clairol account for six months (Wolf, 1992). Losing this kind of lucrative account motivates magazine editors to keep their advertisers in mind, even in preference to presenting the desired changing depictions of women. Consequently, even as women take their place as professionals, magazines continue to portray them as sex objects, wives, and mothers, often lacking in confidence, autonomy, decisiveness, or rationality (Chafetz et al., 1993). Magazines portray women's faces without signs of aging, even on older women, as artists routinely airbrush out flaws or computers generate adjusted images of women. Fashion editors have acknowledged changing the already glamorous images of top models by using the Scitex machine (Wolf, 1992), a computer graphics package, making them appear smoother and more slender than they actually are. As a result, women's magazines continue to create self-doubt and eternally springing hope: they invent cellulite and then cure it (Levine, 1994).

As women view these images and then look in the mirror, they often feel inadequate unless they meet the impossible standards established in the media and accepted by the culture for a woman's figure and face. An increase in plastic surgery to increase breast size, decrease or rearrange fat by liposuction, and produce face lifts has generated a whole new industry within the last fifty years. When women obtain breast implants their nipples cease to feel sensitive. Kilbourne (1996) asks, What if men did this: "Wonder jock for the bulge you've always wanted." Young women disregard the dangers of implants, as well as the physical mutilation associated with them, claiming they do not care and just want larger breasts.

Seeing these unrealistic images and wanting to attain them may trigger eating disorders among women and young girls (Bruch, 1973). The average female model weighs 23 percent less than a normal woman and exhibits a body type present in only 5 percent of the population (Kilbourne, 1996). Advertisers use body parts of more than one model when attempting to portray the "perfect woman" in their ads. The problem then becomes the inability of women to enjoy eating because society does not allow it. When young girls reach puberty and begin to develop physically, they may start expressing feelings of being "too fat."

Girls diet even when not regarded as clinically overweight. The weight loss industry informs the public of its $33 billion success stories. As food becomes the enemy, dieting becomes salvation. Ads promoting diet plans use language evocative of salvation such as *sin, salvation, temptation*—all rhetoric of the diet industry (Kilbourne, 1996). Eating healthy as a regular habit of life differs from dieting, which can be unhealthy. For example, in people predisposed to eating disorders dieting may cause chemical changes that can trigger anorexia and bulimia (Wolf, 1992). The metabolism slows to accommodate less food; consequently when dieters begin to eat normally again, the lowered caloric requirements may cause them to put on more pounds than they lost (Worsnop, 1992). Gott (1994) acknowledges the detrimental effects of rapid weight loss and gain. Steinem (1992) claims, "In this country alone about 150,000 females die of anorexia each year." However, the American Anorexia and Bulimia Association claims Steinem misquoted them. One clinician who had treated fourteen hundred patients over ten years reported that only four had died, all through suicide (Hoff-Sommers, 1994). The National Center for Health Statistics reported 101 deaths from anorexia nervosa in 1983 and 67 deaths in 1988 (FDA, 1986 & 1992). The exaggerated statistics suggest some feminists provided provocative but inaccurate information about women's issues to promote their own agenda; the inaccurate information can be just as damaging to the psyche of women as the distorted magazine images. Further, the conclusions drawn blame a "misogynistic society that demeans women by objectifying their bodies" (Brumberg, 1988, pp. 19, 20). As feminists pit men and women against each other, they portray women as victims, unable to reason on their own, the exact opposite of a healthy image.

An increased number of women in the work force has caused a major cultural shift in the United States. Responding to this shift, advertisers have created new images of women working and shared household task allocation (Roberts & Wortzel, 1984). They have begun to reflect women's new roles and behavior (Saunders & Stead, 1986; Sullivan & O'Connor, 1988) but continue to portray them in terms of traditional stereotypes (Belknap & Leonard, 1988; Lazier-Smith, 1989). More specialized women's magazines that target specific interests of women, such as those appealing to college-educated women between the ages of twenty-five and forty, may introduce less traditional ideas—if they think it financially wise to do so. Since many women in the twenty-first century face the dual tasks of paid employment and housework, many women's magazines support ideas commonly associated with feminism.

MEN IN MAGAZINES

Many men's magazines still tend to address themselves to images of men in terms of action-adventure, do-it-yourself, finance, sports and arts, fashion, or women. The editors seek to arouse the desires and assuage the worries of men, or at least high earners, as they attempt to *reshape* masculinity. "Men want to understand and master their lives" (Levine, 1994), believing masculinity and mastery translate into action and accomplishment. Men's magazines appeal to self-confidence, not self-doubt; they cater to a man who dares to sit in a chair, wearing Calvin Klein aftershave, Ralph Lauren polo shirts, a Rolex watch, while writing with a Mont Blanc pen as he orders the products in the magazines from his home with his major credit card.

The American culture in the twenty-first century also depicts a male body as a sexual object, just as it has the female body for decades. Fabio, spokesmodel for hyperheterosexuality with hard abs and thighs, represents a masculinity icon. However, "he cannot do much of anything except stand there and be looked at" (Kendrick, 1994, p. 130). Pin-up boys typically win that honor as a side effect of fame in some other field, but Fabio began as a pin-up, then "diversified into psuedosinging, pseudoacting, even pseudowriting" (Kendrick, 1994, p. 130). Another magazine ad, which appeared in the summer of 1993, depicted an eye-catching, ravishing naked man, stretched across two pages with his arms raised and his hands behind his head. His handsome head, fashionably shaggy hair, finely chiseled nose, lips, and stubbly chin leaned up against his upraised left arm as he lay on white linen bedsheets. This naked man was intended to transform men into irresistible objects—if they used Zino "eau de toilette." "In the 80's the Marlboro man, allured women by means of strength in action, rather than the languid availability of the Zino hunk" (Kendrick, 1994, p. 126). In the twenty-first century a man cannot afford to get old: men's magazines will not let him. Middle-aged men who see images of fabulous male bodies are beginning to recognize the historical problems imposed on women as sex objects.

Often coded into the text and images of many men's magazines are messages of social transformation. The balance between the hyperheterosexuality and the "regular guy attitude" (code word for homosexual) suggests men want to look good, feel good, read good writing, and have good relationships. Most of the men's magazines do not endorse feminism but seem more comfortable making room for homosexuals. Levine (1994) reports unclear messages that seduce men, women, or homosexuals as filling magazine ads. With gender bending as the rage, even among jocks, the messages vaguely mesh with the homosocial life-style (Levine, 1994). The 1996 Calvin Klein ads exemplified the unclear messages of masculinity; one could not be sure whether the models portrayed in the ads were men or women.

In cartoon jokes of the 90's, irreverent references to women's cutting off the penis of abusive husbands appeared in magazines. Becoming almost incomprehensible at once, such jokes quickly disappeared. In another cartoon bombasting homosexuality, yet discussing it in an ice cream shop, one old women asks her friend, "If homosexuality is inherited, shouldn't it have died out by now?" (Kendrick, 1994, p. 128). In another cartoon, one little boy introduces his friend to a third boy, saying, "This is Donovan. He's pretty sure he's gay, too" (Kendrick, 1994, p. 128). The relevant point behind the jokes is the social transformation occurring in America when old ladies in an ice cream shop talk about homosexuality and little boys think they are gay. It in no way suggests straight Americans have gown tolerant of gays and lesbians.

Magazines have focused on substantive issues to inform both men and women. McElroy (1995) describes a climate of hysteria among feminist groups attempting to politicize the crime of rape and domestic abuse. The article quotes President Clinton, who had announced that rape had increased three times faster than other crimes in the preceding decade, whereas a U.S. Bureau of Justice Statistics study showed that sexual assaults on women declined 20 percent from 1992 to 1993. McElroy (1995) also reported about a survey that showed women are beaten every fifteen seconds but men are beaten every fourteen seconds. Other studies reported in the article also indicate men become victims of violence more often than women. In 1992 American husbands assaulted wives at a rate of 4.6 percent, whereas wives assaulted husbands at a rate of 9.5 percent. The author claimed these statistics rarely were published. Dogmatic attitudes have crippled honest research and reporting about domestic violence, causing zealots to accept propaganda unthinkingly as fact. Still, the battered women syndrome has been used successfully as a defense in murder cases of women who killed abusive husbands while they were asleep.

Articles describing cases of rape also appear in magazines portraying men as monsters, rather than fathers, lovers, or sons. For example, the Violence against Women Act recognized men and women as antagonistic classes to be governed by different standards of law (McElroy, 1995). As feminists pushed for a redefinition of rape, the "no means no" rape law reversed the burden of proof and narrowed the definition of consent. Under this law, sex becomes rape when the man fails to receive consent from the woman or when the woman has consumed drugs or alcohol and subsequently exhibits a "diminished state." The burden of proof now requires men to prove the woman gave her consent, and that is nearly impossible to do. Magazine articles intended to inform both men and women of what the law states have taken the initiative to correct the misguided enthusiasm of disingenuous feminist advocates reporting misinformation. They do so by presenting accurate information on the numbers of actual rapes versus the numbers presented by many feminist activists, and then they provide accurate information about recent legal cases to young men and women who may be engaging in premarital sex.

WOMEN AND MEN IN NEWSPAPERS

About twenty years ago, more women than men read newspapers. Curiously, those newspapers reported information largely targeted at male readers. Personal finance, investments, government, business, the economy, and sports, formerly dominated by men and presented from a male perspective, filled the pages. "Ladies sections" included recipes, fashion, weddings, manners, and so on, and appeared deep within the newspaper. Readership surveys showed women consistently became uninterested in daily newspapers. Critics argued newspapers failed to recognize and react to the changes experienced in the lives of women (as opposed to ladies).

Today, the focus of newspapers is on recapturing their declining female readership. The traditional women's sections have been revamped in many papers to accommodate women's interests such as their children's education and how they learn (rather than the politics of the school board); time and money and how to save both; safety and health issues; issues related to women in the workplace; social concerns, such as homelessness; and family and personal relationships. Women want information with depth that is useful and easy to find. Women do not like reporters to invade privacy or be insensitive to disaster or crime victims. The idea of juggling career, family, time, and money interests women. Newspaper sections that focus on gossip, recipes, tips on housekeeping, parenting, and the like, appear to offer sexist perspectives.

The new leadership in newspapers looks for opportunities to focus on what readers want. Schmidt and Collins (1993) report the *Chicago Tribune* dropped their "ladies' pages" of the 70's and moved to "Womanews," which talks about work-related problems catering to women of the twenty-first century whose lives focus on work, family, and money. Other newspapers run feature stories about superwomen who handle career and family with seeming ease and cause women to believe something is wrong with them when they have more difficulty balancing all of their responsibilities. Instead of covering major institutions, like the Social Security Administration, newspapers have begun to look at covering aging; instead of covering religious denominations, they cover religion and ethics. Instead of covering death row, they cover America's love affair with guns; instead of covering the politics of the school board, they focus on how the action of the school board will affect ordinary families. Women want to know about kinship, workplace relationships, quality of life, and life passages through time. Instead of a crisis approach, newspapers have to inform women of how they can help solve problems. Since women fear violence, instead of using a voyeuristic account of who did what to whom, newspapers need to report whether violent acts are isolated incidents, whether such acts represent a trend, and whether these problems will require women to restrict their movements.

WOMEN AND MEN IN MOVIES

Women in the movies first appeared in strong roles as worldly women. Later they depicted fallen women, who usually experienced some sort of rebuke at the end. Since 1945 female characters have sought to divert male attention from the pursuit of careers, adventure, wealth, or even war or a life of crime, and to channel more energy into domesticity (Rothman, 1995). Most of the female leads remain young, attractive, and motivated by romance. Their goal remains getting the men they care about to behave as a "good" father or husband would. In most of the story plots, men usually succumb to the persuasion of the romantic other in the films and ultimately behave as good guys in the domestic sphere. These light-hearted comedies follow the classical injunction to end with a marriage or pregnancy (if characters are already married) or to smooth out a marital conflict (Rothman, 1995). Usually, however, because men were protagonists in featured roles, women were the target of influence, not influential themselves.

Although women often worked in earlier movies, the work consisted of support roles such as secretary, waitress, wife, nurse, or other occupations usually associated with women of that time. Usually the dominant work role remained that of the male figure in the film; if women became involved with these men, they generally quit their job to fulfill a more domestic role. Women of this period held significantly more traditional domestic roles than nontraditional roles such as those held by men. Not coincidentally, movies before 1965 usually condemned sexual activity outside marriage, which nearly always resulted in some sort of punishment, reinforcing the idea that such activity was morally reprehensible.

Since the sexual revolution of the 70's the gender roles depicted by Hollywood have been modified or even reversed outright. Changes in the depiction of sex have been the most sensational, using sexually explicit material, generally entailing sex outside marriage, as a more and more acceptable notion in films for adults. As this has occurred, roles of women have become increasingly complex. In the early twenty-first century sex rarely leads to marriage or scandal but instead projects an image of increasingly carefree, harmless, nonpunished behavior. Hollywood has endorsed a judgment-free approach to nonmarital sex. In an overheard conversation (by author at an ABC Television affiliates meeting in Los Angeles, June, 1994) Steven Bochco, the producer of *NYPD Blue*, a television police drama, was heard to say, "I will drag the rest of the country kicking and screaming into the Hollywood value mentality, if it's the last thing I do."

The goals of women in films of the twenty-first century more closely align with those of male characters, with the exception that women exhibit less villainous behavior than men in similar situations. Since the mid-70's women have been treated more sympathetically, on the run from the law because of killing a rapist, abuser, or stalker; justifying their actions, portrayals of men include fools, villains, and opportunists who consistently try to take advantage of women. Wealthy men consistently have been portrayed as villains as fewer rich women are shown in such roles. Positive portrayals of businesswomen outnumber those of businessmen by a ratio of more than two to one (Rothman, 1995). Curiously, women play more sympathetic characters than men during a time when business as a whole appears seamier and more corrupt than it had. Yet female characters also have condemnable impulses, such as greed and malevolence, more than ever before. Increasingly, portraying women as using violence has become an important new method for depicting employed women. In a study by Rothman (1995), when the characters of men and women who hold elite jobs are rated in film, it is clear women come out far ahead of men. They have an advantage despite their reliance on negative goals and methods in recent movies.

WOMEN AND MEN ON TELEVISION

From the 50's into the twenty-first century the role of women in prime time television has changed. In the 50's media images of women reflected traditional portrayals of them at home; if they were in work roles, most positions centered on sex-typed jobs or low-status jobs. Earlier depictions of women often presented stereotyped portrayals of them as dependent on men; in support roles, traditional wife roles, helpmate roles; as incompetent; as primary care givers; in domestic roles; as victims; as sex objects; as passive; as decoration; and as dominated by men. In the 60's and 70's women began to move into more glamorous roles and higher status jobs such as doctor, lawyer, police officer, news writer/producer, and rancher. During this time the theme of equality as an ideal became more prominent. In the 80's the trends of the 60's and 70's continued, removing the exclusive role of housewife from prime-time television altogether. During this time women began to play more sexually aggressive roles. Alexis Carrington Colby played by Joan Collins in *Dynasty* and Sable Scott Colby played by Stephanie Beacham in *The Colbys* represented earlier versions of women who unabashedly spoke their mind. Sexual equality in the 80's began to emerge as less of an issue and more of an expectation. At the same time, mixed messages about women's "place" also reinforced traditional ideas about women.

In the 90's prime time programming focused on the battle of the sexes. Rothman (1995) reported one of five episodes depicted the unequal treatment of women, and one in twelve made a specific case for women's rights. Women's roles often displayed assertiveness, on *Roseanne, Grace under Fire, Murphy Brown, ER, Chicago Hope, Dr. Quinn, Mad about You, The Practice*, and *Savannah*, in the mid-90's. Contemporary sitcoms did not depict women as subordinate to men; women characters were twice as likely to display sensitivity to the emotional needs of others, demonstrate more sensible thinking, show more competence, appear more coolheaded and wiser than men three times out of four (Rothman, 1995). Characterizations of men often showed them as philanderers or sex fiends, blustery buffoons, no-good abusive ex-husbands, or immature clowns. In the 90's, images of loverboys usually fell flat, became targets of derision, and tried pickup lines that usually preceded a feminist put down. Rothman (1995) characterized prime time television as depicting predominantly liberal feminist ideologies. The primary reason, Rothman (1995) asserted, was the preponderance of strong Hollywood feminist writers and producers. In contrast to the Rothman (1995) research, Timson (1995) described the portrayal of women on television in the 90's as bimbos, as less-than-intelligent sex kittens. Examples abound on such programs as *Baywatch, Melrose Place, Friends*, and *War and Peace*.

Brinson (1992) described aggression in response to interpersonal conflict on television programs. Having lost a sizable portion of their audience to cable programming, the networks responded by attempting to attract younger audiences, who appeared to enjoy greater buying power than previous generations. These audiences subscribed to life-styles that were consistent with more assertive communication, less passivity and less willingness to withdraw from confrontation. Consequently, television programming appeared to appeal to masculine communication behavior, incongruent with traditional feminine socialization. In other words, female characters of the mid-90's rarely shrank from disagreement and were unwilling to "back down." Good conflict drama, which is difficult to maintain when someone withdraws from argument, required writers and producers themselves to hold fairly progressive views in order to portray action-packed programming. Bate (1992) claimed that before the 80's and 90's stereotypical women would not use compelling and persuading strategies and stereotypical men would not use avoiding/accommodating styles. Rarely did women characters engage in arguments with one another. One exception was a "cat fight" between the actresses Linda Evans and Joan Collins on *Dynasty*, which compelled viewers to watch just to see these two women engaged in hand-to-hand combat. In 90's dramas, women did use compelling and persuading to resolve conflicts. Television appeared to require a winner and a loser to enhance the dramatic tension so if women were to play lead roles in conflict, they no longer could back down (Brinson, 1992, p. 99). Further, the male-female argument, often depicted in promotions for programs, stimulated viewers to watch because of this new and curious role for women.

Rapping (1994) claimed the women who made the headlines on the major networks did not represent most of the women in America. Popular television narratives minimized the problems of men and women as they attempted to carve out new identities for themselves during times of turbulent social and corporate change (Press & Strathman, 1993). While Zoe Baird struggled with the servant issue, Hillary Clinton misplaced most of her records, and the queen of England struggled with royal-family dysfunction, the majority of women in America coped with less glamorous, more mundane issues. The main female characters of *Cosby*, *Mary Tyler Moore*, and *Murphy Brown* were well educated, upper-middle-class women. Even the Stepford-like wives played by Donna Reed and Barbara Billingsly (June Cleaver) of the 50's represented the life of the "ideal" woman rather than that which most working-class American families struggled with every day.

Rapping (1994, p. 37) describes the character *Roseanne* as representing the real life of a "fat, sloppy, foul-mouthed, bossy," unrepentantly combative, proud of her gender and social class woman who spoke out for the dignity and rights of working-class women; who often worked two jobs; who reared rebellious, unmotivated children; and who burned casseroles: women who used rough language, worked dead-end minimum-wage jobs, lashed out at the kids because they were stressed out from work, and duked it out with their husbands over power issues. Rapping (1994) claims sitcoms represent liberal values, often preaching about tolerance and personal freedom. *Roseanne* represented the outsider who sneaked into the polite world of television and exposed its hypocrisy and phoniness.

Press and Strathman (1993) describe prime time television in the mid-80's to the early 90's as the "postfeminist" age, defining *postfeminism* as an interpretation of traditional family life after only the briefest application of feminist representations in earlier television with a character such as that in *Maude*. Skill and Robinson (1994) describe families on television during the 50's through mid-1990. They found that extended families dominated prime time television after the 60's, whereas the nuclear family dominated all programming during the twentieth century, followed closely by the single-parent family. Yet, feminist critics argue, television minimizes the problems of single women and working-class single mothers. Television's earlier "feminist" images had portrayed women in solidarity with other women to combat male authority or react in opposition to their families or husbands; Press and Strathman (1993) argued these images had vanished in "postfeminist" programming. Postfeminist images depict women working but highlight women's traditional nurturing roles within the family unit. Consequently in postfeminist programming, when women have trouble, they solve their problems by calling up strength from within, competence and intelligence, rather than by bonding with other women.

WOMEN AND MEN IN POPULAR MUSIC

Even if you do not listen to popular music, young people *do* spend half or more of their waking hours hearing it at some level. The frequent exposure to music, the repetitive aspects of music lyrics, the sociocultural power of music, all combine to create a strong influence on gender identities (Stewart et al., 1996). Some might even describe it as brainwashing. Butruille and Taylor (1987) describe three recurring images of women in popular music: the witch/sinner/whore, the victim, and the madonna/saint. Up until about the 70's women musical performers frequently constituted about 10 in 268 acts. As this began to change, "women's music," produced and distributed by female-operated companies, tended to be acoustic, folk-based, feminist, with an emphasis on sisterhood, explicitly lesbian themes, and often an antimale bias (Denisoff & Bridges, 1982). Other groups of female artists who recorded more for mainstream record companies appealed to more of a mixed-sex audience. Their music varied more in theme, used more humor, and expressed more mainstream values. Stewart (1989) describes the emergence of a new biting, aggressive, emotionally intense, often unpleasant music, making a declaration of independence from stereotypical female roles. Portrayals of men as friends, coworkers, successful breadwinners, or relatives took second place to more popular depictions of men as perfect lovers or unfaithful or abusive partners.

The unusual, intertextual depictions of men in rap music and music videos often unsettle the formal images of men. Black masculinity, for example, was often depicted in terms of the use of drugs, sexism, pleasure, excess, nihilism, defiance, pride, and "the cool pose of disengagement designed to challenge hegemonic constructions of whiteness" (Gray, 1995, p. 6). "The menacing black male criminal body is also the object of adolescent intrigue, fascination, and adulation" (Gray, 1995, p. 6). Gray (1995) says capitalizing on the white idea of policing black men, rappers have exploited the threat and dread of black men. This figure of black masculinity stands as a threat to disturb dominant white representations of black men but also conflicts with images of middle-class, rational black men idealized in the civil rights movement of family and nation. This negative image of black men may have prompted some police departments to use "profiling," a system of stereotyping black men as potential criminals.

The influence of misogynous rap music on sexual aggression against women is consistent with that indicated by research on pornographic materials that also encourage sexually abusive and degrading treatment of women (Mayerson & Taylor, 1987). Pornographic depictions of sexual aggression against women lead some men who regularly look at it to believe women enjoy it, society sanctions it, and it is justified, not deviant behavior (Hall & Hirschman, 1991). Considerable evidence suggests regular users of pornographic depictions of sexual aggression against women show an increased acceptance of violence against women, such as rape and spousal abuse (Malamuth & Briere, 1986). Some musical lyrics express the same messages as those found in pornographic depictions of women, including those of coercive sexual activity, as enjoyable for women. Society regulates pornographic materials, which are available to men eighteen or under; not so, misogynist rap music. St. Lawrence and Joyner (1991) found an increase in sex role stereotyping and negative attitudes toward women among men who exposed themselves to heavy-metal rock music, irrespective of lyrical content. Although the lyrics in heavy-metal rock music may be difficult to discern and not the central focus, in rap music the lyrics act as the central focus of attention. If rap music has an important role in shaping the attitudes of its listeners, it may produce a whole generation of individuals who view women as of little worth. In fact, Barongan and Hall (1995) suggest a strong relationship exists between sexually aggressive behavior and listening to misogynist music. Not all rap music contains references to sex or violence; much of it concerns itself with the problems of social injustice faced by African Americans in America in the twenty-first century.

Another genre of popular music, the "murder ballad," portrays women as victims of murder by a man whom they usually "done wronged." "This type music also incorporates stalking and threats sung directly to the target" (Hamerlinck, 1995, p. 23). The stalking entails pure terror rather than mind games. The MTV generation has embraced the depiction of woman-killing video/popular music. Even Johnny Cash sings a song called "Delia's

Gone," which features Cash digging a grave for his victim. The victims portrayed in this type of music are overwhelmingly women, who primarily defend themselves with a restraining order or a wooden door between them and the perpetrator of the crime. Clearly, these songs depict power and control, not love.

CONCLUSION

The standards depicted in the media have a history of representing women as an underclass of victims, dependent on men for just about everything, whereas men's magazines appeal to male self-confidence. Men want to understand and master their lives, believing masculinity and mastery translate into action and accomplishment. With gender bending as the rage, even among jocks, the messages vaguely mesh with the homosocial lifestyle, often using models who look like either young men or women at the same time.

Newspapers used to cater mostly to men, but in the twenty-first century with the falling off of readership, editors have attempted to gain new subscribers by acknowledging similar interests among both male and female readers. Males still prefer to read stories about hard news and important decision makers, whereas females prefer to read stories with a more human interest. Newspapers have attempted to incorporate the female viewpoint.

A gradual change in the portrayal of men and women in the movies reflects changes in society. The goals of women and men in films of the twenty-first century are related to work and home. However, positive portrayals of businesswomen outnumber those of businessmen by a ratio of more than 2 to 1.

Since the 50's, men and women's images of dominance and submission on television have been reversed. Whereas in the early 50's women were depicted as the targets of influence, submissive, and of lower status, gradually over time their portrayal has become more closely aligned with that of male characters. Women were twice as likely to be depicted as sensitive to the needs of others and as wiser than men. Men were more often shown as sexual predators, abusive ex-husbands, or comical buffoons. The lover boy image of the 90's became obvious and obnoxious. As the twentieth century drew to a close, a resurgence of nineteenth-century British characters, with refined manners in all things including sexual restraint, became popular. Movies based on the stories of Jane Austen, such as *Pride and Prejudice*, *Emma*, and *Sense and Sensibility* received high praise.

In popular music, women were depicted as very bad, very good, or as victim, whereas men, especially in rap music and music videos, took on increasingly violent images. For men, images of hedonistic behavior, rebellion from and defiance of social norms, and drug use disturbed society, especially civil rights advocates. Sexual aggression against women in rap music correlated with findings of research about the effects of using pornographic materials. Researchers are alarmed by these findings of negative attitudes toward women among men who listen to rap music. Thus, although the images of women in the media have generally improved over time, the exception has been women in music.

References

Abbey, A. (1982). Sex differences in attributions for friendly behavior: Do males misperceive females friendliness? *Journal of Personality and Social Psychology*, 42, 830–838.

Adams, M. (1985). Female emotion and feminist logic. In Francis Baumli (Ed.), *Men freeing men: Exploding the myth of the traditional male*. Jersey City, NJ: New Atlantis.

Addington, D. W. (1968). The relationship of selected vocal characteristics to personality perceptions. *Speech Monographs*, 35, 492–503.

Adkins, L. (1984, October). Divorce: Upping the ante for executives. *Dun's Business Month*, pp. 74–75.

Adler, R., & Towne, N. (1978). *Looking out/looking in*. New York: Holt, Rinehart, & Winston.

Albright, D. G., & Chang, A. F. (1976). An examination of how one's attitudes toward women are reflected in one's defensiveness and self-esteem. *Sex Roles*, 2, 195–198.

Alfonso, R., & Trigilio, J. (1997, Summer). Surfing the third wave: A dialogue between two third wave feminists. *Hypatia*, 12 (3), 7.

Alinsky, S. (1971). *Rules for radicals: A practical primer for realistic radicals*. New York: Random House.

Allen, F. (1981, December 17). Executives' wives describe effects of husbands' careers on children. *Wall Street Journal*, p. 27.

Allen, M. (1982). The Hindu view of women. In M. Allen and S. N. Mukherjee (Eds.), *Women in India and Nepal*. Canberra: Australian National University.

Allis, S. (1990). What do men really want? *Time*, 136 (19), 80–82.

Allport, G., & Ross, J. M. (1967). Personal religious orientation and prejudice. *Journal of Personality and Social Psychology, 5*, 432–443.

American Association of University Women. (1991). Shortchanging girls, shortchanging America. Washington, DC: AAUW.

Andeline, H. (1975). *Fascinating womanhood.* New York: Bantam Books.

Andrews, P. H. (1987). Gender differences in persuasive communication and attribution of success and failure. *Human Communication Research, 13* (3), 372–385.

Ankerberg, J., & Weldon, J. (1993). *The facts on sex education.* Eugene, OR: Harvest House.

Antill, J. K. (1983). Sex role complementarity versus similarity in married couples. *Journal of Personality and Social Psychology, 45*, 145–155.

Anzaldua, G. (1983). La Prieta. In C. Moraga & G. Anzaldua (Eds.), *This bridge called my back: Writings by radical women of color.* New York: Kitchen Table.

Argyris, C. (1962). *Interpersonal competence and organizational effectiveness.* Homewood, IL: Irwin Dorsey Press.

Aries, E. J. (1982). Verbal and nonverbal behavior in single-sex and mixed-sex groups: Are traditional sex roles changing? *Psychological Reports, 51*, 127–134.

Aristotle. (1951). Metaphysics. In P. Wheelwright (Ed. and Trans.), *Aristotle: Selections.* New York: Odyssey Press.

Arkin, R. M. (1988). Self-presentation strategies and sequelae. In S. L. Zelen (Ed.), *Self-representation: The second attribution-personality theory conference, California School of Professional Psychology-LA.* New York: Springer-Verlag.

Arliss, L. (1991). *Gender communication.* Englewood Cliffs, NJ: Prentice Hall.

Arnovitch, C. D. (1976). The voice of personality: Stereotyped judgments of the relation to voice quality and sex of speaker. *Journal of Social Psychology, 99*, 207–220.

Atkinson, D. L. (1987). Names and titles: Maiden name retention and the use of Ms. *Women and Language, 10*, 37.

Averill, J. R. (1982). *Anger and aggression: An essay on emotion.* New York: Springer-Verlag.

Babb, L. A. (1975). *The devine hierarchy: Popular Hinduism in central India.* New York: Columbia University Press.

Baber, A. (1995). Why men need the Women's Freedom Network. In J. Rita Simon (Ed.), *Neither victim nor enemy* (pp. 153–159). Lanham, MD: University Press of America.

Bains, G. (1983). Explanations and the need for control. In M. Hewstone (Ed.), *Attribution theory: Social and functional extensions.* Oxford: Basil Blackwell.

Baker, D., & Terpstra, D. (1986). Locus of control and self-esteem vs. demographic factors as predictors of attitudes toward women. *Basic and Applied Social Psychology, 7*, 163–172.

Baker, M. J. (1981). The impact of physically attractive models on advertising evaluations. *Journal of Marketing Research, 14*, 538–555.

Baldridge, J. V. (1971). *Power and conflict in the university*. New York: John Wiley & Sons.

Balswick, J., & Avertt, C. P. (1977, February). Differences in expressiveness: Gender, interpersonal orientation, and perceived parental expressiveness as contributing factors. *Journal of Marriage and the Family*, pp. 121–127.

Bardwick, J. M. (1973). Androgyny and humanistic goals. Unpublished manuscript.

Barnard, C. I. (1938). *The functions of the executive*. Cambridge, MA: Harvard University Press.

Barnes, N. S. (1987). Buddhism. In A. Sharma (Ed.), *Women in world religions*. New York: SUNY Press.

Barnett, R. C., & Baruch, G. K. (1978). *The competent woman*. New York: Irvington.

Barnett, R. C., & Rivers, C. (1992). *She works/he works: How two-income families are happier, healthier and better off*. San Francisco: Harper.

Barnett, R. C., & Rivers C. (1992, February). *Working women*. New York: Irvington.

Barongan, C., & Hall, G. C. N. (1995). The influence of misogynous rap music on sexual aggression against women. *Psychology of Women Quarterly, 19,* 195–207.

Barron, N. (1970). Grammatical case and sex role: Language differences in interaction. Unpublished doctoral dissertation, University of Missouri, Columbia.

Bartol, K. M., & Butterfield, D. A. (1976). Sex effects in evaluating leaders. *Journal of Applied Psychology, 61,* 446–454.

Bascow, S. A. (1992). *Gender: stereotypes and roles* (3rd Ed.). Pacific Grove, CA: Brooks/Cole.

Bate, B. (1992). *Communication and the sexes*. Prospect Heights, IL: Waveland Press.

Beck, M. N. (1996). *Flight from the iron cage: LDS women's responses to the paradox of modernization*. Englewood Cliffs, NJ: Prentice Hall.

Beckwith, L. (1972). Relationships between infants: Social behavior and their mothers' behavior. *Child Development, 43,* 397–411.

Beh, H. C. (1994). Gender rivalry and attitudes toward sex roles: Changes over a fifteen year period. *Psychological Reports, 74,* 188–190.

Belenky, M. F., Clinchy, B. N., Goldberger, N. R., & Tarule, J. M. (1986). *Women's ways of knowing: The development of self, voice, and mind*. New York: Basic Books.

Belknap, P., & Leonard, W. M. (1991). A conceptual replication and extension of Erving Goffman's study of gender advertisements. *Sex Roles, 25,* 103–118.

Bell, A. P., & Weinberg, M. S. (1978). *Homosexualities: A study of diversity among men and women*. New York: Simon & Schuster.

Bell, R. A., & Buerkel-Rothfuss, N. L. (1990). S(he) loves me, s(he) loves me not: Predictors of relational information-seeking in courtship and beyond. *Communication Quarterly, 38,* 64–82.

Bem, S. (1974). The measure of psychological androgyny. *Journal of Consulting and Clinical Psychology, 42,* 155–162.

Bem, S. (1975). Sex-role adaptability: One consequence of psychological androgyny. *Journal of Personality and Social Psychology, 31,* 634–643.

Bem, S. (1979). Theory and measurement of androgyny: A reply to the Pedhazur-

Tetenbaum and Locksley-Colten critiques. *Journal of Personality and Social Psychology, 37,* 1047–1054.

Bem, S. L., & Bem, D. J. (1973). Does sex-biased job advertising aid and abet sex discrimination? *Journal of Applied Social Psychology, 3,* 6–18.

Bem, S. L., & Lenney, E. (1976). Sex-typing and the avoidance of cross-sex behavior. *Journal of Personality and Social Psychology, 33,* 48–54.

Bem, S. L., Martyna, W., & Watson, C. (1976). Sex typing and androgyny: Further explorations of the expressive domain. *Journal of Personality and Social Psychology, 34,* 1016–1023.

Bendroth, M. L. (1993). *Fundamentalism and gender: 1875 to the present.* New Haven, CT: Yale University Press.

Bennis, W. G. (1969). *Organization development: Its nature, origins and prospects.* Reading, MA: Addison-Wesley.

Berger, C. R. (1968). Sex differences related to self-esteem factor structure. *Journal of Consulting and Clinical Psychology, 32,* 442–446.

Berger, J., Cohen, J. B., & Zelditch, M., Jr. (1972). Status characteristics and social interaction. *American Sociological Review, 37,* 241–255.

Berger, J., & Fisek, M. H. (1974). A generalization of the status characteristics and expectation states theory. In J. Berger, T. L. Conner, & M. H. Fisek (Eds.), *Expectations states theory: A theoretical research program* (pp. 163–205). Cambridge, MA: Winthrop.

Berger, J., Fisek, H. M., Norman, R. Z., & Zelditch, M., Jr. (1977). *Status characteristics and social interaction: An expectation states approach.* New York: American Elsevier.

Berger, J., Rosenholtz, S. J., & Zelditch, M., Jr. (1980). Status organizing processes. In A. Inkeles, N. J. Smelser, & R. H. Turner (Eds.), *Annual Review of Sociology* (Vol. 6, pp. 479–508). Palo Alto, CA: Annual Reviews.

Berger, L. S. (1973). Use of power, Machiavellianism, and involvement in a simulated industrial setting. Unpublished doctoral dissertation, Temple University.

Berkovits, E. (1978). The status of women within Judaism. In Menachem Mark Kellner (Ed.), *Contemporary Jewish ethics.* New York: Schocken Books.

Berlo, D. K., Lemert, J. B., & Mertz, R. J. (1969–1970). Dimensions for evaluating the acceptability of message sources. *Public Opinion Quarterly, 33,* 563–576.

Berman, P. W., & Smith, V. L. (1984). Gender and situational differences in children's smiles, touch, and proxemics. *Sex Roles, 10,* 347–356.

Berne, R. W. (1995). Women can have it all. In Jonathan S. Petrikin (Ed.), *Male/female roles: Opposing viewpoints* (p. 131). San Diego, CA: Greenhaven Press.

Berryman, C. L., & Wilcox, J. R. (1980). Attitudes toward male and female speech: Experiments on the effects of sex-typical language. *The Western Journal of Speech Communication, 44,* 50–59.

Berryman-Fink, C. (1993). Preventing sexual harassment. In G. Kreps (Ed.), *Sexual harassment: Communication implications* (pp. 267–280) Cresskill, NJ: Hampton Press.

Bettelheim, B. (1943). Individual and mass behavior in extreme situations. *Journal of Abnormal and Social Psychology, 38,* 417–452.

Biaggio, M. K. (1980). Assessment of anger arousal. *Journal of Personality Assessment, 4,* 289–298.

Birdwhistell, R. L. (1970). *Masculinity and femininity as display: Kinesics and Context.* Philadelphia: University of Pennsylvania Press.

Birdwhistell, R. L. (1983). Masculinity and femininity as display. In A. M. Katz and V. T. Katz (Eds.), *Foundations of nonverbal communication: Readings, exercises, and commentary* (pp. 81–86). Carbondale: Southern Illinois University Press.

Bischoping, K. (1993). Gender differences in conversation topics, 1922–1990. *Sex Roles: A Journal of Research, 28* (1–2), 1.

Blake, R. R., & Mouton, J. S. (1964). *The managerial grid.* Houston: Gulf.

Blaskovich, J., & Tomaka, J. (1989). Measures of self-esteem. In J. R. Robinson & P. R. Shaver (Eds.), *Measures of social psychological attitudes* (3rd Ed.). Ann Arbor, MI: Institute for Social Research.

Blier, M. J., & Blier-Wilson, L. A. (1989). Gender differences in self-rated emotional expressiveness. *Sex Roles, 21,* 287–295.

Blumstein, P., & Schwartz, P. (1983). *American couples.* New York: William Morrow.

Bly, R. (1990). *Iron John.* New York: Addison-Wesley.

Bly, R. (1995). Thoughts on reading this book. In M. Kimmel (Ed.), *The politics of manhood.* Philadelphia: Temple University Press.

Bohan, J. (1973, Fall). Age and sex differences in self concept. *Adolescence, 8* (31), 379–384.

Boskind-Lodahl, M. (1976). Cinderella's stepsisters: A feminist perspective on anorexia nervosa and bulimia. *Signs: Journal of Women in Culture and Society, 2,* 342–356.

Bowlby, J. (1952). *Maternal care and mental health.* Geneva: World Health Organization.

Bradley, P. H. (1981). The folk-linguistics of women's speech: An empirical examination. *Communication Monographs, 48,* 73–90.

Brain, R. (1979). *The decorated body.* New York: Harper & Row.

Brass, D. J. (1985). Men's and women's networks: A study of interaction patterns and influence in an organization. *Academy of Management Journal, 28,* 327–343.

Brend, R. (1975). Male-female intonational patterns in American English. In B. Thorne, & N. Henley (Eds.), *Language and sex: Difference in dominance.* Rowley, MA: Newbury House.

Brenner, O. C., & Tomkiewicz, J. (1982). Sex differences among business graduates on fear of success and fear of appearing incompetent as measured by objective instruments. *Psychological Reports, 51,* 179–182.

Brinson, S. L. (1992). TV Fights: Women and men in interpersonal arguments on prime-time television dramas. *Argumentation and Advocacy, 29* (2), 89–105.

Broca, S. (1868). Broca on anthropology. *Anthropological Review 6,* 45–46.

Brouwer, D., Gerritsen, M., & DeHaan, D. (1979). Speech differences between women and men: On the wrong track? *Language in Society, 8,* 33–50.

Broverman, I. K., Vogel, S. R., Broverman, D. M., Clarkson, F. E., & Rosenkrantz,

P. S. (1972). Sex role stereotypes: A current appraisal. *Journal of Social Issues, 128,* 59–78.

Brown, L. D. (1986). Power outside organizational paradigms: Lessons from community partnerships. In S. Srivastva and Associates (Eds.), *Executive power: How executives influence people and organizations.* San Francisco: Jossey-Bass.

Brown, R. M. (1984). In defense of traditional values: The anti-feminist movement. *Marriage and Family Review, 7* (3/4), 19–35.

Brown, S. M. (1979). Male versus female leaders: A comparison of empirical studies. *Sex Roles, 5,* 595–611.

Brownmiller, S. (1975). *Against our will: Men, women and rape.* New York: Simon & Schuster.

Bruch, H. (1973). *Eating disorders.* New York: Basic Books.

Brumberg, J. J. (1988). *Fasting girls: The emergence of anorexia nervosa as a modern disease.* Cambridge, MA: Harvard University Press.

Buechler, S. M. (1990). *Women's movements in the United States.* New Brunswick, NJ: Rutgers.

Bunch, C. (1975). *Lesbianism and the women's movement.* Oakland, CA: Diana Press.

Burchardt, C. J., & Serbin, L. A. (1982). Psychological androgyny and personality adjustment in college and psychiatric populations. *Sex Roles, 8,* 835–851.

Burgoon, J. K. (1983). Nonverbal violations of expectations. In J. M. Wiemann & R. P. Harrison (Eds.), *Nonverbal interaction* (pp. 77–111). Beverly Hills, CA: Sage.

Burgoon, J. K., Buller, D. B., Hale, J. L., & deTurck, M. A. (1982, April). *Relational messages associated with immediacy behaviors.* Paper presented at the International Communication Association Convention, Boston.

Burgoon, J. K., Buller, D. B., & Woodall, W. G. (1988). *Nonverbal communication: The unspoken dialogue.* New York: Harper & Row.

Burgoon, J. K., & Saine, T. (1978). *The unspoken dialogue: An introduction to nonverbal communication.* Boston: Houghton Mifflin.

Burgoon, M., Dillard, J. P., & Doran, N. E. (1983). Friendly or unfriendly persuasion: The effects of violations of expectations by males and females. *Human Communication Research, 10* (2), 283–194.

Burgoon, M., Jones, S., & Steward, D. (1974). Toward a message centered theory of persuasion: Three empirical investigations. *Human Communication Research, 1,* 240–248.

Burleson, B. R., & Denton, W. H. (1997, November). The relationship between communication skill and marital satisfaction: Some moderating effects. *Journal of Marriage and Family, 59* (4) 884.

Burris, B., Barry, K., Moore, T., Delor, J., Parreut, J., & Stadelman, C. (1973). The fourth world manifesto. In A. Koedt (Ed.), *Radical feminism.* New York: Quadrangle Press.

Busby, L. (1975). Sex-role research on the mass media. *Journal of Communication, 25* (4), 107–131.

Business and Professional Women's Foundation. (1992, April). *You can't get there from here: Working women and the glass ceiling.* Washington, DC.

Butler, K. (1988). *It's all in your mind: A student's guide to learning style*. Columbia, CT: The Learner's Dimension.

Butrille, S. G., & Taylor, A. (1987). Women in American popular song. In L. P. Stewart & S. Ting-Toomey (Eds.), *Communication, gender, and sex roles in diverse interaction contexts* (pp. 179–188). Norwood, NJ: Ablex.

Cadden, M., & Galifianakis, N. (1995, May 12). USA Snapshots: Women, work and home. *USA TODAY*, p. 01B.

Calden, G., Lundy, R. M., & Schlafer, R. J. (1959). Sex differences in body concepts. *Journal of Consulting Psychology, 27*, 115–222.

Caldera, Y. M., Huston, A. C., & O'Brien, M. (1989). Social interactions and play patterns of parents and toddlers with feminine, masculine, and neutral toys. *Child Development, 60*, 70–76.

Cameron, D. (1985). *Feminism and linguistic theory*. New York: St. Martin's Press.

Campbell, H. (1891). *Differences in the nervous organisation of man and woman*. London: H. K. Lewis.

Campbell, K. K. (1973). The rhetoric of women's liberation: An oxymoron. *Quarterly Journal of Speech, 59*, 74–86.

Campbell, K. K. (1989). *Man cannot speak for her: A critical study of early feminist rhetoric*. New York: Praeger Publishers.

Canary, D. J., Cunningham, E. M., & Cody, M. J. (1988). Goal types, gender, and locus of control in managing interpersonal conflict. *Communication Research, 15*, 426–446.

Canary, D. J., & Hause, K. S. (1993). Is there any reason to research sex differences in communication? *Communication Quarterly, 41*, 129–144.

Canavan, F. (1995). The sexual revolution is immoral. In C. Cozic (Ed.), *Sexual Values: Opposing Viewpoints* (pp. 29–36). San Diego, CA: Greenhaven Press.

Cann, A., & Siegfried, W. D. (1990). Gender stereotypes and dimensions of effective leader behavior. *Sex Roles, 23* (7/8), 413–419.

Capra, F. (1983). *The tao of physics*. Boulder, CO: Shambhala.

Carli, L. L. (1981, August). *Sex differences in small group interaction*. Paper presented at the 89th Annual Meeting of the American Psychological Association, Los Angeles.

Carli, L. L. (1989). Gender differences in interaction style and influence. *Journal of Personality and Social Psychology, 56*, 565–576.

Carmody, D. L. (1987). Judaism. In A. Sharma (Ed.), *Women in world religions*. New York: SUNY Press.

Carroll, J. L., Volk, K. D., & Hyde, J. S. (1985). Differences between males and females in motives for engaging in sexual intercourse. *Archives of Sexual Behavior, 14*, 131–139.

Chafetz, J. S. (1974). *Masculine/feminine or human*. Itasca, IL: F. E. Peacock Publishers.

Chafetz, J. S., Lorence, J., & Larosa, C. (1993). Gender depictions of the professionally employed: A content analysis of trade publications, 1960–1990. *Sociological Perspectives, 36* (1), 63–82.

Chasler, S. (1985, January 13). I need to know you. *Parade Magazine*, p. 8.

Cherry, L., & Lewis, M. (1978). Differential socialization of girls and boys: Implications for sex differences in language development. In N. Waterson & C.

Snow (Eds.), *The development of communication* (pp. 189–197). New York: John Wiley & Sons.

Chiauzzi, E., Heimberg, R. G., & Doty, D. (1982). Task analysis of assertiveness behavior revisited: The role of situational variables with female college students. *Behavioral Counseling Quarterly, 2,* 42–50.

Chodorow, N. J. (1978). *The reproduction of mothering: Psychoanalysis and the sociology of gender.* Berkeley: University of California Press.

Chopra, D. (1991). *Unconditional life.* New York: Bantam Books.

Christensen, F. M. (1990). *Pornography: The other side.* Westport, CT: Praeger Publishers.

The Christian Century. (1997). PK message strikes close to home. *The Christian Century, 114* (35), 1151.

Clarke, E. (1874). *Century of American medicine, 1776–1876.* New York: B. Franklin.

Clarke-Stewart, K. A. (1973). Interactions between mothers and their young children: Characteristics and consequences. *Monographs of the Society for Research in Child Development, 38* (6–7), Serial No. 153.

Clatterbaugh, K. (1997). *Contemporary perspectives on masculinity: Men, women, and politics in modern society.* Boulder, CO: Westview Press.

Coates, J. (1988). Introduction. In J. Coates & D. Cameron (Eds.), *Women in their speech communities: New perspectives on language and sex* (pp. 63–73). New York: Longman.

Colbert, K. R., & Biggers, T. (1986). Why should we support debate. *Journal of the American Forensics Association, 21,* 237–240.

Cole, E. L. (1982). *Maximized manhood: A guide to family survival.* Springdale, PA: Whitaker House.

Collins, P. H. (1986). Learning from the outsider within. *Social Problems, 33,* 514–532.

Condry, J., & Condry, S. (1976). Sex differences: A study of the eye of the beholder. *Child Development, 47,* 812–819.

Cook, S. P. (1985). *Psychological androgyny.* New York: Pergamon Press.

Crawford, M. (1977). What is a friend? *New Society, 42,* 116–117.

Crosby, F., & Nyquist, L. (1977). The female register: An empirical test of Lakoff's hypothesis. *Language in Society, 6,* 313–322.

Crosby, F. J. (1991). *Juggling: The unexpected advantages of balancing career and home for women and their families.* New York: Simon & Schuster.

Crowley-Long, K. (1998). Making room for many feminisms. *Psychology of Women Quarterly, 22,* 112–130.

Culbert, S. A., & Renshaw, J. R. (1972). Coping with the stresses of travel as an opportunity for improving the quality of work and family life. *Family Processes, 11,* 321–337.

Cush, D. (1997). Buddhism. In C. Richards (Ed.), *The illustrated encyclopedia of world religions.* Rockport, MA: Element Books Limited.

Daly, M. (1968). *The church and the second sex.* New York: Harper & Row.

Daly, M. (1992). *Outercourse: The bedazzling voyage.* San Francisco: Harper.

Darwin, C. (1900). *The descent of man, and selection in relation to sex.* New York: P. F. Collier & Son.

Davidman, L. (1991). *Tradition in a rootless world: Women turn to Orthodox Judaism.* Berkeley: University of California Press.

Davidson, M. J., & Cooper, C. L. (1986). Executive women under pressure. *International Review of Applied Psychology, 35,* 301–326.

Davis, A. (1982). *Women, race and class.* London: The Women's Press.

Deaux, K. (1976). *The behavior of men and women.* Monterey, CA: Brooks/Cole.

Deaux, K., & Lewis, L. L. (1983). Components of gender stereotypes. *Psychological Documents, 13* (25), Ms. No. 2583.

Denisoff, R. S., & Bridges, J. (1982). Popular music: Who are the recording artists? *Journal of Communication, 32* (1), 132–142.

Densmore, D. (1970). *Speech is a form of thought.* Pittsburgh, PA: KNOW.

Deutsch, F. M., LeBaron, D., & Fryer, M. M. (1987). What is in a smile? *Psychology of Women Quarterly, 11,* 341–352.

Devor, H. (1989). *Gender blending: Confronting the limits of duality.* Bloomington: Indiana University Press.

Dittes, J. (1959). Effect of changes in self-esteem upon impulsiveness and deliberation in making judgments. *Journal of Abnormal and Social Psychology, 58,* 348–356.

Dittman, A. T. (1972). Developmental factors in conversational behavior. *Journal of Communication, 22,* 404–423.

Dobson, J. (1982). *Marriage and sexuality: Dr. Dobson answers your questions.* Wheaton, IL: Tyndale House.

Dobson, J. C. (1991). *Straight talk to men and their wives.* Dallas: Word Publishing.

Dobson, J. C. (1994). *Pornography: Addictive, professive, and deadly.* VCR, available from Focus on the Family, Word, Inc.

Donnell, S. M., & Hall, J. (1980, Spring). Men and women as managers: A significant case of no significant difference. *Organizational Dynamics, 8,* 60–77.

Donovan, J. (1985). *Feminist theory: The intellectual traditions of American feminism.* New York: Frederick Ungar.

Doyle, J. A. (1989). *The male experience* (2nd Ed.). Dubuque, IA: William C. Brown.

Dransfield, A. (1984, August 20). The uneasy life of the corporate spouse. *Fortune,* pp. 26–32.

Drummond, R. J., McIntire, W. G.,& Ryan, C. W. (1977). Stability and sex differences on the Coppersmith Self-esteem Inventory for students in grades two to twelve. *Psychological Reports, 40,* 943–946.

Dubin, R. (1951). *Human relations in administration.* Englewood Cliffs, NJ: Prentice-Hall.

Dulin, B. (1993). Founding project challenges young feminists. *New Directions for Women, 21* (1), 33.

Dyson, M. E. (1995). Words unsaid. *The Christian Century, 112* (34), 1100.

Eagly, A. H. (1978). Sex differences in influenceability. *Psychological Bulletin, 85,* 86–116.

Eagly, A. H., & Carli, L. L. (1981). Sex of researchers and sex-typed communications as determinants of sex differences in influenceability: A meta-analysis of social influence studies. *Psychological Bulletin, 90,* 1–20.

Eagly, A. H., & Johnson, B. T. (1990). Gender and leadership style: A meta-analysis. *Psychological Bulletin, 108* (2), 233–256.

Eagly, A. H., & Karau, S. J. (1991). Gender and the emergence of leaders: A meta-analysis. *Journal of Personality and Social Psychology, 60* (5), 685–710.

Eagly, A. H., & Steffen, V. J. (1984). Gender stereotypes stem from the distribution of women and men into social roles. *Journal of Personality and Social Psychology, 46,* 735–754.

Eakins, B. W., & Eakins, R. G. (1978). *Sex differences in human communication.* Boston: Houghton Mifflin.

Ebeling, K. (1991, Summer). Ecofeminists andpagan politics. *The Human Life Review,* 1–6.

Edelsky, C. (1979). Question intonation and sex roles. *Language in Society, 8,* 15–32.

Ehrenreich, B. (1989). A feminist's view of the new man. In M. Kimmel and M. Messner (Eds.), *Men's lives.* New York: Macmillan.

Ehrhardt, A. A. (1984). Gender differences: A biosocial perspective. In T. B. Sonderegger (Ed.), *Psychology and gender* (pp. 37–57). Lincoln: University of Nebraska Press.

Eisler, R. (1987). *The chalice and the blade: Our history, our future.* San Francisco: Harper & Row.

Ekman, P., & Friesen, W. V. (1967). Head and body cues in the judgment of emotion: A reformulation. *Perceptual and Motor Skills, 24,* 711–724.

Encyclopaedia Britannica (1979). *History of World Religions.* Chicago: William Benton/Helen Hemingway Benton.

Erdwins, D. J., Tyer, Z. E., & Mellinger, J. C. (1982). Achievement and affiliation needs of young adult and middle-aged women. *The Journal of Genetic Psychology, 141,* 219–224.

Etaugh, C. (1975). Biographical predictors of college students' attitudes toward women. *Journal of College Student Personnel, 16,* 273–276.

Evans, G. W., & Howard, R. B. (1973). Personal space. *Psychological Bulletin, 80,* 334–344.

Fagenson, E. A. (1993). *Women in management: Trends, issues, and challenges in managerial diversity.* Newbury Park, CA: Sage.

Faludi, S. (1991). *Backlash: The undeclared war against American women.* New York: Crown.

Farrell, W. (1974). *The liberated man.* New York: Random House.

Farrell, W. (1991, May/June). *Men as success objects.* Utne Reader, pp. 81–84.

Farrell, W. (1993). *The myth of male power.* New York: Simon & Schuster.

Farwell, M. (1973). Women and language. In J. R. Leppaluoto (Ed.), *Women on the move.* Pittsburgh: KNOW.

Fassinger, R. E. (1990). Casual models of career choice in two samples of college women. *Journal of Vocational Behavior, 36,* (2), 225–248.

Fast, J. (1970). *Body language.* New York: Pocket Books.

FDA Consumer. (1986, May and 1992, March.) The report is based on figures provided by the National Center of Health Statistics (NCHS).

Feather, N. T. (1967). Some personality correlates of external control. *Australian Journal of Psychology, 19,* 253–260.

Feingold, A. (1994). Gender differences in personality: A meta-analysis. *Psychological Bulletin, 11* (116), 429–456.

Ferber, R. (1995). Is speakers' gender discernible in transcribed speech? *Sex Roles, 32* (3/4), 209–223.

Festinger, L. (1957). *A theory of cognitive dissonance.* Stanford, CA: Stanford University Press.

Findlen, B. (1995). *Listen up: Voices from the next feminist generation.* Seattle: Seal Press.

Fischer, P. C., Smith, R. J., Leonard, E., Fuqua, D. R., Campbell, J. L., & Masters, M. A. (1993, March/April). Sex differences on affective dimensions: Continuing examination. *Journal of Counseling and Development, 71,* 440–443.

Fisher, S. (1975). Body decoration and camouflage. In L. M. Gurel & M. S. Beeson (Eds.), *Dimensions of dress and adornment: A book of readings.* Dubuque, IA: Kendall Hunt Publishing.

Fishman, P. M. (1978). Interaction: The work women do. *Social Problems, 25,* 397–406.

Fiske, S. T. (1993). Controlling other people. *American Psychologist, 48* (6), 621–628.

Fiske, S. T., Goodwin, S. A., Rosen, L., & Rosenthal, A. (1993). Romantic outcome dependency and the (in) accuracy of impression formation: A case of clouded judgment. Unpublished doctoral dissertation, University of Massachusetts at Amherst.

Fitzpatrick, M. A. (1988). *Between husbands and wives.* Newbury Park, CA: Sage.

Frankenhaeuser, M., Lundberg, U., Frederikson, M., Melin, B., Tuomisto, M., & Myrsten, A. (1989). Stress on and off the job related to sex and occupational status in white collar workers. *Journal of Organizational Behavior, 10,* 321–346.

Freedman, C. (1985). *Manhood redux: Standing up to feminism.* Brooklyn, NY: Samson Publishers.

Freedman, J. L., Levy, A. S., Buchanan, R. W., & Price, J. (1972). Crowding and human aggressiveness. *Journal of Experimental Social Psychology, 8,* 528–548.

Freeman, B., & Lanning, W. (1989). A multivariate analysis of the relationship between social power motivation and personality characteristics in college students. *Journal of College Student Development, 30* (6), 522–527.

French, J. R. P., & Raven, B. H. (1959). The bases of social power. In D. Cartwright (Ed.), *Studies in Social Power.* Ann Arbor, MI: Institute for Social Research.

Freud, S. (1957). *The ego and the id* (J. Riviere, Trans.). London: Hogarth Press.

Freud, S. (1963). *Dora: An analysis of a case of hysteria.* New York: Collier Books.

Friedan, B. (1963). *The feminine mystique.* New York: Dell.

Friedan, B. (1981). *The second stage.* New York: Summit Books.

Friedberg, B. A., & Friedberg, R. D. (1985). Locus of control and religiosity in college students. *Psychological Reports, 56,* 757–758.

Friedman, S. (1983). *Men are just desserts.* New York: Warner Books.

Frieze, I. H., Parsons, J. E., Johnson, P. B., Ruble, D. N., & Zellman, G. L. (1978). *Women and sex roles: A social psychological perspective.* New York: W. W. Norton.

Frodi, A., Macauley, J., & Thorme, P. R. (1977). Are women less aggressive than men? A review of the experimental literature. *Psychological Bulletin, 84,* 634–660.

Funabiki, D., Bologna, N. C., Pepping, M., & Fitzgerald, K. C. (1980, April). Revisiting sex differences in the expression of depression. *Journal of Abnormal Psychology, 89* (2), 194–202.

Gamson, W. A. (1968). *Power and discontent.* Homewood, IL: Dorsey.

Gecas, V., & Schwalbe, M. L. (1986). Parental behavior and adolescent self-esteem. *Journal of Marriage and the Family, 48,* 37–46.

Gelbort, K. R., & Winer, J. L. (1985). Fear of success and fear of failure: A multitrait-multimethod validation study. *Journal of Personality and Social Psychology, 48* (4), 1009–1014.

Gigy, L. L. (1990). Self-concept of single women. *Psychology of Women Quarterly, 5,* 321–340.

Gilbert, Neil. (1995). Violence against women: Social research and sexual politics. In R. J. Simon (Ed.), *Neither victim nor enemy.* Lanham, MD: University Press of America.

Gilder, G. (1995). The glass ceiling is not what limits women at work. In *Male/female roles: Opposing viewpoints* (pp. 92–99). San Diego, CA: Greenhaven Press.

Giles, H., Mulac, A., Bradac, J. J., & Johnson, P. (1987). Speech accommodation theory: The first decade and beyond. *Communication Yearbook #10,* 13–48.

Giles, H., Scherer, K. R., & Taylor, D. M. (1979). Speech markers in social interaction. In K. R. Scherer & H. Giles (Eds.), *Language and social psychology* (pp. 45–65). Oxford: Basil Blackwell.

Gill, D. L. (1988). Gender differences in competitive orientation and sport participation. *International Journal of Sport Psychology, 19,* 145–159.

Gilley, H. M., & Summers, C. S. (1970). Sex differences in the use of hostile verbs. *The Journal of Psychology, 76,* 33–37.

Gilligan, C. (1982). *In a different voice: Psychological theory and women's development.* Cambridge, MA: Harvard University Press.

Gilligan, C., Ward, J. V., Taylor, J. M., & Bardige, B. (Eds.) (1988). *Mapping the moral domain.* Cambridge, MA: Harvard University Press.

Gimbutas, M. (1982). *Goddesses and gods of old Europe, 7000–3500 B.C.* Berkeley: University of California Press.

Glass, D. C. (1977). *Behavior patterns, stress, and coronary disease.* Hillsdale, NJ: Lawrence Erlbaum.

Gleason, J. B., & Weintraub, S. (1978). Input language and the acquisition of communicative competence. In K. E. Nelson (Ed.), *Children's language* (Vol. 1, pp. 171–222). New York: Gardner Press.

Glenn, S. (1990). *Daughters of the Shtetl: Life and labor in the immigrant generation.* Ithaca, NY: Cornell University Press.

Gold, A. R., Brush, L. R., & Sprotzer, E. R. (1980). Developmental changes in self-perceptions of intelligence and self-confidence. *Psychology of Women Quarterly, 5,* 231–239.

Goldberg, H. (1976). *The hazards of being male: Surviving the myth of masculine privilege.* New York: Signet.

Goldberg, P. (1968). Are women prejudiced against other women? *Transaction, 5*, 28–30.

Goldberg, P., & Lewis, M. (1969). Play behavior in the year-old infant: Early sex differences. *Child Development, 40*, 21–31.

Golding, J. M., & Singer, J. L. (1983). Patterns of inner experience: Daydreaming styles, depressive moods, and sex roles. *Journal of Personality and Social Psychology, 45*, 663–675.

Goodman, E. (1979, May 20). Mork and Mindy are just pals. *The Utica Observer Dispatch*, 9A.

Goodwin, M. H. (1988). Cooperation and competition across girls' play activities. In S. Fisher & A. D. Todd (Eds.), *Gender and discourse: The power of talk* (pp. 55–94). Norwood, NJ: Ablex.

Googins, B., & Burden, D. (1987). Vulnerability of working parents: Balancing work and home roles. *Social Work, 32*, 295–300.

Gorman, C., Nash, J., and Ehrenreich, B. (1992, January 20). Sizing up the sexes. *Time, 139* (3), 42–50.

Gott, N.E.A. (1994, November 29). Banding surgery should be last resort for weight loss, *Park City Daily News*, p. 6-A.

Gottfredson, G. D. (1976). A note on sexist wording in interest measurement. *Measurement and Evaluation of Guidance, 8*, 221–223.

Gottschalk, L. A., & Hambidge, G., Jr. (1995). Verbal behavior analysis: A systematic approach to the problem of quantifying psychologic processes. *Journal of Porj, Technology, 19*, 387–409.

Grant, G., & Horne, M. A. (1993). *Legislating morality: The homosexual movement comes out of the closet*. Chicago: Moody Press.

Gray, H. (1995). Black masculinity and visual culture. *Callaloo, 18* (2), 401–406.

Gray, J. (1992). *Men are from Mars, women are from Venus*. New York: HarperCollins.

Gray, L., White, M., & Libby, R. W. (1978). A test and reformulation of reference group and role correlates of premarital sexual permissiveness theory. *Journal of Marriage and Family, 40*, 79–91.

Graybill, D. (1978). Relationship of maternal child-rearing behaviors to children's self-esteem. *The journal of Psychology, 100*, 45–47.

Greeley, A., & Durkin, M. (1984). *Angry Catholic women*. Chicago: Thomas Moore Press.

Greenglass, E. R. (1987). Type A behavior and coping strategies in female and male supervisors. *Applied Psychology: An International Review, 37*, 271–288.

Gregorc, A. (1982). *An adult's guide to style*. Columbia, CT: Gregorc Associates.

Griffin, C. L. (1996). A web of reasons: Mary Wollstonecraft's *A vindication of the rights of woman* and the re-weaving of form. *Communication Studies 47*, 272–288.

Griffore, R. J., Kallen, D. J., Popovich, S., & Powell, V. (1990). Gender differences in correlates of college students' self-esteem. *College Student Journal, 24*, 287–291.

Gross, J. (1990, September 2). Navy is urged to root out lesbians despite abilities. *New York Times*, p. A24.

Guisso, R. W. (1981). Thunder over the lake: The five classics and the perception of woman in early China. In R. W. Guisso and S. Johannesen (Eds.), *Women in China: Current directions in historical scholarship.* Youngstown, OH: Philo Press.

Guisso, R. W., & Johannesen, S. (1981). *Women in China: Current Directions in Historical Scholarship.* Youngstown, OH: Philo Press.

Gump, J. P. (1972). Sex role attitudes and psychological well-being. *Journal of Social Issues, 28,* 79–92.

Haas, A. (1979). *Teenage sexuality.* New York: Macmillan.

Hackman, M. A., & Johnson, C. E. (1991). *Leadership: A communication perspective.* Prospect Heights, IL: Waveland Press.

Halberstadt, A. G., Hayes, C. W., & Pike, M. (1988). Gender and gender role differences in smiling and communication consistency. *Sex Roles, 19,* 589–604.

Hall, C. N., & Hirschman, R. (1991). Toward a theory of sexual aggression: A quadripartite model. *Journal of Consulting and Clinical Psychology, 59,* 662–669.

Hall, E. T. (1959). *The silent language.* Greenwich, CT: Fawcett Publications.

Hall, E. T. (1968). Proxemics. *Current Anthropology, 9,* 83–108.

Hammen, C., & Padesky, C. (1977, December). Sex differences in the expression of depressive responses on the Beck depression inventory. *Journal of Abnormal Psychology, 86* (6), 609–614.

Hammerlinck, J. (1995, July–August). Killing women: A pop-music tradition. *The Humanist, 55* (4), 23–24.

Hao, J. Y. (1993). Religious beliefs, affects, and values toward supporting women's pastoral leadership. Doctoral dissertation, Fuller Theological Seminary, Pasadena, CA. *Dissertation Abstracts* #9169153/1072.

Harding, S. (1991). *Whose science? Whose knowledge? Thinking from women's lives.* Ithaca, NY: Cornell University Press.

Harper, N. L., & Hirokawa, R. Y. (1988, Spring). A comparison of persuasive strategies used by female and male managers: An examination of downward influence. *Communication Quarterly, 36* (2), 157–168.

Harris, M. B. (1977). The effects of sender masculinity, femininity and trait favorability on evaluations of students. *Contemporary Educational Psychology, 2,* 253–263.

Harrison, B. G., Guy, R. F., & Lupfer, S. L. (1981). Locus of control and self-esteem as correlates of role orientation in traditional and nontraditional women. *Sex Roles, 7,* 1175–1187.

Hartlage, L. C. (1980, March). *Identifying and programming for differences.* Paper presented at the parent and professional conference on young children with special needs, Cleveland, Ohio.

Hartman, M. (1976). A descriptive study of the language of men and women born in Maine around 1900 as it reflects the Lakoff hypotheses in "Language and women's place." In B. L. Dubois & I. Crouch (Eds.), *The sociology of the languages of American women* (pp. 81–90). San Antonio, TX: Trinity University.

Hartnett, J. J., Bailey, K. G., & Gibson, F. W., Jr. (1970). Personal space as influenced by sex and type of movement. *Journal of Psychology, 76,* 139–144.

Harvey, P. D. (1995). Censoring pornography harms society. In C. Cozic (Ed.),

Sexual values: Opposing viewpoints (pp. 136–144). San Diego, CA: Greenhaven Press.

Hegstrom, T. G. (1979). Message impact: What percentage is nonverbal? *Western Journal of Speech Communication, 43*, 134–142.

Heiss, J. S. (1962). Degree of intimacy and male-female interaction. *Sociometry, 25*, 197–208.

Helgesen, S. (1990). *The female advantage: Women's ways of leadership.* New York: Doubleday Currency.

Henley, N. M. (1973). Status and sex: Some touching observations. *Bulletin of the Psychonomic Society, 2*, 91–93.

Henley, N. M. (1977). *Body politics: Power, sex and nonverbal communication.* Englewood Cliffs, NJ: Prentice-Hall.

Henning, M., & Jardim, A. (1976). *The managerial woman.* New York: Pocket Books.

Henrichsen, J. J., Follansbee, D. J., & Ganellen, R. (1981). Sex-role related differences in self-concept and mental health. *Journal of Personality Assessment, 45*, 584–599.

Hertz, S. H. (1977). The politics of the Welfare Mothers Movement: A case study. *Signs: Journal of Women in Culture and Society, 2*, 600–611.

Hertzberg, F. (1966). *Work and the nature of man.* New York: John Wiley & Sons.

Heunemann, R. I., Shapiro, L. R., Hampton, M. C., & Mitchell, B. W. (1966). A longitudinal study of gross body composition and body conformation and their association with food activity in a teenage population. *American Journal of Clinical Nutrition, 18*, 325–338.

Hewlett, S. A. (1991). *When the bough breaks: The cost of neglecting our children.* New York: Basic Books.

Hiatt, M. P. (1977). *The way women write: Sex and style in contemporary prose.* New York: Teachers College Press, Columbia University.

Hillestad, R. C. (1974). A schematic approach to a theoretical analysis of dress as nonverbal communication. Ph.D. dissertation, Ohio State University, Columbus.

Hinckley, G. B. (1995, September 23). The family: A proclamation to the world. Message delivered at the General Relief Society Meeting, Salt Lake City, Utah. Available at http://www.lds.org/Policy/Family.html

Hite, S. (1981). *The Hite report on male sexuality.* New York: Alfred Knopf.

Hjelle, L. A., & Butterfield, R. (1974). Self-actualization and women's attitudes toward their roles in contemporary society. *Journal of Psychology, 87*, 225–230.

Hochschild, A. (1989). *The second shift: Working parents and the revolution at home.* New York: Viking.

Hochschild, A. R. (1983). *The managed heart: Commercialization of human feeling.* Berkeley: University of California Press.

Hoff-Sommers, C. (1994). *Who stole feminism?* New York: Simon & Schuster.

Hoff-Sommers, C. (2000). *The war against boys.* New York: Simon & Schuster.

Hogg, M. A., & Abrams, D. (1988). *Social identifications: A social psychology of intergroup relations and group processes.* London: Routledge.

Holmwood, R. (1997). Christianity. In C. Richards (Ed.), *The illustrated encyclopedia of world religions.* Rockport, MA: Element Books Limited.

hooks, b. (1990). Definitions of difference. In D. L. Rhode (Ed.), *Theoretical perspectives on sexual difference* (pp. 185–193). New Haven, CT: Yale University Press.

Hopkins, H. R., & Klein, H. A. (1993). Multidimensional self-perception: Linkages to parental nurturance. *The Journal of Genetic Psychology, 154,* 465–473.

House, J. S., Landis, K. R., & Umberson, D. (1988). Social relationships and health. *Science, 241,* 540–545.

Hoy, W. K., & Miskel, C. G. (1982). *Educational administration: Theory, research, and practice* (2nd Ed.). New York: Random House.

Hubbard, R. (1990). *The politics of women's biology.* New Brunswick, NJ: Rutgers University Press.

Hudak, M. A. (1993). Gender schema theory revisited: Men's stereotypes of American women. *Sex Roles, 28,* 279–293.

Hudson, L., & Jacot, B. (1992). *The way men think.* New Haven, CT: Yale University Press.

Hunt, M. (1974). *Sexual behavior in the 1970's.* Chicago: Playboy Press.

Hunter, J. D. (1991). *Culture wars: The struggle to define America.* New York: Basic Books.

Ide, S., Hon, M., Kawasaki, A., Ikuta, S., & Haga, H. (1985). *Forms and functions of honorifics used by women.* Tokyo: Nippon Women's University Press.

Infante, D. A. (1981). Trait argumentativeness as a predictor of communicative behavior in situations requiring argument. *Central States Speech Journal, 32,* 265–272.

Infante, D. A. (1985). Inducing women to be more argumentative: Source credibility effects. *Journal of Applied Communication Research, 13,* 33–44.

Infante, D. A. (1986). Aggressiveness and interpersonal communication. In J. C. McCroskey, & J. A. Daly (Eds.), *Personality and interpersonal communication.* Beverly Hills, CA: Sage Publications.

Infante, D. A. (1989). Response to high argumentatives: Message and sex differences. *The Southern Communication Journal, 54,* 159–170.

Infante, D. A., Chandler, T. A., & Rudd, J. E. (1989). Test of an argumentative skill deficiency model of interspousal violence. *Communication Monographs, 56,* 163–177.

Infante, D. A., & Gorden, W. I. (1991). How employees see the boss: Test of an argumentative and affirming model of superiors' communicative behavior. *Western Journal of Speech Communication, 55,* 294–304.

Infante, D. A., & Rancer, A. S. (1982). A conceptualization and measure of argumentativeness. *Journal of Personality Assessment, 46,* 72–80.

Infante, D. A., Sabourin, T. C., Rudd, J. E., & Shannon, E. A. (1990). Verbal aggression in violent and nonviolent marital disputes. *Communication Quarterly, 38,* 361–371.

Infante, D. A., Trebing, J. D., Shepherd, P. E., & Seeds, D. E. (1984). The relationship of argumentativeness to verbal aggression. *Southern Speech Communication Journal, 50,* 67–77.

Infante, D. A., Wall, C. H., Leap, C. J., & Danielson, K. (1984). Verbal aggression as a function of the receiver's argumentativeness. *Communication Research Reports, 1,* 33–37.

Infante, D. A., & Wigley, C. J., III. (1986, March). Verbal aggressiveness: An interpersonal model and measure. *Communication Monographs, 54,* 61–69.

Ivancevitch, J. M., & Matteson, M. T. (1986). Organizational level stress management interventions: A review and recommendations. *Journal of Organizational Behavior Management, 8,* 229–248.

Ivancevitch, J. M., Matteson, M., Breedman, S., & Philips, J. (1990). Worksite stress management interventions. *American Psychology, 45* (2), 252–261.

Ivey, D. K., & Backlund, P. (1994). *Exploring gender speak.* New York: McGraw-Hill.

Jackson, J. M. (1964). The organization and its communication problems. In H. J. Leavitt and L. R. Pondy (Eds.), *Readings in managerial psychology.* Chicago: University of Chicago Press.

Jacobs, J. S. (1980). Divorce: The price of success. *Industry Week, 205* (5), 76–82.

Jaggar, A. M. (1983). *Feminist politics and human nature.* Totowa, NJ: Rowman & Allanheld.

Jaggar, A. (1988). *Feminist politics and human nature.* Totowa, NJ: Rowman & Littlefield.

James, D., & Drakich, J. (1993). Understanding gender differences in amount of talk: A critical review of research. In D. Tannen (Ed.), *Gender and conversational interaction* (pp. 281–312). New York: Oxford University Press.

Janeway, E. (1971). *Man's world, woman's place.* New York: William Morrow.

Janis, I., & Field, P. (1959). Sex differences and personality factors related to persuasibility. In C. Hovland and I. Janis (Eds.), *Personality and persuasibility.* New Haven, CT: Yale University Press.

Jerome, A. (2000). *Scarlett's transformation: An analysis of gender role transcendence theory's presence in the film "Gone with the Wind."* Paper presented at the Central States Communication Convention, Detroit, MI.

Jick, R. D., & Mitz, L. F. (1985). Sex differences in work stress. *Academy of Management Review, 10,* 408–420.

Johnson, C., & Gilmore, S. (1993). *Differences between men and women sex talk.* Paper presented at the meeting of the organization for the study of communication, language, and gender, Tempe, AZ.

Johnson D. W., & Johnson, R. T. (1979). Conflict in the classroom: Controversy and learning. *Review of Educational Research, 49,* 51–70.

Jones, S. E. (1984). *An exploratory study of sex differences in tactile communication.* Paper presented at the annual meeting of the Speech Communication Association, Chicago.

Jones, W. H., Chernovetz, M. E., & Hansson, R. O. (1978). The enigma of androgyny: Differential implications for males and females? *Journal of Clinical and Consulting Psychology, 46,* 298–313.

Jourard, S. M., & Rubin, J. E. (1968). Self-disclosure and touching: A study of two modes of interpersonal encounter and their inter-relation. *Journal of Humanistic Psychology, 8,* 39–48.

Judd, L. R., & Smith, C. B. (1974). A study of variables influencing self-concept and ideal self-concept among students in the basic speech course. *Speech Teacher, 23,* 215–221.

Julty, S. (1995). Mens lives are changing for the better. In J. Petrikin (Ed.), *Male/*

female roles: Opposing viewpoints (pp. 146–150). San Diego, CA: Greenhaven Press.

Kaats, G. R., & Davis, E. E. (1970). The dynamics of sexual behavior of college students. *Journal of Marriage and Family, 32,* 390–399.

Kadoduala, D. (1997). Hinduism. In C. Richards (Ed.), *The illustrated encyclopedia of world religions.* Rockport, MA: Element Books Limited.

Kagan, J., & Moss, H. A. (1983). *Birth to maturity: A study in psychological development* (2nd ed). New Haven, CT: Yale University Press.

Kalelkar, K. (1960). *Bapu's letters to Ashram sisters.* Ahmedabad: Navajivan Publishing House.

Kanter, R. (1977). *Men and women of the corporation.* New York: Basic Books.

Kaplan, A. (1986). The "self-in-relation": Implications for depression in women. *Psychotherapy, 23,* 234–242.

Katz, L. (1995). Censoring pornography harms society. In C. Cozic (Ed.), *Sexual Values: Opposing Viewpoints* (p. 141). San Diego, CA: Greenhaven Press.

Katz, R. (1982). *Boiling Energy.* Cambridge, MA: Harvard University Press.

Katz, S. M. (1979). American purdah: An examination of the role of executives' wives. Doctoral dissertation, Golden Gate University. *Dissertation Abstracts International, 40,* 2162A.

Kaufman, D. (1991). *Rachel's daughters: Newly orthodox Jewish women.* New Brunswick, NJ: Rutgers University Press.

Kawaguchi, Y., (1990, May 14–20). Do women really speak more politely than men in Japan? *The Japan Times Weekly International Edition,* p. 17A.

Keating, C. F. (1985). Human dominance signals: The primate in us. In S. L. Ellyson & J. R. Dovidio (Eds.), *Power, dominance, and nonverbal behavior* (pp. 89–108). New York: Springer-Verlag.

Kelleher, T. (1987). Confucianism. In A. Sharma (Ed.), *Women in world religions.* New York: SUNY Press.

Keller, E. F. (1985). *Reflections on gender and science.* New Haven, CT: Yale University Press.

Kelly, C. M. (1987). The interrelationship of ethics and power in today's organizations. *Organizational Dynamics, 16* (1), 5–18.

Kelly, J. A., O'Brien, G. G., & Hosford, R. (1981). Sex roles and social skills considerations for interpersonal adjustment. *Psychology of Women Quarterly, 5,* 758–765.

Kendrick, W. (1994, Winter-Spring). Here's looking at you. *Salmagundi,* (101–102), 124–132.

Kerens, C. L. (1989). Determinants of feminism: A longitudinal study. Doctoral dissertation at Cornell University, Ithaca, New York. *Dissertation Abstracts.* #850499/2211.

Kersten, K. (1997, November–December). Male models. *The American Enterprise, 8* (6), 161.

Kilbourne, J. (1996). Slim hopes: Advertising and the obsession with thinness, eating disorders and anorexia. *Journalism History, 23* (4), 175–176.

Kimmel, M. S., & Kaufman, M. (1994). Weekend warriors: The new men's movement. In H. Brod & M. Kaufman (Eds.), *Theorizing masculinities* (pp. 259–288). Thousand Oaks, CA: Sage.

Kimura, D. (1987). Are men's and women's brains really different? *Canadian Psychology, 28,* 133–147.

Kincaid, M. B. (1977). Changes in sex-role attitudes and self-actualization of adult women following a consciousness-raising group. *Sex Roles, 3,* 329–336.

King, A. (1987). *Power and Communication.* Prospect Heights, IL: Waveland Press.

Kipnis, A. (1995). The postfeminist men's movement. In M. Kimmel (Ed.), *The politics of manhood.* Philadelphia: Temple University Press.

Kipnis, D. (1972). Does power corrupt. *Journal of Personality and Social Psychology, 24,* 33–41.

Kipnis, D., Castell, P. J., Gergen, M., & Mauch, D. (1976). Metamorphic effects of power. *Journal of Applied Psychology, 61* (2), 127–135.

Kirkendall, A. L., & Sibley, W. R. (1966). Interpersonal relationship—crux of the sexual renaissance. *The Journal of Social Issues, 22,* 45–49.

Klein, H. A., O'Bryant, K., & Hopkins, H. R. (1996, March). Recalled parental authority style and self-perception in college men and women. *Journal of Genetic Psychology, 157* (1), 5–13.

Knapp, M. L. (1978). *Nonverbal communication in human interaction* (2nd Ed.). New York: Holt, Rinehart, & Winston.

Knapp, M. L. (1980). *Essentials of nonverbal communication.* New York: Holt, Rinehart, & Winston.

Knapp, M. L. (1984). *Interpersonal communication and human relationships.* Newton, MA: Allyn & Bacon.

Knowles, E. S. (1973). Boundaries around group interaction: The effect of group size and member status on boundary permeability. *Journal of Personality and Social Psychology, 25,* 327–331.

Koffman, S., & Lips, H. M. (1980). Sex differences in self-esteem and performance expectancies in married couples. *Social Behavior and Personality, 8,* 57–63.

Kogut, D., Langley, T., & O'Neal, E. C. (1992). Gender role masculinity and angry aggression in women. *Sex Roles, 26* (9/10), 355–368.

Kohlberg, L. (1958). *The development of modes of thinking and moral choice in the years 10–16.* Unpublished doctoral dissertation, University of Chicago.

Kohn, A. (1986). *No contest: The case against competition.* Boston: Houghton Mifflin.

Kolbenschlag, M. (1979). *Kiss sleeping beauty goodbye.* New York: Bantam.

Konsky, C. (1978). *Male-female language attributions in the resolution of conflict.* Paper presented at the meeting of the Speech Communication Association, Minneapolis, MN.

Kopper, B. A. (1993). Role of gender, sex role identity, and type A behavior in anger expression and mental health functioning. *Journal of Counseling Psychology, 40* (2), 232–237.

Korda, M. (1975). *Power! How to get it, how to use it.* New York: Ballantine.

Koss, M. (1988). Hidden rape: Sexual aggression and victimization in a national sample of students in higher education. In A. W. Burgess (Ed.), *Rape and Sexual Assault II.* New York: Garland Publishing.

Kramarae, C. (1981). *Women and men speaking.* Rowley, MA: Newbury House.

Kramer, C. (1977). Perceptions of female and male speech. *Language and Speech, 20,* 151–161.

Kramer, C. (1978). Women's and men's ratings of their own and ideal speech. *Communication Quarterly, 26,* 2–11.

Labov, W. (1972). *Sociolinguistic patterns.* Philadelphia: University of Pennsylvania Press.

LaCroix, A. Z., & Hayness, S. G. (1987). Gender differences in the health effects of workplace roles. In R. C. Barnett, L. Beiner, & G. K. Baruch (Eds.), *Gender and stress* (pp. 96–121). New York: Free Press.

Ladner, J. (1987). Introduction to tomorrow's tomorrow: The black woman. In S. Harding (Ed.), *Feminism and methodology: Social science issues.* Milton Keynes: Open University Press.

LaFrance, M., & Mayo, C. (1978). *Moving bodies: Nonverbal communication in social relationships,* (pp. 155–170). Monterey, CA: Brooks/Cole.

LaFrance, M., & Mayo, C. (1979). A review of nonverbal behaviors of women and men. *Western Journal of Speech Communication, 43,* 96–107.

LaHaye, B. (1976). *The spirit-controlled woman.* Eugene, OR: Harvest House.

Lakoff, R. (1973). Language and woman's place. *Language in Society, 2,* 45–80.

Lakoff, R. (1975). *Language and women's place.* New York: Harper & Row.

Lancaster, B. (1997). Judaism. In C. Richards (Ed.), *The illustrated encyclopedia of world religions.* Rockport, MA: Element Books Limited.

Langer, E. J. (1979). The illusion of incompetence. In L. Perlmutter & R. Monty (Eds.), *Choice and perceived control.* Hillside, NJ: Lawrence Erlbaum Associates.

Langer, E. J., & Benevento, A.(1978). Self-induced dependence. *Journal of Personality and Social Psychology, 36,* 886–893.

Lawler, K. A., Rixse, A., & Allen, M. T. (1983). Type A behavior and psychophysiological responses in adult women. *Psychophysiology, 20,* 343–350.

Lawless, E. (1988). *Handmaidens of the Lord: Pentecostal women preachers and traditional religion.* Philadelphia: University of Pennsylvania Press.

Lawson, C. (1989, June 15). Toys: Girls still apply make-up, boys still fight wars, *New York Times,* pp. C1, C10.

Lazier-Smith, L. (1989). *Demographics vs. demigoddesses: A new generation of advertising images to women.* Paper presented at the annual meetings of the Association for Education in Journalism and Mass Communications, Washington, DC.

Leathers, D. G. (1986). *Successful nonverbal communication: Principles and applications* (pp. 232–247). New York: Macmillan.

Lefcourt, H. M. (1973). The function of the illusions of control and freedom. *American Psychologist, 28,* 417–425.

Leiberman, P. (1977). *On the origins of language: An introduction to the evolution of human speech.* New York: Macmillan.

Leigh, B. C. (1989). Reasons for having and avoiding sex: Gender, sexual orientation, and relationship to sexual behavior. *Journal of Sex Research, 26,* 199–209.

Lenney, E. (1991). Sex roles: The measurement of masculinity, femininity, and androgyny. *Measures of personality and social psychological attitudes.* New York: Academic Press.

Leo, J. (1997, November 3). Men behaving well. *U.S. News & World Report,* p. 16.

Lerner, G. (Ed.). (1972). *Black woman in white America: A documentary history.* New York: Pantheon.

Lesak, M. (1976). *Neuropsychological assessment.* New York: Oxford University Press.

Levine, J. (1988, March). Thinking about sex. *Tikkun Magazine,* pp. 16–18.

Levine, J. (1994). The man in the mirror: The image of the American male as it emerges from Esquire, GQ, Men's Journal and Details. *Columbia Journalism Review, 32* (6), 27–32.

L'Heureux-Barrett, T., & Barnes-Farrell, J. L. (1991). Overcoming gender bias in reward allocation. *Psychology of Women Quarterly, 15,* 127–139.

Liebkind, K. (1992). Ethnic identity—challenging the boundaries of social psychology. In G. M. Breakwell (Ed.), *Social Psychology of identity and the self concept.* London: Surrey University Press.

Lienesh, M. (1993). *Redeeming America: Piety and politics in the new Christian right.* Chapel Hill: University of North Carolina Press.

Limbaugh, Rush. (1992). *The way things ought to be.* New York: Simon & Schuster.

Lips, H. (1981). *Women, men and the psychology of power.* Englewood Cliffs, NJ: Prentice-Hall.

Litewka, J. (1977). The socialized penis. In J. Snodgrass (Ed.), *For men against sexism* (pp. 16–35). Albion, CA: Times Change Press.

Loden, M. (1985). *Feminine leadership or how to succeed in business without being one of the boys.* New York: Times Books.

Loeb, R. C., & Horst, L. (1978). Sex differences in self and teachers' reports of self-esteem in pre-adolescents. *Sex Roles, 4,* 779–788.

Logan, D. (1985). Some thoughts about my feelings. In Francis Baumli (Ed.), *Men freeing men: Exploding the myth of the traditional male.* Jersey City, NJ: New Atlantis.

Logon, D. D., & Kaschak, E. (1980). The relationship of sex, sex role, and mental health. *Psychology Lynn of Women Quarterly, 4,* 573–579.

Lombroso, C. (1894). *The man of genius.* London: Walter Scott.

Lord, S. (1993, June). The mild ones. *Vogue,* pp. 119–124.

Lukes, S. (1974). *Power: A radical view.* New York: Macmillan.

Lyman, S. M., & Scott, M. B. (1967). Territoriality: A neglected sociological dimension. *Social Problems, 15,* 236–249.

Lynch, C. M., & Strauss-Noll, M. (1987, January). Mauve washers: Sex differences in freshman writing. *English Journal,* 90–94.

Maccoby, E. E., & Jacklin, C. N. (1974). *The psychology of sex differences.* Stanford, CA: Stanford University Press.

Maccoby, M. (1976). *The gamesman.* New York: Simon & Schuster.

Mackey, W. C. & White, U. (1993). The abrading of the American father. In *The Family in American.* Rockford, IL: The Rockford Institute.

Major, B. (1980). Gender patterns in touching behavior. In C. Mayo & N. M. Henley (Eds.), *Gender and nonverbal behavior* (pp. 3–37). New York: Springer-Verlag.

Malamuth, N. M., & Briere, J. (1986). Sexual violence in the media: Indirect effects on aggression against women. *Journal of Social Issues, 42,* 75–92.

Malandro, L. A., & Barker, L. (1983). *Nonverbal communication* (pp. 210–239). Reading, MA: Addison-Wesley.

Manning, C. J. (1995). Coming to terms with feminism: A study of evangelical Protestant, conservative Catholic and orthodox Jewish women. University of California, Santa Barbara. Dissertation Abstracts #9168351/1071.

Margargee, E. I. (1969). Influence of sex roles on the manipulation of leadership. *Journal of Applied Psychology, 53,* 377–382.

Martin, J. (1916). *Feminism: Its fallacies and follies. Book 2.* New York: Dodd, Mead.

Martin, J., & Martin, P. (1916). *Feminism: Its fallacies and follies.* New York: Dodd, Mead.

Martin, J. N., & Craig, R. T. (1983). Selected linguistic sex differences during initial social interactions of same-sex and mixed-sex student dyads. *Western Journal of Speech Communication, 47,* 16–28.

Maslow, A. H. (1970). *Motivation and personality* (2nd Ed.). New York: Harper & Row.

Maspero, H. (1981). *Taoism and Chinese religion* (F. A. Kierman, Jr., Trans.). Amherst: University of Massachusetts Press.

Mayerson, S. E., & Taylor, D. A. (1987). The effects of rape myth pornography on women's attitudes and the mediating role of sex role stereotyping. *Sex Roles, 17,* 321–338.

McCarrick, A. K., Manderscheid, R. W., & Silbergeld, S. (1981). Gender differences in competition and dominance during married-couples group therapy. *Social Psychology Quarterly, 44* (3), 164–177.

McClelland, D. C. (1970). The two faces of power. *Journal of International Affairs, 24,* 29–47.

McClelland, D. C. (1985). *Human motivation.* Glenview, IL: Scott Foresman.

McConnell-Ginet, S. (1983). Intonation in a man's world. In B. Thorne, C. Kramarae, & N. Henley (Eds.), *Language, gender and society.* Rowley, MA: Newbury House.

McCroskey, J. C., Richmond, V. P., Plax, T. G., & Kearney, P. (1985). Power in the classroom: Behavior alteration techniques, communication training and learning. *Communication Education, 34,* 214–226.

McDannell, C. (1989). Catholic domesticity, 1960–1970. In Karen Kennelly (Ed.), *American Catholic women: A historical exploration* (pp. 48–80). New York: Macmillan.

McElroy, W. (1995). The unfair sex? *National Review, 47* (8), 74–76.

McFarlane, S. (1997). Confucianism. In C. Richards (Ed.), *The illustrated encyclopedia of world religions.* Rockport, MA: Element Books Limited.

McGregor, D. (1960). *The human side of enterprise.* New York: McGraw-Hill.

McMillan, J. R., Clifton, A. K., McGrath, C., & Gale, W. S. (1977). Women's language: Uncertainty or interpersonal sensitivity and emotionality: *Sex Roles, 3,* 545–559.

Mead, G. H. (1934). *Mind, self, and society.* Chicago: University of Chicago Press.

Mead, M. (1963). *Sex and temperament in three primitive societies.* New York: Dell.

Megargee, E. E. (1969). Influence of sex roles on the manifestation of leadership. *Journal of Applied Psychology, 53,* 377–382.

Merabian, A. (1971). *Silent messages: Implicit communication of emotion and attitudes* (2nd Ed.). Belmont, CA: Wadsworth.

Mercer, W. G. & Kohn, P. M. (1979). Gender differences in the integration of conservatism, sex urge, and sexual behaviors among college students. *Journal of Sex Research, 15*, 129–142.

Messner, M. (1995). Changing men and feminist politics in the United States. In M. Kimmel (Ed.), *The politics of manhood*. Philadelphia: Temple University Press.

Messner, M. (1997). *Politics of masculinities*. Thousand Oaks, CA: Sage.

Millar, F. E., & Rogers, L. E. (1987). Relational dimensions of interpersonal dynamics. In M. E. Roloff & G. Millar (Eds.), *Interpersonal processes* (pp. 117–139). Newbury Park, CA: Sage.

Miller, A., Gurin, P. & Gurin, G. (1980). Social cleavage in the United States. Doctoral dissertation, The University of Michigan, Ann Arbor.

Miller, C., & Swift, K. (1972, Spring). De-sexing the English language. *Ms.*, Preview issue, 13–14.

Miller, C., & Swift, K. (1976). Women and the language of religion. *Christian Century, 93*, 353–358.

Miller, J. B. (1976). *Toward a new psychology of women*. Boston: Beacon Press.

Miller, J. B. (1986). *Toward a new psychology of women* (2nd Ed.). Boston: Beacon Press.

Milroy, L. (1980). *Language and social networks*. Oxford: Basil Blackwell.

Minnigerode, F. (1976). Attitudes toward women, sex-role stereotyping, and locus of control. *Psychological Reports, 38*, 1301–1302.

Mischel, H. N. (1974). Sex bias in the evaluation of educational achievements. *Journal of Educational Psychology, 66*, 157–166.

Mischel, W. (1966). A social learning view of sex differences in behavior. In E. E. Macoby (Ed.), *The development of sex differences* (pp. 93–106). Stanford, CA: Stanford University Press.

Mlachak, N. N. (1984). Life with the CEO: Glamour and junkets or heroic patience. *Industry, 223* (6), 74–80.

Moir, A., & Jessel, D. (1991). *Brain sex: The real difference between men and women*. New York: Carol Publishing Group.

Mollay, J. T. (1981). The executive spouse. *Cosmopolitan, 191* (6), 142.

Montague, A. (Ed.). (1971). *Touching: The significance of the human skin*. New York: Harper & Row.

Montgomery, C. L., & Burgoon, M. (1980, March). The effects of androgyny and message expectations on resistance to persuasive communication. *Communication Monographs, 47*.

Moore, D. (1984). It's either me or your job: Working couples. *Working Woman, 9* (4), 108–111.

Moore, H. T. (1922). Further data concerning sex differences. *Journal of Abnormal Psychology, 17*, 210–214.

Moore, R., & Gillette, D. (1992). The Warrior within: Accessing the knight in the male psyche. New York: William Morrow.

Morales, R. (1983). I am what I am. In C. Moraga & G. Anzaldua (Eds.), *This bridge called my back: Writings by radical women of color*. New York: Kitchen Table.

Morgan, M. (1973). *The total woman*. New York: Pocket Books.

Morrison, A. M., & Von Glinow, M. A. (1990). Women and minorities in management. *American Psychologist, 45,* 200–208.

Muelenhard, C. L., & Hollabaugh, L. C. (1988). Do women sometimes say no when they mean yes? The prevalence and correlates of women's token resistance to sex. *Journal of Personality and Social Psychology, 54,* 872–879.

Mulac, A., Bradac, J. J., & Mann, S. K. (1985a). Male/female language differences and attributional consequences in children's television. *Human Communication Research, 11* (4), 481–506.

Mulac, A., Incontro, C. R., & James, M. R. (1985b). Comparison of the gender-linked language effect and sex role stereotypes. *Journal of Personality and Social Psychology, 49* (4), 1098–1109.

Mulac, A., & Lundell, T. L. (1980). Differences in perceptions created by syntactic-semantic productions of male and female speakers. *Communication Monographs, 47,* 111–118.

Mulac, A., & Lundell, T. L. (1986). Linguistic contributors to the gender-linked language effect. *Journal of Language and Social Psychology, 5,* 81–102.

Mulac, A., Lundell, T. L., & Bradac, J. J. (1986, June). Male/female language differences and attributional consequences in a public speaking situation: Toward an explanation of the gender-linked language effect. *Communication Monographs, 53,* 115–129.

Mulac, A., Wiemann, J. M., Widenmann, S. J., & Gibson, T. W. (1988). Male/female language differences and effects in same-sex and mixed-sex dyads: The gender-linked language effect. *Communication Monographs, 55,* 315–335.

Mullin, V. (1983). *Midlife women and power: An exploratory study*. Unpublished doctoral dissertation, California School of Professional Psychology, Los Angeles.

Murdy, A., & Hayse, C. (1995). Teenagers should learn how to have safe sex. In C. Cozic (Ed.), *Sexual values: Opposing viewpoints* (pp. 206–212). San Diego, CA: Greenhaven Press.

Murray, J. (1973). Male perspective in language. *Women: A Journal of Liberation, 3,* 45–50.

Neeman, J., & Harter, S. (1986). *Manual for the self-perception profile for college students*. Denver; CO: University of Denver.

Neitz, M. J. (1987). *Charisma and community: A study of religious commitment within the Charismatic Renewal*. New Brunswick, NJ: Transaction Books.

Nelson, D. L. & Quick, J. C. (1985). Professional women: Are distress and disease inevitable? *Academy of Management Review, 10,* 206–218.

Nguyen, T., Heslin, R., & Nguyen, M. L. (1975). The meanings of touch: Sex differences. *Journal of Communication, 25* (3), 92–103.

Nicotera, A. M. & Rancer, A. S. (1994). The influence of sex on self-perceptions and social stereotyping of aggressive communication predispositions. *Western Journal of Communication, 58,* 283–307.

Nord, W. R. (1969). Social exchange theory: An integrative approach to social conformity. *Psychological Bulletin, 71,* 174–208.

Norwood, R. (1985). *Women who love too much*. New York: Pocket Books.

Novaco, R. C. (1976). The function and regulation of the arousal of anger. *American Journal of Psychiatry, 133*, 1124–1128.

Nugent, C. R., & Spong, J. S. (1995). Homosexuality does not erode moral values. In C. Cozic (Ed.), *Sexual values: Opposing viewpoints*. San Diego, CA: Greenhaven Press.

Nylander, I. (1971). The feeling of being fat and dieting in a school population: Epidemiologic, interview investigation. *Acta Sociomedica Scandinavia, 3*, 17–26.

Obeyesekere, G. (1984). *The cult of the goddess Pattini*. Chicago: University of Chicago Press.

Olson, B. (1999). *Hell to pay*. Washington, DC: Regnery.

O'Malley, P. J., & Bachman, J. G. (1979). Self-esteem and education: Sex and cohort comparisons among high school seniors. *Journal of Personality and Social Psychology, 37*, 1153–1159.

Onyekwere, E. O., Rubin, R. B., & Infante, D. A. (1991). Interpersonal perception and communication satisfaction as a function of argumentativeness and ego-involvement. *Communication Quarterly, 39*, 35–47.

O'Reilly, T. A. (1988). The Zelen-O'Reilly Locus of Control Scale. Unpublished doctoral dissertation, California School of Professional Psychology, Los Angeles.

Orlofsky, J. L. (1977). Sex-role orientation, identity formation, and self-esteem in college men and women. *Sex Roles, 3*, 561–575.

Orr, C. (1997a). *Wollstonecraft's Daughters: Woomanhood in England and France, 1780–1920*. Manchester and New York: Manchester University Press.

Orr, C. (1977b). Charting the currents of the third wave. *Hypatia, 12* (3), 29.

Otto, H. (1988). America's youth: A changing profile. *Family Relations, 37*, 385–391.

Paglia, C. (1992). *Sex, art, and American culture*. New York: Random House.

Palazzoli, M. P. (1974). *Anorexia nervosa*. London: Chaucer.

Paludi, M. A. (1992). *The Psychology of Women*. Dubuque, IA: William C. Brown.

Panghorn, K. (1985). The murdered husband: Fmaily violence and women's lib. In Francis Baumli (Ed.), *Men freeing men: Exploding the myth of the traditional male*. Jersey City, NJ: New Atlantis.

Papanek, H. (1973). Men, women, and work: Reflections on the two-person career. *American Journal of Sociology, 78*, 852–872.

Parr, J. (1977). *The superwives*. New York: Avon Books.

Parsons, T. (1953). *The theory of action*. New York: Free Press.

Patterson, G. R., & Cobb, J. A. (1973). Stimulus control for classes of noxious behaviors. In J. F. Knutson (Ed.), *The control of aggression: Implications from basic research* (pp. 145–194). Chicago: Aldine.

Paul, E., & White, K. (1990). The development of intimate relationships in late adolescence. *Adolescence, 25*, 375–400.

Payne, K. (1988). Executive wives: A study of interpersonal and organizational relationships. Doctoral Dissertation, Vanderbilt University, Nashville, TN. *Dissertation Abstracts International*.

Payne, K. (1996). *Voice and diction*. New York: McGraw-Hill.

Payne K., & Payne-Houchen, H. (1999). *In search of a gender connection: A study in gender communication.* A paper presented at the National Communication Association, Chicago.

Pearcey, N. (1995). Women cannot have it all. In J. Petrikin (Ed.), *Male/Female roles: Opposing Viewpoints* (pp. 136–142). San Diego, CA: Greenhaven Press.

Pearson, J. C., Turner, L. H., & Todd-Mancillas, W. (1991). *Gender and communication.* Dubuque, IA: William C. Brown.

Peck, S. M. (1978). *The road less traveled.* New York: Simon & Schuster.

Peplau, L. A. (1981). What homosexuals want in relationships. *Psychology Today, 15,* 28–37.

Peplau, L. A. (1983). Roles and gender. In H. H. Kelley, (Ed.), *Close relationships.* San Francisco: W. H. Freeman.

Peplau, L. A., & Gordon, S. L. (1983). The intimate relationships of lesbians and gay men. In E. R. Allgeier & N. B. McCormick (Eds.), *Changing boundaries: Gender roles and sexual behavior.* Palo Alto, CA: Mayfield.

Peplau, L. A., Rubin, Z., & Hill, C. T. (1977). Sexual intimacy in dating relationships. *Journal of Social Issues, 33,* 86–109.

Perry, M. O., Schutz, H. G., & Rucker, M. H. (1983). Clothing interest, self-actualization, and demographic variables. *Home Economics Research Journal, 11,* 280–288.

Peterson, G. K., Kiesler, S. B., & Goldberg, P. A. (1971). Evaluation of the performance of women as a function of sex, achievement, and personal history. *Journal of Personality and Social Psychology, 19,* 114–118.

Peterson, P. (1976). An investigation of sex differences in regard to nonverbal body gestures. In B. W. Eakins, R. G. Eakins, & B. Lieb-brilhart (Eds.), *Siscom '75: Women's (and men's) communication.* Falls Church, VA: Speech Communication Association.

Pfost, K. S., & Fiore, M. (1990). Pursuit of nontraditional occupations: Fear of success or fear of not being chosen? *Sex Roles, 23* (1–2), 15–24.

Piaget, J. (1965). *The moral judgment of the child.* New York: Free Press.

Piliavin, J. A., & Martin, R. R. (1978). The effects of the sex composition of groups on the style of social interaction. *Sex Roles, 4,* 281–296.

Plax, T. G., Kearney, P., & Downs, T. M. (1986). Communicating control in the classroom and satisfaction with teaching and students. *Communication Education, 35,* 379–388.

Pleck, J. H. (1977). Men's power with women, other men, and society: A men's movement analysis. In D. Hiller and R. Sheets (Eds.), *Women and Men: The consequences of power.* Cincinnati: Office of Women's Studies, University of Cincinnati.

Pogash, C. (1992, April). Women at work. *Working Woman,* p. 104.

Poire, B. A., Burgoon, J. K., & Parrott, R. (1992). Status and privacy restoring communication in the workplace. *Journal of Applied Communication Research, 4,* 419–436.

Polhemus, T., & Procter, L. (1978). *Fashion and anti-fashion: Anthropology of clothing and adornment.* London: Thames & Hudson.

Pomerleau, A., Bolduc, D., Malcuit, G., & Cossette, L. (1990). Pink or blue: Environmental stereotypes in the first two years of life. *Sex Roles, 22,* 359–367.

Poupko, C. K., & Wohlgelernter, D. L. (1976). Women's liberation: An orthodox response. *Tradition, 15* (4), 45–52.

Powell, G. N. (1988). *Women and men in management.* Beverly Hills, CA: Sage.

Powell, G. N. (1993) *Women and men in management* (2nd Ed.). Newbury Park, CA: Sage.

Prager, K. J. (1983). Identity status, sex-role orientation, and self-esteem in adulthood. *International Journal of Aging and Human Development, 12,* 129–138.

Press, A., & Strathman, T. (1993). Work, family, and social class in television images of women: Prime-time television and the construction of postfeminism. *Women and Language, 16* (2) 7–9.

Price, M. (1979). Distress of corporate damsel (wives of executives). *Industry Week, 203* (3), 79.

Procter, L. (1978). *Fashion and anti-fashion.* London: Cox & Wyman.

Pugliesi, K. (1988). Employment characteristics, social support, and the well-being of women. *Women and Health, 14,* 35–58.

Putnam, L. L. (Ed.) (1988). Communication and conflict styles in organizations. *Management Communication Quarterly, 1* (3) 293–301.

Putnam, L. L., & Wilson, C. E. (1982). Communicative strategies in organizational conflicts: Reliability and validity of a measurement scale. *Communication Yearbook VI,* 629–652. Beverly Hills, CA: Sage.

Quinn, D. M. (1997). *The Mormon Hierarchy: Extensions of power.* Salt Lake City: Signature Books in Association with Smith Research Association.

Ragan, S. L. (1989). Communication between the sexes: A consideration of differences in adult communication. In J. R. Nussbaum (Ed.), *Life-span communication* (pp. 179–193). Hillsdale, NJ: Lawrence Erlbaum.

Rahim, M. A. (1989). Relationships of leader power to compliance with supervision: Evidence from a national sample of managers. *Journal of Management, 15* (4), 545–556.

Raimy, V. C. (1948). Self-reference in counseling interviews. *Journal of Consulting Psychology, 12,* 153–163.

Rancer, A. S. Baukus, R. A., & Amato, P. P. (1986). Argumentativeness, verbal aggressiveness, and marital satisfaction. *Communication Research Reports, 3,* 28–32.

Rancer, A. S., Kosberg, R. L., & Baukus, R. A. (1992). Beliefs about arguing as predictors of trait argumentativeness: Implications for training in argument and conflict management. *Communication Education, 41,* 375–387.

Rapping, E. (1994). In praise of Roseanne. *The Progressive, 58* (7), 36–38.

Rategan, C. A. (1993). He said, she said: Good talk with good friends. *Current Health, 2* (20), n1, 4–6.

Raven, B. H. (1974). The comparative analysis of power and power preference. In J. Tedeschi (Ed.), *Perspectives on social power.* Chicago: Aldine.

Raven, B. H., Centers, R., & Rodriguez, A. (1975). The bases of conjugal power. In R. E. Cromwell & D. H. Olson (Eds.), *Power in families* (pp. 217–232). New York: John Wiley & Sons.

Recely, N. L. (1973). Level of self-esteem and conformity to sex-role stereotypes Doctoral dissertation at University of Colorado. *Dissertation Abstracts International, 34* (4-B), 1757–1758.

Reed, B. (1987). Taoism. In A. Sharma (Ed.), *Women in world religions*. New York: SUNY Press.

Reed, E. (1970). Women: Caste, class, or oppressed sex? In E. Reed (Ed.), *Problems of women's liberation* (pp. 64–76). New York: Pathfinder Press.

Reissman, A. (1990). Intimacy in same sex friendships. *Sex Roles, 23*, 65–81.

Rekers, G. A. (1991). Psychological foundations for rearing masculine boys and feminine girls. In Piper and W. Grudem (Eds.), *Recovering Biblical manhood and womanhood* (pp. 292–311). Wheaton, IL: Crossway Books.

Rekers, G. A. (1996). Gender identity disorder. *The Journal of Human Sexuality. 5* (4), 243–249.

Renshaw, J. R. (1974). Explorations at the boundaries of work and family life. Doctoral dissertation, University of California at Los Angeles. *Dissertation Abstracts International, 35*, 600A.

Renshaw, J. R. (1976). An exploration of the dynamics of the overlapping worlds of work and family. *Family Process, 15*, 143–165.

Rich, E. (1977). Sex-related differences in color vocabulary. *Language and Speech, 20*, 404–409.

Ringer, R. (1973). *Winning through intimidation*. New York: Fawcett Crest Books.

Roberts, M. L., & Wortzel, L. H. (1984). *Marketing to the changing household*. Cambridge, MA: Ballinger.

Roberts, R. C. (1993). The dilemma of self-esteem: The cross and Christian confidence. *Christianity Today, 37* (7), 37.

Rogers, C. R., & Dymond, R. (Eds.) (1954). *Psychotherapy and personality change*. Chicago: University of Chicago Press.

Roloff, M. E., & Greenberg, B. S. (1979). Sex differences in choice of modes in conflict resolution in real-life and television. *Communication Quarterly, 27*, 3–12.

Roof, W. C. (1993). *A generation of seekers: The spiritual journeys of the baby boom generation*. San Francisco: HarperCollins.

Rosenberg, M. (1985). Self-concept and psychological well-being in adolescence. In R. L. Leahy (Ed.), *The development of the self* (pp. 205–246). Orlando, FL: Academic.

Rosenberg, M. (1989). *Society and the adolescent self-image*. Princeton, NJ: Princeton University Press.

Rosenfeld, L. B., & Fowler, G. D. 1976. Personality, sex, and leadership style. *Communication Monographs, 43*, 320–324.

Rothman, S. (1995). Was there ever a backlash against women: The presentation of gender in the mass media. In R. J. Simon, (Ed.), *Neither Victim nor Enemy*. Lanham, MD: University Press of America.

Rousseau, M. (1991). Pope John Paul II's teaching on women. In R. McInerny (Ed.), *The Catholic Woman* (pp. 11–13). San Francisco: Ignatius Press.

Rowe, E. (1985). *New age globalism*. Herndon, VA: Growth Publishing.

Ruble, D. N., Balaban, T., & Cooper, J. (1981). Gender constancy and the effects of sex-typed televised toy commercials. *Child Development, 52*, 667–673.

Ruble, D. N., Boggiano, A. K., Feldman, N. S., & Loeble, J. H. (1980). Developmental analysis of the role of social comparison in self-evaluation. *Developmental Psychology, 16*, 105–115.

Ruble, R. L. (1983). Sex stereotypes: Issues of change in the 1970s. *Sex Roles, 9*, 397–402.

Ruddick, S. (1989). *Maternal thinking: Towards a politics of peace.* Boston: Boston Press.

Rudofsky, B. (1972). *The unfashionable human body.* New York: Doubleday.

Ruether, R. R. (1987). Christianity. In A. Sharma (Ed.), *Women in world religions.* New York: SUNY Press.

Russell, G. M., & Jorgenson, D. O. (1978). Religious group membership, locus of control, and dogmatism. *Psychological Reports, 42*, 1099–1102.

Russell, J. A., & Mehrabian, A. (1974). Distinguishing anger and anxiety in terms of emotional response factors. *Journal of Consulting and Clinical Psychology, 42*, 79–83.

Ryan, B. (1989). Ideological purity and feminism: The U.S. women's movement from 1966–1975. *Gender and Society, 3*, 239–257.

Ryckman, R., Marten, J., Rodda, W., & Sherman, M. (1972). Locus of control and attitudes toward women's liberation in a college population. *Journal of Social Psychology, 87*, 157–158.

Sabourin, T. C., Infante, D. A., & Rudd, J. E. (1993). Verbal aggression in marriages: A comparison of violent, distressed but nonviolent, and non distressed couples. *Human Communication Research, 20*, 58–65.

Sagan, Eli. (1985). *At the dawn of tyranny: The origins of individualism, political oppression, and the state.* New York: Alfred A. Knopf.

Sanday, P. R. (1981). *Female power and male dominance: On the origins of sexual inequality.* London: Cambridge University Press.

Sanger, M. (1920). *Woman and the new race.* New York: Brentano's.

Sassen, G. (1980). Success anxiety in women: A constructivist interpretation of its source and its significance. *Harvard Educational Review, 50* (1), 13–24.

Saunders, C. S., & Stead, B. A. (1986). Women's adoption of a business uniform: A content analysis of magazine advertisements. *Sex Roles, 15*, 197–205.

Sause, E. F. (1976). Computer content analysis of sex differences in the language of children. *Journal of Psycholinguistic Research, 5*, 3.

Schalon, C. (1968). Effect of self-esteem upon performance following failure stress. *Journal of Consulting and Clinical Psychology, 32*, 497.

Scheidel, T. M. (1963). Sex and persuasibility. *Speech Monographs, 30*, 353–358.

Schmidt, C. C. (1994, September 7–14). Promise keepers: Message to men. *Christian Century*, pp. 805–806.

Schmidt, K., & Collins, C. (1993). Showdown at gender gap. *American Journalism Review, 15* (6), 39–43.

Schroeder, P. (1991, April 21). *Gender Equity in Education Act* Testimony before the House Education and Labor Committee Subcommittee on Elementary, Secondary, and Vocational Education. (H.R. 1793).

Schwartz, H. (1983). Sex differences in social competence among androgynous: The influence of sex-role blending, nonverbal information processing, and social cognition. Unpublished doctoral dissertation, Emory University.

Segrin, C., & Fitzpatrick, M. A. (1992). Depression and verbal aggressiveness in different marital couple types. *Communication Studies, 43*, 79–91.

Seligman, D. (1988). The case of the profane lady. *Fortune, 118* (2), 11.

Selle, R. (1995). Pornography harms society. In C. Cozic (Ed.), *Sexual values: Opposing viewpoints* (pp. 128–135). San Diego, CA: Greenhaven Press.

Sexton, P. M., Leak, G. & Toenies, F. (1980). Relationship of locus of control and modernity to certainty of religious beliefs. *Psychological Reports, 46*, 1285–1286.

Sharkin, B. S. (1993). Anger and gender: Theory, research, and implications. *Journal of Counseling and Development, 71*, 386–389.

Shastri, S. R. (1969). *Women in the Vedic Age*. Bombay: Bharatiya Vidya Bhavan.

Sheehy, G. (1974). *Passages*. New York: E. P. Dutton.

Sherif, C., Sherif, M., & Nebergall, R. E. (1965). *Attitude and attitude change: The social judgment-involvement approach*. Philadelphia: W. B. Saunders.

Shields, S. (1987). The dilemma of emotion. In P. Shave & C. Hendrick (Eds.), *Sex and gender*. NewBury Park, CA: Sage.

Shimanoff, S. B. (1975). *English lexical gender and the perception of sex markedness*. Paper presented at the Western Speech Communication Association Convention, Newport Beach, CA.

Shinar, C. H. (1978). Person perception as a function of occupation and sex. *Sex Roles, 4*, 679–693.

Shrauger, J., & Rosenberg, S. (1970). Self esteem and the effects of stress and failure feedback on performance. *Journal of Personality, 33*, 404–414.

Simmons, B., & Whitfield, E. (1979). Are boys victims of sex role stereotyping? *Childhood Education, 56*, (2), 75–79.

Simon, H. A. (1951). *Administrative behavior*. New York: Macmillan.

Sistrunk, F., & McDavid, J. W. (1971). Sex variable in conforming behavior. *Journal of Personality and Social Psychology, 17*, (2), 200–207.

Skill, T., & Robinson, J. D. (1994, Fall). Four decades of families on television: A demographic profile, 1950–1989. *Journal of Broadcasting & Electronic Media*.

Slater, P. (1970). *The pursuit of loneliness*. Boston: Beacon Press.

Smith, C. A., & Ellsworth, P. C. 1985. Patterns of cognitive appraisal in emotion. *Journal of Personality and Social Psychology, 48*, 813–838.

Smith, J. I. (1987). Islam. In A. Sharma (Ed.), *Women in world religions* (pp. 235–250). New York: SUNY Press.

Smokler, C. B. (1974). The development of self-esteem and femininity in early adolescence. Doctoral dissertation, University of Michigan. *Dissertation Abstracts International, 35*, (7-B), 3599–3600.

Smythe, M. J., & Meyer, J. (1994). On the origins of gender-linked language differences: Individual and contextual explanations. In Lynn H. Tuner & H. M. Sterk (Eds.), *Differences that make a difference* (pp. 51–60). Westport, CT: Bergin & Garvey.

Sobran, J. (1995). The wanderer. In C. Cozic (Ed.), *Sexual values: Opposing viewpoints* (p. 32). San Diego, CA: Greenhaven Press.

Sorokin, P. A., & Lundin, W. A. (1959). *Power and morality: Who shall guard the guardians?* Boston: Sargent.

Spence, J. T. (1983). Comment on Lubinski, Tellegen & Butcher's masculinity, femininity, and androgyny viewed and assessed as distinct concepts. *Journal of Personality and Social Psychology, 4*, 440–446.

Spence, J. T., Deaux, K., & Helmreich, R. L. (1985). Sex roles in contemporary

American Society. In G. Lindzey & E. Aronson (Eds.), *Handbook of social psychology* (3rd Ed.). New York: Random House.

Spencer, H. (1897). *The principles of sociology* (Vol. 1). London: D. Appleton.

Stacey, J. (1990). *Brave new families: Stories of domestic upheaval in late twentieth century America*. New York: Basic Books.

Staley, C. (1978). Male-female use of expletives: A heck of a difference in expectations. *Anthropological Linguistics 20*, 367–380.

Stanley, L., & Wise, S. (1983). *Breaking out: Feminist consciousness and feminist research*. London: Routledge & Kegan Paul.

Steinem, G. (1992). *Revolution from within: A book of self-esteem*. Boston: Little, Brown.

Stewart, L. P., Cooper, P. J., Stewart, A. D., & Friedley, S. A. (1996). *Communication and Gender*. Scottsdale, AZ: Gorsuch Scarisbrick.

Stogdill, R. M., & Coons, A. E. (Eds.) (1957). Leader behavior: Its description and measurement. *Research Monograph, 88*. Columbus, Ohio: Bureau of Business Research, The Ohio State University.

Stotland, E., & Blumenthal, A. L. (1964). The reduction of anxiety as a result of the expectation of making a choice. *Canadian Journal of Psychology, 8*, 139–145.

Strodtbeck, F. L., & Mann, R. D. (1956). Sex role differentiation in jury deliberations. *Sociometry, 29*, 3–11.

Stroh, L. K., & Brett, J. M. (1994, October 16). Dual-earner dads versus traditional dads: Can we account for differences in salary progression? *New York Times*, p. A3.

Study links men's cognitive abilities to seasonal cycles. (1991, November 11). *Raleigh News and Observer*, p. A3.

Stunkard, A. J. (1975). From explanation to action in psychosomatic medicine: The case of obesity: Presidential address, 1974. *Psychosomatic Medicine, 37*, 195–236.

Suchoki, M. (1994). The idea of God in feminist philosophy. *Hypatia, 9* (4), 1–7.

Sullivan G. L., & O'Conner, P. J. (1988). Women's role portrayals in magazine advertising: 1958–1983. *Sex Roles, 18*, 181–188.

Swain, S. (1989). Covert intimacy: Closeness in men's friendships. In B. J. Risman & P. Schwartz (Eds.), *Gender and intimate relationships*. Belmont, CA: Wadsworth.

Tajfel, H. (Ed.) (1978). *Differentiation between social groups*. New York: Academic Press.

Tang, A. (1999, October 20). Fewer men are working as home duties beckon. New York Times, Section G.

Tannen, D. (1984). *Conversational style: Analyzing talk among friends*. Norwood, NJ: Ablex.

Tannen, D. (1986). *That's not what I meant! How conversational style makes or breaks your relations with others*. New York: William Morrow.

Tannen, D. (1991). *You just don't understand*. New York: Ballantine Books.

Tannen, D. (1994). *Talking from 9–5: How women's and men's conversational styles affect who gets heard, who gets credit, and what gets done at work*. New York: William Morrow.

Tavris, C. (1982). *Anger: The misunderstand emotion.* New York: Simon & Schuster.

Tavris, C. (1992). *The mismeasure of woman.* New York: Simon & Schuster.

Taylor, M. C., & Hall. J. A. (1982). Psychological androgyny: Theories, methods and conclusions. *Psychological Bulletin, 92,* 347–366.

Thomas, D. A., & Rexnikoff, M. (1984). Sex role orientation, personality structure, and adjustment in women. *Journal of Personality Assessment, 48,* 28–36.

Thomas, I., & Raj, H. S. (1985). A factor analytical study on the antecedents of self-esteem. *Psychological Studies, 30,* 97–101.

Thomas, S. (1989). Gender differences in anger expression: Health implications. *Research in Nursing and Health, 12* (6), 389–398.

Thompson, V. (1917). *Woman.* New York: E. P. Dutton.

Thorne, B., Henley, N. (1975). Differences and Dominance: An overview of language, gender and society. *Language and Sex: Difference and dominance.* Rowley, MA: Newbury House.

Timson, J. (1995). Bimbo-watch. *McLean's, 108* (48), 52–54.

Tomalin, C. (1974). *The life and death of Mary Wollstonecraft.* New York: Harcourt Brace Javanovich.

Topley, M. (1975). Marriage resistance in rural Kwangtung. In M. Wolf & R. Witke (Eds.), *Women in Chinese Society.* Stanford, CA: Stanford University Press.

Tuchman, G. (1979). Women's depiction by the mass media. *Signs: Journal of Women in Culture and Society, 4* (3), 528–542.

Tannen, D. (1994). *Talking 9 to 5.* New York: William Morrow.

Urbanski, M. M. O. (1980). *Margaret Fuller's women in the nineteenth century: A literary study of form and content of sources and influence.* Westport, CT: Greenwood.

Vaux, A. (1988). Social and emotional loneliness: The role of social and personal characteristics. *Personality and Social Psychology Bulletin, 14,* 722–734.

Walker, A. (1995). *In search of our mothers' garden.* London: The Women's Press.

Walsh, K. (1978). *Neuropsychology.* Edinburgh and London: Churchill Livingstone.

Watson, O. M. (1970). *Proxemic behavior: A cross-cultural study.* The Hague: Mouton.

Weaver, R. L. (1995, February 11). Leadership for the future: A new set of priorities. *Vital Speeches of the Day,* pp. 438–439.

Webster, M., & Foschi, M. (1988). *Status generalization: New theory and research.* Palo Alto, CA: Stanford University Press.

Webster's II. (1984). *New Riverside University Dictionary.* Boston: Houghton Mifflin.

Weedon, C. (1987). *Feminist practice and poststructuralist theory.* New York: Basil Blackwell.

Weissman, D. (1976). Bais Yaakov: A historical model for Jewish feminists. In Elizabeth Kolthun (Ed.), *The Jewish woman: New perspectives* (pp. 139–148). New York: Schocken Books.

Weitz, R. (1982). Feminist consciousness-raising, self-concept, and depression. *Sex Roles, 8,* 231–241.

Weitz, S. (1976). Sex difference in nonverbal communication. *Sex Roles, 2,* 175–184.

Wells, J. W. (1990). The sexual vocabularies of heterosexual and homosexual males and females for communicating erotically with a sexual partner. *Archives of Sexual Behavior, 19,* 139–147.

Wells, L. E., & Marwell, G. (1976). *Self esteem: Its conceptualization and measurement.* Beverly Hills, CA: Sage Publications.

Welter, B. (1966). The cult of true womanhood: 1820–1960. *American Quarterly, 18,* 151–174.

West, C., & Fenstermaker, S. (1995). Doing difference. *Gender and Society, 9,* 8–37.

Whaley, A. B. (1982). Televised violence and related variables as predictors of self-reported verbal aggression. *Central States Speech Journal, 33,* 490–497.

Wheelwright, P. (1960). *The way of philosophy.* New York: Odyssey Press.

Whitehead, G. E., & Tawes, S. L. (1976). Dogmatism, age, and educational level as correlates of feminism for males and females. *Sex Roles, 2,* 401–405.

Whitley, B. E., Jr. (1983). Sex role orientation and self-esteem: A critical meta-analytic review. *Journal of Personality and Social Psychology, 44,* 765–778.

Whitley, B. E., Jr. (1984). Sex-role and psychological well-being: Two meta-analysis. *Journal of Sex Roles, 12,* 207–221.

Whitley, B. E., Jr. (1988). The relation of gender-role orientation to sexual experience among college students. *Sex Roles, 19,* 619–638.

Whyte, W. H., Jr. (1951). The wives of management. *Fortune.* pp. 86–89, 150–158.

Wiegers, R. M., & Frieze, I. H. (1977). Gender, female traditionality, achievement level, and cognitions of success and failure. *Psychology of Women Quarterly, 2,* 125–137.

Wiles, K. (1955). *Supervision for better schools.* Englewood Cliffs, NJ: Prentice-Hall.

Willis, F. N., Jr. (1966). Initial speaking distance as a function of the speakers' relationship. *Psychonomic Science, 5,* 221–222.

Wilson, P. R. (1968). Perceptual distortion of height as a function of ascribed academic status. *Journal of Social Psychology, 74,* 97–102.

Wittig, M. (1979). *One is not born a woman.* Paper delivered at the Second Sex Conference: New York Institute for the Humanities.

Wolf, N. (1992). *The Beauty Myth: How images of beauty are used against women.* New York: Doubleday.

Women & Work. (1995). *Facts and Figures, 16* (2), 12–14.

Wood, J. (1982). Communication and relational culture: Bases for the study of human relationships. *Communication Quarterly, 30,* 2.

Wood, J. (1994). *Gendered lives: Communication, gender, and culture.* Belmont, CA: Wadsworth.

Wood, J. (1997). *Gendered lives: Communication, gender, and culture* (2nd Ed.). Belmont, CA: Wadsworth.

Woodworth, R. (1958). *Dynamics of behavior.* New York: Holt, Rinehart & Winston.

Worsnop, R. L.(1992, December, 18). Eating disorders. *CQ Researcher,* pp. 1099–1119.

Wright, P. H. (1982). Men's friendships, women's friendships, and the alleged inferiority of the latter. *Sex Roles, 8,* 1–20.

Wylie, R. (1974). *The self-concept* (Vol. I). Lincoln: University of Nebraska Press.

Wyre, Ray. (1995). Pornography causes: sexual violence. In C. Cozic (Ed.), *Sexual values: Opposing viewpoints* (pp. 145–152). San Diego, CA: Greenhaven Press.

Yamada, M. (1983). Asian Pacific American women and feminism. In C. Moraga and G. Anzaldua (Eds.), *This bridge called my back: Writings by radical women of color.* New York: Kitchen Table.

Young, E. P., & Wiedemann, F. L. (1987). *Female authority: Empowering women through psychotherapy.* New York: Guilford Press.

Young, K. K. (1987). Hinduism. In A. Sharma (Ed.), *Women in world religions.* Albany: State University of New York Press.

Yukl, G. A. (1981). *Leadership in organizations.* Englewood Cliffs, NJ: Prentice Hall.

Zahn, C. (1989). The bases for differing evaluations of male and female speech: Evidence from ratings of transcribed conversation. *Communication Monographs, 56,* 59–74.

Zander, A., Cohen, A. R., & Stotland, E. (1959). Power and the relations among the professions. In D. Cartwright (Ed.), *Studies in social power.* Ann Arbor, MI: Institute for Social Research.

Zelditch, M., Jr. (1955). Role differentiation in the nuclear family: A comparative study. In T. Parsons & R. F. Bales (Eds.), *Family socialization and interaction process* (pp. 307–352). New York: Free Press.

Ziller, R., Hagey, F., Smith, M., & Long, B. (1969). Self-esteem: A self-social construct. *Journal of Consulting and Clinical Psychology, 33,* 84–95.

Zimmerman, D. H., & West, C. (1975). Sex roles, interruptions and silences in conversation. In B. Thorne & N. Henley (Eds.), *Language and sex: Difference and dominance* (pp. 105–129). Rowley, MA: Newbury House.

Index

About the Author

KAY E. PAYNE is a Professor in the Department of Communication at
Western Kentucky University.